OUR VIETNAM WARS

VOLUME 3

As Told by Still More Veterans
Who Served

William F. Brown

DEDICATION

First and foremost, this book is dedicated to the 2,709,918 men and women who served in Vietnam, the 211,454 who were wounded, and the 58,220 who made the ultimate sacrifice there. Second, it is dedicated to my fellow Veterans who opened up to leave a record of their lives, experiences, and very personal memories in hope they may be of help to others.

First, I want to thank the best set of proofreaders a writer can have: my wife Fern here in Florida, Elisabeth Hallett in far-away Montana, Loren Vinson in San Diego, Reg Thibodeaux, also in Montana, Wayne Burnop in Texas, John Russ in Alabama, John Brady in Baton Rouge, Ken Friedman in Orlando, and Craig Smedley, the farthest away of all, in Melbourne, Australia.

I also want to thank Hitch, Barb, and the staff of Booknook Biz in Phoenix and Toronto for their usual marvelous advice and help with processing and conversion of this manuscript and its photographs into "Kindle-Speak." And I want to thank Todd Hebertson at My Personal Artist in Salt Lake City, for the outstanding cover art he has provided for my books. As you can see, it takes a very geographically diverse village to produce a book these days.

And finally, a special "hats off" to the folks at Together We Served, and their website for Vets of all wars to post their memories and experiences, to VVA Chapter 1036, to The Villages Band of Brothers, and to Ed Burke for sending me all those Marines. Ed's most memorable story as well as John Russ's can be found further on in the book.

PREFACE

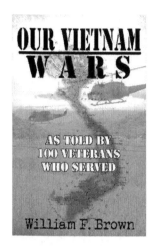

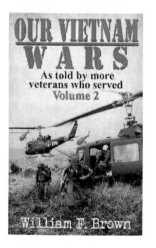

This is **Volume 3** of *Our Vietnam Wars*. Like the first two volumes, it is not simply another "war book," nor is it fiction. Together, they contain the stories of over 200 Veterans who served in that war some fifty years ago. They are short vignettes told by the men and women who were there, where we came from, our jobs and training, our experiences and memories of that country, and what we did after we came back home. Why did I do all these interviews and write their stories? And why did so many Vets open up to me, many for the first time since they left country? I think it is because we are all 70 now, give or take, and our ranks are now rapidly thinning, partly due to the natural effects of age and partly due to the very unnatural effects of Agent Orange, PTSD, and numerous Vietnam-related diseases and illnesses they brought home with them. Those are the names you will not find inscribed on "The Wall" in Washington DC.

The stories in this book are from U.S. Army, Marines, Air Force, Navy, and Coast Guard Veterans, as well as our Australian and New Zealand brothers who also served in that war. The stories are presented in chronological order according to the date the soldier arrived in-country, as the stories were in the first two volumes of the series. What I hope they demonstrate is regardless of where we served, or our service, branch, unit, job, rank, race, or sex, the Vietnam War dominated our generation. And for all too many of us, it still does.

Many of our kids and grandkids only know the Vietnam War from films like Oliver Stone's *Platoon* or the handful of better books written on the war. If they even know where

Vietnam is, many are left with the impression that all of us were low crawling through the jungle on the Cambodian border smoking dope. Oliver was there and that may have been his war, but it wasn't mine or that of most of the men and women who served.

Some of the men and women in these volumes are genuine war heroes, but most were simply targets and survivors. As in most wars, fewer than twenty percent of the troops

"in-country" were actually out in the field in combat putting "boots on the ground." The rest served in support units of one type or another, and Vietnam was no different. My goal was to cover all those experiences from infantrymen to truck drivers, medics, clerk typists, helicopter pilots, nurses, artillerymen, cooks, and aircraft mechanics.

In this volume, you will find a few more West Point-trained Army officers, a few more Special Ops and Recon guys, more corpsmen and medics, and more Australians and New Zealanders. I didn't set out to find them, they managed to find me; and they help fill a few voids in the first two books and add some different perspectives.

Several things surprised me as I wrote these books. First, I'm the first person many of these Veterans have talked to about their experiences in fifty years or more, including their wives, children, and friends. Given the hostile reception many received when they arrived home, who can blame them? No one wanted to hear about the war, and they soon learned not to talk about it. Besides, if you weren't there, you wouldn't understand anyway, not even friends or loved ones. They were the Vets who forced me to bring the books out as paperbacks, not just as e-books, and bought six, eight, even ten copies, so they could personally hand them to their children and grandchildren and say, "You asked me what I did in the war and I never wanted to talk about it, so here! Read it!"

I've also been surprised by the many comments I've received from other Vets, personally and in reviews, about how much the stories have helped them cope with their own issues, to break the ice with family, and to know they weren't alone; and from their wives and children who now understand what their husbands or fathers went

through. Obviously, the stories struck a chord and have done some good, and that's a very humbling experience for any writer.

As I encountered in the interviews for the first and second books, there were more instances this time around where once guys began talking, their eyes seemed to glaze over, and I knew to sit back, keep quiet, and let my recorder keep running. They had stories to tell and things they needed to say. I'm not a trained therapist, but they made me a better listener.

Many of the Veterans in this volume and the earlier ones experienced multiple tours, many were in the worst combat, and many were wounded or are still suffering from the scourges of PTSD and serious Agent Orange-related diseases. That's why these stories are fewer but longer than in *Volume 2*, which were fewer but longer than the ones in *Volume 1*, more personal, more emotional, and more intense. They are presented in chronological order with many marvelous "then and now" photographs, which add a real poignancy to each story.

In the end, the truest words that were written those of us who went and served in Vietnam came from the late Mel Tillis in his song, "Ruby," as sung by Kenny Rogers:

> "It wasn't me that started that old crazy Asian war,
> But I was proud to go and do my patriotic chore."

William F. Brown

TABLE OF CONTENTS

WAYNE ROBSON'S WAR

Royal New Zealand Artillery Regiment, Gunner and Radioman, 161 Battery, attached to the US 173rd Infantry Brigade and the 1st and 6th Battalions of the Royal Australian Regiments, Bien Hoa and Nui Dat, 1965-66

I grew up in Hawera, New Zealand, a small town of 10,000 people back then, in the Taranaki Region on the North Island. This is fairly flat cattle and dairy country and we make a lot of cheese there. New Zealand's population was only 2.6 million when the Vietnam War started, about 4.8 million today, so our military is structured very differently from the United States. It is a small, volunteer force, highly trained and organized into Infantry, Artillery, Engineer, Medical and other units. A draft was politically out of the question, and our entire armed forces only totaled 3,900 men back then. Of those numbers, 187 men were wounded and 37 killed in action in Vietnam.

We all went in the Army as very young cadets and advanced up through the ranks on our own. In my case, I attended a local technical high school until I was 16, and then quit and joined the New Zealand Army Regular Force Cadet School. It was a bit like military college, and I graduated into the Regular Force in January 1961 at 18 years of age.

All New Zealand recruits went to basic training at the Waiouru Military camp, a rugged piece of ground in the center of the North Island. I graduated and went on into the more specialized training in the Royal New Zealand Artillery Regiment in late 1962. I later passed the selection course for training in the New Zealand SAS, modeled after the British commandos, from 1964-1965 before going to Vietnam. We had a long-standing mutual support treaty with the United States, and New Zealand had routinely cooperated with the Australians and British, in some cases with joint units, going back to World War I and World War II.

The US requested that both New Zealand and Australia provide troops for a multinational force in Vietnam. We had a very strong antiwar movement in New Zealand, sending combat troops was very controversial, budgets were tight, and our military resources were already stretched very thin with our commitments in Malaya. However, the government felt that Cold War concerns and its treaty obligations to the US were very important. In May 1965, our Prime Minister announced we were sending medical units, engineers, and an artillery unit, the "161 Battery," as it was called, of the Royal New Zealand Artillery Regiment, to help in the war effort. This consisted of nine officers and 101 enlisted men, which may not seem like very much, but it was a very big deal for our country. For the first nine months in-country, we were under the command of the US 173rd Airborne Brigade at Bien Hoa near Saigon. When the 1st Australian task force was established at Nui Dat in Phouc Tuy province around Vung Tau southeast of Saigon near the coast, we were transferred and became part of that.

Importantly, this was the first war in which New Zealand troops were not fighting as part of a British command or as part of a Commonwealth contingent. Our national commitment to the Vietnam War came in very small steps, beginning with advisors in 1962 and then a small civilian medical detachment in 1963. I went over as the Forward Observer radio operator with the original 161 Battery. In the beginning, we were armed with

four lightweight Italian L-5 pack howitzers. They were very mobile, could be broken down and carried by men on foot in packs, but they weren't very durable and proved unsatisfactory for our mission. One nice thing about them was that they could be put in the back of an APC and moved around with us, which came as a surprise to the VC when they didn't know artillery was around. The number of guns in the battery was later increased to six, and the Italian guns were soon replaced with the more rugged American M2A2 105mm howitzers.

Infantry units were added in May 1967, when New Zealand sent Victor 2, a 182-strong infantry company from the 1st Battalion of the Royal New

Zealand Infantry Regiment. In December, it was joined by "Whiskey 2 Company." These units were superbly trained in counterinsurgency warfare and well-experienced in jungle fighting from their years in Borneo and Malaysia. The 4th Troop from the New Zealand Special Air Service, consisting of one officer and 25 enlisted arrived the following year. They were placed under the 1st Australian Task Force's command, as part of the Royal Australian Regiment's 2nd Battalion, and were primarily deployed on infantry operations in Phuoc Tuy province. The infantry companies were from the Regiment in Malaya were rotated in and out of Vietnam several times, usually after 12-month tours of duty. Eventually, the infantry companies were withdrawn without replacement in November 1970 and in December 1971. We also had as many as 20 Air Force personnel attached to various American units, a small contingent of Navy personnel assigned to the USS *Kitty Hawk* and a destroyer, some Armored personnel assigned to the US 4th Cavalry and several other units, and Signal Corps personnel in-country. While most of these were attached to American units, they also rotated in and out of Thai and South Korean units.

The American 173rd Airborne Brigade we were attached to was light infantry, and we provided them with artillery support, along with one of their own batteries. When we arrived, it was summer. There was nothing there, just scrub brush and dead grass, and we lived in tents on dry, bare dirt. We adapted quickly to working with and being co-locat-

ed with the Americans and relied on them for ammunition and food. One thing that was very good was the US C-rations we were given. They consisted of individual meals, and even contained packs of cigarettes! Australian field rations were intended to last for an entire day and were very spartan, primarily rice. On the other hand ours were much more lightweight, so that we could carry a week's worth in our packs when we went to the field. We did not expect to be resupplied. As a result, we were very disciplined with water, ammunition, and food. That wasn't the way the American troops operated. With their fleets of helicopters and control of the sky, they relied on frequent resupply of those items, and they even received the occasional hot meal when they were in the bush.

My first nine months in-country I worked on a gun crew as an artillery crewman. We were assigned to the south sector of the perimeter. The 173rd was a very active unit and always had companies and battalions out on sweeps, patrolling. We fired our guns every day and fired a lot of "Harassing and Interdictory," or H&I rounds, at night to places where it was suspected that the enemy was located or could be concentrating or traveling. It kept them on edge. It also meant that we never got a full night's sleep. We would be woken several times in the night for a fire mission.

As the war expanded and more troops were brought in, the joint Australian and New Zealand command, ANZAC, was given operational control of Phouc Tuy Province southeast of Saigon on the coast as its own area of operations. In June 1966, we moved there, to Nui Dat, attached to the 6th Royal Australian Regiment. Similar to Bien Hoa, there was nothing at Nui Dat when we arrived. Phouc Tuy Province had been a major VC stronghold for years, and we set up camp in the middle of "their turf." Eventually, we made our compound comfortable as the regiment continued to add facilities. The worst part about that location, however, was mosquitoes. They were so bad that we had to wear long-sleeved shirts.

After a few months there, the big highlight was to be given a three-day in-country R&C to the Australian recreation center at Vung Tau. I was also entitled to one trip out of the country on leave (R&R) every six months. I got one trip to Bangkok and two to Hong Kong.

When I arrived in Nui Dat, there was a sudden need for radio operators from the artillery battery to go out with the Australian infantry during their operations to act as FAC's or Forward Artillery Controllers to call in fire missions to our battery. Someone looked through all the personnel files in our unit and discovered that I was a qualified FAC radio operator in addition to a trained gunner, and that was all it took to end my pleasant existence in camp with the battery. Instead, one officer and two radio operators were assigned to each infantry company. So, while the facilities at the base steadily improved, I had little occasion to enjoy them because I was always out on patrol with the infantry. Every New Zealand soldier regardless of branch had been trained to be an infantryman in our Basic Training course, so I had no problem adapting to the disciplined patrol techniques used by the Australian infantry companies.

When we were in the field, each man was assigned a plastic sheet, which was like a shelter half. You could use it to make an individual lean-to or put two pieces together and make a small tent. However, we only put them up if it was going to rain. Most nights we slept on the ground in the open. Typically, I would go out on patrol for two or three nights, sometimes for a week. The radio I carried was the standard American field backpack model, the AN PRC-25. I also carried what was then the standard New Zealand infantry rifle, the Belgian 7.62 FN. It had a lot of stopping power, but it was heavy, like the American

M-14. The ammunition was very heavy too, so we carried less of it than you would be able to carry with, say, the M-16.

I was assigned to various companies of the Australian Infantry Regiment as a radioman. In early August I was working with B Company. Our compound had been mortared the night before, and the company was sent out as a quick reaction force to locate the enemy. Unfortunately, we were understrength and had no rations with us. We located the enemy's tracks and followed them toward the Long Tan rubber plantation, until it was decided by higher-ups that D Company would be sent out to relieve us and continue the hunt, while we pulled back and were resupplied.

D Company had around 120 men, and we had far fewer than that. It did not appear that the VC were expecting a major battle, and neither were we, when on August 18, 1966, D Company ran into a strong enemy force five kilometers east of Nui Dat, and all hell broke loose. It turned out that the enemy was a combined NVA and Viet Cong force of regimental size, comprised of the VC 275th Regiment,  the D445 Mobile Battalion, and a number of other units, estimated to be 1500-2000 men, which had been massing for a major attack on Nui Dat itself. If our much smaller B Company had run into the ambush, the outcome would have been quite different, and I would not be here typing this story. But that's how the cookie crumbles sometimes.

D Company was in serious trouble. Headquarters immediately turned B Company around, sent in APCs, armored personnel carriers, armed with their heavy .50-caliber machine guns, and unleashed the guns of our 161 Battery plus three Australian batteries back at Nui Dat. The task was made more difficult by a heavy rainstorm, which began early in the two-day engagement. During the ensuing battle, D Company held off repeated NVA and VC attacks. Our Forward Observer parties from the 161 Battery ended up pinned down in the rubber plantation with the infantry, where we were able to direct devastating artillery fire on the enemy and break up their repeated attacks.

Back at Nui Dat, the Battery was still using the lightweight Italian pack howitzers. By that time we had six guns, however, and that night they fired over 3500 rounds, a phenomenal amount and rate. Normally, you would expect a howitzer to overheat and its barrel to warp with that amount of firing, but we were doing it in a rainstorm, which did help cool down the barrels. The firing was so intense that trucks full of artillery shells were arriving nonstop from the ammunition dump and port at Vung Tao. Even the cooks and clerks from headquarters were called out to uncrate shells and feed them to the gun crews. There is no good place to be when an artillery round goes off near you, but the trees in the rubber plantation were a very bad place to hide for the enemy. In addition to the flying steel, the air was full of flying wood and splinters, adding to the carnage. Unfortunately, eighteen Australian soldiers were also killed in the battle, but the nonstop artillery fire from 161 Battery was key in breaking up the attacks and handing the VC a major defeat.

The Italian pack howitzers weren't meant to sustain the rate of firing they did during that battle. Shortly after I rotated out at the end of the year, they were replaced with the heavier, more rugged American 105s. Later, the battery also played important roles during the Tet Offensive and the Battle of Coral Balmoral in 1968. More than 750 men served with the Battery until it was finally withdrawn from Vietnam after providing virtually continuous fire support for six years to American, Australian, and New Zealand infantry units. The infantry companies and tri-service medical teams were withdrawn in November and December 1970, and the SAS Troop and the 161 Battery in February 1971. We have the distinction of being awarded a United States Meritorious Unit commendation while serving under the American 173rd Airborne brigade.

Every Veteran has some memories of their time on operations – a particular firefight,

a near miss, or maybe a comrade killed in action. Victor 3 Company Veteran Bruce Goodall put it best. "The trouble with contact with the enemy is that the first time it is great. The second one is not so bad. By the third one, you know what's going to happen. And the fourth time, you're starting to shit yourself. You start getting very wary, particularly when you are 'short,' and the time is coming to go home."

The war in Vietnam was fought at close range in jungle terrain negotiated inch by inch. The ever-shifting "front line" and an elusive enemy made for tentative soldiering and little downtime on operations. While the war was ultimately lost by the Allied coalition, the objective to seize the initiative in the Phuoc Tuy province was largely achieved, with provincial enemy forces rendered largely ineffective without outside support.

Antiwar protests were loud and very pronounced in New Zealand from the very beginning of our commitment. After the last troops were withdrawn, Veterans faced continuing struggles to obtain the care and support that many felt they needed. As with US forces, many of our illnesses can be attributed to the use of the "Agent Orange" defoliant. From 1962 until 1987, the 2,4,5T herbicide was manufactured at an Ivon Watkins-Dow Chemical plant in Paritutu, New Plymouth, New Zealand, and was then shipped to U.S. military bases in South-East Asia for spraying. In 1984, Agent Orange manufacturers paid New Zealand, Australian and Canadian Veterans an out-of-court settlement, and in 2004 Prime Minister Helen Clark's government apologized to Vietnam War Veterans who had been exposed to Agent Orange or other toxic defoliants, following a New Zealand Health Select Committee's inquiry into its use on New Zealand servicemen and its effects. In 2005, the New Zealand government confirmed that it had supplied Agent Orange chemicals to the United States military during the conflict.

I left the New Zealand Army at end of my contract in February 1967 and went to work for the New Zealand government in law enforcement where I stayed for 43 years until my retirement in September 2010.

DAN SULLIVAN'S WAR

U.S. Marine Corps, Lance Corporal and Ambulance Driver, C Company, 3rd Medical Battalion, 3rd Marine Division, Dong Ha, Chu Lai, Khe Sanh, Hue, Quang Tri, and Phu Bai, two tours, 1966-68

I was born in Boston City Hospital and grew up in nearby Dorchester. I enlisted in the Marines at the age of 17 in November 1964. After boot camp at Parris Island and ITR, or advanced infantry training, at Camp Lejeune, I became an MOS 3500 Motor Transport Operator, or truck driver.

My first tour in Vietnam was nine months long, from January to September 1966. I was assigned to a Marine Corps aviation unit, VMFA 314, "the Black Knights," at Da Nang and Chu Lai. They were a fighter-attack squadron that flew F-4 Phantoms to provide close air support for the Marine ground troops in I and II Corps. During my second tour, a year later, from September 1967 to August 1968, I was assigned as an ambulance driver to "Charlie Med," C Company of the 3rd Medical Battalion. It was based at Phu Bai but had companies spread all across I Corps supporting the 3rd Marine Division. As an ambulance driver, my job was to get wounded Marines from the battlefield to one of our medical facilities for treatment as quickly as possible.

It was during that second tour that I was assigned as an ambulance driver at Khe Sanh during the 77-day siege of the base, from January 21, 1968 to April 7, 1968. Basically, there were 6,000 Marines on the Khe Sanh combat base and its surrounding hills, like Hill 861, 881S, and 881N, each of which had bloody battles of their own. Surrounding us were three North Vietnamese divisions with over 20,000 men, complete with rockets and very large artillery.

Two days I'll never forget are Day 44 and Day 45 of the Siege. I still have vivid memories of them. It was about mid-morning on Day 44 when I heard rockets headed our way from the southwest, but we had never heard anything like this sound before. It was twice as loud as the usual 122-millimeter rockets the NVA fired at us and scared the hell out of us like death from above. The first one landed between Graves Registration and what was called "the Ponderosa" bunkers. The impact made the ground quiver like it was an earthquake. The crater was about twelve feet deep and twenty feet wide in the red clay.

I turned to a Marine named Roberts and said, "I hope those assholes don't have any more of whatever that was!" Roberts yelled back to me, "Incoming!" That was the only answer to my question I needed, and pretty soon everyone was coming out of their bunkers to see what type of shit they were throwing at us now. Evidently, all they had were just those two. Thank God, because we never saw any more of them at Khe Sanh. Later, we heard they were 210-millimeter missiles. But they still had lots of other rockets and mortars.

I couldn't believe after forty-four days those assholes hadn't run out of shit to throw at us, but they hadn't. A short time later I was eating C-rations with Ralph Shelly, waiting for our usual mid-morning entertainment. The B52s would come overhead and kick ass on the NVA, and you couldn't watch a good show like that on an empty stomach. You needed lots of energy to cheer on the B52s. At no time did I ever feel sorry for the NVA. Picking up dead Marines on the airstrip for a couple of months had that deadening effect on me.

The next day was Day 45 of the siege. We were in the bunker playing cards most of the night and paid no attention to the Incoming falling all around us, trying to block out the sounds and learn to live with them. Some nights we were better at that than others. That night's group conversation dealt with Robert Kennedy. We were discussing if he were elected, would he get us the hell out of South Vietnam? Most of the group said, "No way, Bobby was just trying to get JFK's old job."

Shortly after midnight, the "Charlie Med" field phone rang. I picked it up and heard a voice cracking with emotion as he said to me, "Gray Sector, Marine down, come quickly." Corpsman Ralph Shelly and I jumped into my ambulance and we made our way there. Shelly and I ran over with a stretcher, but nothing could be done. A nineteen-year-old Marine lay dead with a very large part of his body missing. A hand grenade had exploded in his pocket, and I felt like shit. This was an accidental death that should not have happened; and I thought of all the pain we would be sending home to his parents.

At Twentynine Palms in California a year earlier, I drove an officer and a chaplain to the home of the parents of a fallen Marine to inform them of their son's death. His parents were working in their yard. Before we even came to a complete stop, I saw the mother collapse on the grass. Her husband's face turned pure white with tears falling down his cheeks. We did what we could for them, which was next to nothing, and left them with their pain, grieving for the loss of their son. With that memory still in my head, Corpsman Ralph Shelly and I placed the Marine in my ambulance and took him to Graves Registration.

It seemed the guys at 113-A Battery never slept; and if they couldn't sleep, no one else was going to either, because they fired lots of artillery rounds at the Gooks. It was 3:00 a.m. and I spent two hours pretending to sleep. I picked up my "E tool," a fold-up shovel, and went looking for revenge for being awoken. I found it in the form of a rat in my bunker. It was as big as a cat and it took me three hard whacks to take that SOB out. The rats at Khe

Sanh had been living off the corpses of dead Gooks on the south side of the base since the beginning of the siege. Even rats had to eat you know, but not in my bunker! One of the Corpsmen was awoken by the noise I was making and was really scared that I might have killed his pet rat. I told him no. This rat had blue eyes and looked like his girlfriend. He said okay and went back to sleep. Rats don't have blue eyes, of course, but he didn't know that. Anywhere else, the two of us would have been shipped out to a nut house, but here we were. We were the "Kings of the crazy people."

Around 0700, it was C-ration time again. Oh boy, I lived for ham and lima beans. Oh God, did I really, really, miss the old mess hall. The damn Gooks had blown ours up on the 21st of January. That was when the ground started shaking again and we were treated to more good entertainment courtesy of the B52s. It might have been a little early, but if I had to eat ham and lima beans again, then let those Gooks eat five-hundred-pound bombs by the hundreds. Showtime lasted ten to fifteen minutes.

A short time later a CH-46 helicopter landed in front of Charlie Med with four dead men from the hills. We took them to Graves Registration to be bagged and tagged. This never got any easier for us. What was always in the back of my mind was that I no longer had any hope of getting out of this siege at Khe Sanh alive, and I truly believed that. My luck would only last so long, so I no longer gave a shit about anything except doing my job. That attitude helped me, and I became less afraid and colder.

At noon, I was having "whiskey nips," miniature bottles of alcohol, thanks to Dr. Finnegan, who gave them out to us a couple times a week. At least there were some benefits to being assigned to a Navy unit. A corpsman started yelling "Incoming!" It sounded like artillery this time, and ten minutes later wounded began coming into Charlie Med from all over the combat base. A gun pit crew had taken a direct hit. Three out of four of them were dead, and the only one left alive might lose both legs and his left arm. Two doctors and a Corpsman worked feverishly on this Marine until they got him stable. He was awake and he kept saying, "I want to live!"

Corpsman Allen called for a Medevac flight, and ten minutes later all of the wounded would be on their way to Delta Medical, the Forward Casualty Receiving Facility for the 3rd

Marine Division in Dong Ha, six miles from the DMZ, where we sent a lot of our casualties. Carl Ebert and I were at Charlie Med when the Marine from the gun pit came out of surgery. Carl asked the triage doctor for an update on the Marine's condition, but the doctor shook his head in the negative. Both of his legs had been removed above his knees and his left arm had been amputated. I turned around, looked at him, and saw him stop breathing. They tried to revive him, but they could not.

The next day, I was going to cheer much louder and longer for the Air Force and their B52s. It seemed that the only payback we were going to get around there was from them. It was 1400 hours and it had been a little bit quiet for about thirty minutes.

The Medevac helicopters were on their way in to pick up a second flight of wounded from Khe Sanh. Twenty or more wounded Marines and stretcher-bearers were standing around waiting at the helipad. I was headed for the Charlie Med triage bunker thinking that was too many people in one area at the same time. Within a millisecond of that thought, as I was on the second step down, I felt the concussion of a large blast.

I turned around, ran back out, and only saw one man on the helipad who could stand on his own. That was Hospitalman Second Class Carl Ebert. Miraculously, he wasn't hurt. I couldn't believe I had found someone alive. Carl was a damn good Corpsman, and I considered him a good friend of mine since I came to Charlie Med in November. Carl was trying to help move our Catholic priest, Walter Driscoll, to the triage bunker before we got more Incoming, but he needed a stretcher for Father Driscoll. By the looks of things, Father Driscoll would never walk again. One of the doctors came out of the bunker to help Carl, so I started to look for more stretchers.

A lot of the Marines on the ground weren't breathing. I began C.P.R on one of them, but I got nowhere with him. A Corpsman came up from the bunker and helped me get that Marine onto a stretcher. We moved him into the triage unit; but when we got to the bottom of the walkway, we saw Dr. Magilligan and Dr. Wolfe working on Jonathan "Nat" Spicer. They had his chest open and were trying to remove a very small piece of steel from Nat's heart. I can't remember how many times I had reminded Nat to keep his flak jacket closed.

It took another fifteen minutes to get the rest of the wounded down into triage, but the main triage bunker was almost filled to capacity with casualties. All of the Corpsmen and four doctors were working at a frantic pace to save as many as they could and get the wounded ready for the evacuation flight to Delta Medical at Dong Ha. Carl Ebert and I carried Nat Spicer to the CH-46 "Sea Knight" helicopter. We were trying to get everyone on board, but it was filled to capacity. Nat's stretcher was halfway into the helicopter and I was standing on the helicopter ramp when an incoming round exploded next to the chopper. Debris went flying all around us but missed me. I lucked out again, I told Carl, "looks like those assholes missed us again."

That was when the helicopter did what seemed to be a full power lift, with me still standing on the ramp. We were gaining altitude very fast, and Carl and I weren't supposed to be on the flight at all. We got Nat all the way into the helicopter and placed his stretcher on the floor. Seconds later, the helicopter lost power and Carl and I were thrown to the floor with him. The CH 46 was falling fast, and

it wasn't auto-rotating. Carl said we must have been hit, but I said nothing. I continued to watch my life flash in front of me. I tried to raise my head, but that seemed very hard to do and I saw the horizon coming up fast. These last couple of days had really been a bitch and I figured this was going to top it. It wouldn't be long now, I thought.

Suddenly, the chopper's engine started up and we began gaining altitude again. This time, I believed we survived by living off of Carl Ebert's lucky day. No one in the helicopter said a word. There was dead silence, because it was a long way to Dong Ha. Carl checked on Nat. He was still unconscious. We dropped him off at the Delta Medical triage about 30 minutes later and Carl and I finally got a chance to sit down and have a hot meal at their mess hall. Shortly after that, it began getting hit by incoming rockets, six or seven of them, but who was counting. The assholes were either following us or we were getting very unlucky. The next morning we hopped a helicopter back to Khe Sanh.

Three weeks later we learned Nat died in the hospital in Japan of an infection.

All in all, my Charlie Company medical unit treated more than 2,500 casualties and even participated in the birth of a local baby girl during that time.

I was awarded a Bronze Star with "V" for valor. It is my favorite medal, because it was for helping Marines. The Citation read:

"For meritorious achievement in connection with operations against the enemy in the Republic of Vietnam while serving as Motor Vehicle Operator with Company C, Third Medical Battalion, Third Marine Division from 27 January to 15 February 1968. Throughout this period, Corporal SULLIVAN'S unit was deployed at the Khe Sanh Combat Base, which frequently came under intense enemy mortar, rocket and artillery fire. Disregarding his own safety, Corporal SULLIVAN repeatedly exposed himself to hostile fire in order to transport casualties to the medical facility, saving the lives of numerous Marines. On 5 February 1968, a C-123 aircraft sustained severe battle damage from hostile ground fire and crashed on the Khe Sanh airfield. Although the site was under an intense rocket and mortar attack, Corporal SULLIVAN unhesitatingly maneuvered his ambulance across the fire-swept terrain to the location of the downed aircraft. Observing one of the crewmen standing in the hatch of the aircraft with his clothing ablaze, he ran to the man, assisted him from the aircraft and rapidly extinguished the flames with his bare hands. Moments after he moved the airman from the hazardous area, the aircraft exploded. His heroic and timely actions inspired all who observed him and prevented the man from sustaining severe injuries. Corporal SULLIVAN'S courage, sincere concern for the welfare of his comrades and unwavering devotion to duty in the face of great personal danger were in keeping with the highest traditions of the Marine Corps and of the United States Naval Service."

Corporal SULLIVAN is authorized to wear the Combat "V."

FOR THE PRESIDENT

I rotated out after that second tour was over in August 1968 and was discharged the next month. In addition to the Bronze Star with "V," I received a Purple Heart for a wound to my hand, and a healthy dose of PTSD.

After leaving the Corps, I went to work with ATT Long Lines in Boston, where I worked as a central office technician. I retired from the phone company in 2001 after thirty-two years. My wife and I have been married for the past forty-eight years and reside in Massachusetts. We have two daughters and eight grandchildren, and I enjoy painting in my free time.

If you liked this story, Dan has also written an excellent book on his time in the Marines at Khe Sanh, titled Teen Marine, *which is also available at Amazon and on Kindle. It goes into much more detail about his time as an ambulance driver at Khe Sanh.*

DAVE COLE'S WAR

U.S. Navy, Seaman Apprentice E-2, Operations Control, *USS Oriskany* CVA 34, Dixie and Yankee Stations, 1966

I grew up in Englewood, Colorado, a suburb near Denver, with flying in my blood. My mom and dad had met in 1937 while both were enrolled in a flight school. WWII stopped their flying, but I heard about their adventures growing up. After my first airplane ride at age six, I was hooked and earned my private pilot license while in high school (this was even before I had a driver's license), working as a busboy to pay for it. I enrolled in the University of Colorado as an ROTC cadet, and studied aerospace engineering for two years. While working nights to earn tuition and struggling to maintain passing grades, I learned that the Navy had an Aviation Cadet Program, NAVCAD, which only required two years of college, so I enlisted in January 1966. Unfortunately, no sooner was I in boot camp than I found out that the Navy had shut the program down.

Directly following boot camp, I joined the "Ships Company" aboard the USS *Oriskany* as a Seaman Apprentice E-2 "non-assigned personnel." That was about as low on the totem pole as you could get, assigned as a cook's assistant and toilet cleaner working twelve-hour shifts as we headed for WESTPAC (Western Pacific) and Vietnam. After stays in Honolulu and Yokosuka, Japan, we arrived at Dixie Station off the coast of South Vietnam on June 27 and began flight operations, shifting to Yankee Station in the Gulf of Tonkin off the

coast of North Vietnam on July 8. So I went from boot camp to the ship to Vietnam all in six months.

I wanted to get as close as I could to aviation, so I requested and was reassigned to the Operations Center (the OC Division), which provided Air Traffic Control for the ship's airplanes. While there I taught myself how to type, prepared weather reports, learned radar, and got very good at writing backward on the big, clear plastic "status board" with a grease pencil. I would write down the pilots' names, aircraft numbers, and fuel status of our aircraft returning from air strikes against North Vietnam so that the officer in charge could determine which would refuel in the air, divert to South Vietnam, or return to the ship to refuel.

The *Oriskany* was an Essex class aircraft carrier, a "long hull" version with a wooden deck, home-ported in San Diego. Construction of the ship began in 1945 and it was commissioned in 1950, the last of that class still in service when I went aboard. It had done two combat tours during the Korean War and did an eventual five in Vietnam. It was used for the filming of *The Bridges of Toko-Ri* in 1954. The *Oriskany* was actually involved in bombing bridges in North Korea during that war, and we got to watch this movie while we were at sea.

Typically, we worked twelve hours on and twelve hours off. Our division's sleep compartment bunked 30 to 40 men stacked four high, located just below the #2 or #3 catapult wires, which made it very hard to sleep. The officers' quarters had air conditioning, while the enlisted compartments did not, so during a port call in Japan, a number of us chipped in and bought an air conditioning unit for our space. It could draw in outside air, and we added a plywood door to keep the cool air inside the compartment. As events unfolded, that air conditioner and the plywood door were soon to prove critical.

On October 26, 1966, at 0730 a fire broke out in the magnesium flare locker forward of and below our level in the hangar bay. It proved to be the worst ship fire in the U.S. Navy since World War II. Forty-four men died, most of whom were pilots.

I had been to the dentist the previous afternoon and had all four of my wisdom teeth removed. During the extractions, one tooth broke off at the gum line and had to be dug out. My face was all swollen, and I was supposed to keep ice on it. Unfortunately, the average temperature outside was 100° and there was no ice available. I had been lying in my rack all night in pain trying to sleep when the fire alarm klaxons went off all over the ship.

There was nothing new about hearing klaxons or fire drills. Fire was the worst hazard any ship faced, and we were used to having frequent drills. They would always begin, "This is a drill, this is a drill – Fire at the..." This time, however, the voice on the intercom began "This is a dr..." Probably out of habit and continued with the real "Fire at the...," which was a critical mistake. Unfortunately, many people only heard the "This is a…" Assumed it was a drill, and tuned out the rest. That was especially true of the pilots. We had been doing continuous air operations for over three months, they were all exhausted, and their quarters were dangerously close to the flare locker. Many of them died of asphyxiation. Only one crewman died of burns.

What had happened was that a sailor accidentally pulled the trigger lanyard on one of the magnesium parachute flares in the starboard side locker on the forward hangar bay under the flight deck, during a downloading process after the strike had been cancelled. Not thinking, he threw the flare inside the compartment with the 700 others, closed the door, and they all went off. These are intensely hot and set off dangerous chemicals stored in the elevator bay. It is impossible to extinguish a magnesium fire with water. The fire penetrated down five decks before it was brought under control.

Because our air conditioner was running and our plywood door closed, we did not smell the smoke until we exited our space, which was almost too late. I heard several levels of fire warnings. As the three of us were not on any of the fire crews, we did not react until the speakers sounded "General Quarters (Battle Stations)!" That got everyone's attention. We got dressed and headed for the door. The Operations Center (our battle station) was several decks below our quarters. When we opened the door, there was thick smoke in the corridors and stairwells, which quickly got worse.

We all had memorized the route from our berthing quarters to our General Quarters (Battle Stations) and found our way blocked by some locked hatches, which forced us to find an alternative route. I remembered seeing an elevator machinery access door next to the toilets of our head, which allowed us to get down to the hangar deck. While were moving across the deck on our way to the OC division, an officer ordered us to carry five-gallon buckets of animal blood to the foaming equipment fighting the fire in the forward hangar bay, which was what the machinery used to make foam. It was frightening to see flames rising above our heads, to see jet airplanes scorched black, to see crew men frantically moving airplanes to other areas of the flight deck to get them out of danger, and to see men pushing steaming bombs overboard before they exploded. Two other carriers, the *Constellation* and the *Franklin D. Roosevelt* had sailed nearby to give aid.

The "Prepare to Abandon Ship" order was given over the 1MC (the ship's PA system) and I was then told to go to the mess and begin distributing life preservers. A number of thoughts began racing through my head. Two at the forefront were, "How well can I swim under oil-slicked waves on fire?" and "What is the fastest way to jump ship?"

The mess halls were shut down, so they broke out old WW II C-rations for us to eat around lunchtime. It wasn't long before one sailor became ill from eating out of one of the cans which had swollen. It was announced to us that the food inside had gone bad, usually from botulism, which could get you very sick and even kill you. We were told we should not eat contents of any cans that were bulging, and anyone who had should report immediately to the sick bay.

Eventually, they got the fire under control, but so much water had been pumped inside the ship that it was now riding dangerously low in the water, bow-down. Normally the bow was fifty feet above the surface of the ocean, but it was now down by the bow twenty feet. Many flooded compartments below deck had battery-powered emergency lights that were dim or out by nightfall. Twelve hours after the fire began, I was ordered to join a bucket brigade to remove water from flooded compartments well below sea level. With no electricity, the normal water pumps would not function. While going further below decks to do this, moving along dark passageways with water up to our knees, I saw electricity arcing behind us. That was very scary.

When the fire was finally put out, we sailed for Cubi Point Naval Air Station Bay in the Philippines, where the airplanes and munitions were offloaded, and on to San Diego, arriving on November 16. By March 23, all of the repairs to the ship had been completed; and on June 16 the ship returned to WESTPAC and on to Vietnam. On July 14 the ship commenced bombing operations on Yankee Station off North Vietnam. Ironically, on July 26 the *Oriskany* provided help with the fire on the USS *Forestall*.

The Navy interviewed everyone who had been aboard that day. Five crewmen were eventually court-martialed, but the charges were dismissed. Those of us who were involved in fighting the fire received letters of commendation for what we did. It allowed us to pick a school we wished to attend. I chose the basic Air Traffic Controller School at NAS Glynco in Brunswick, Georgia, and left the *Oriskany* in December, enjoying a Christmas stop in Denver on the way to school. Unlike high school, by now I was really motivated, and did very well, placing #1 in each class, and attending all three of the air traffic control schools available – Basic ATC, Ground Controlled Approach, and Tower Controller. I joined the Navy aero club on the base, completed my advanced pilot and flight instructor certification at my own expense and during my off-duty hours.

The Navy assigned me to remain at the Naval Air Station at Glencoe Georgia as an Air Traffic Controller. I was released early from my military service in October 1969. I was an E-5 when I was discharged and received the usual array of Navy medals and ribbons. My only diagnosed disability was tinnitus, ringing of the ears, but suffered from PTSD as a result of the chaos, frenzy and life-threatening terror of being nearly trapped below decks during the fire. During my transfer from the West coast to Georgia, I had stayed at my parents' house over Christmas and woke them up night after night with my screaming. I thought that it was normal until I realized recently that it had a name: PTSD.

My BS degree was completed at Metro State College in Denver, during which time I taught flying. Because of all the pilot certificates I had accumulated, I was able to receive almost a year of college credit by exam. In fact, because of my background I ended up writing a few of the exams and teaching an Instrument Instructor Simulator class to receive its credit because they had not scheduled a class instructor.

During the completion of college I flew in Madagascar and West Germany commercially. As I completed my degree in June of 1973, Frontier Airlines hired me. Due to re-organization, bankruptcy, and restructuring, my piloting career took turns at Peoples Express, Continental, and as a FAA Aviation Safety Inspector. United Airlines recruited me from the FAA as an instructor and line pilot for their Boeing 737, 747-400, 757, 767, and Airbus A-320. I found it interesting that a few of the Navy pilots onboard the *Oriskany*, whose names I had written on the status board, later became my copilots in the airline business. I had been the younger Seaman Apprentice E-2, just up from cook's assistant and toilet cleaner, who couldn't get into the NAVCAD program, while they were the commissioned officer pilots who later became my airline copilots due to their longer time commitments before they could get out of the Navy and the airline's seniority system, which gave me an edge.

I retired from the airlines in 2005 and went on to run a Colorado College flight program. My flying continues flying private jets and turboprops. Additional interests include life memberships in the VFW, American Legion, performing contra-dance and bluegrass violin music, and volunteering in Church outreach.

EDSON BELLIS'S WAR

**U.S. Marine Corps, Corporal, Rifleman, Radioman, and
Fire Team Leader, H Company, 2nd of the 3rd, 3rd Marine Division,
Danang, Camp Carroll, Khe Sanh, and the DMZ, 1966–67**

I was born in Canandaigua, NY, the fourth of five brothers. My father was a hired man on a dairy farm, a hard-working family man who believed in education and honesty. We lived in the tenant house with no running water, a hand pump, no central heat, and an outhouse. The living room had a large, black, pot-belly stove for heating and the kitchen had a wood-burning stove. On a dairy farm, you work seven days a week and cows need to be milked twice each day. Sunday was a day of rest; we milked morning and afternoon but had no work in between.

My Uncle Bob was a Marine who had been severely wounded at Sugar Loaf on Okinawa in WW II. I always held him in high regard. There was a war on, I felt an obligation to serve, so in June 1965 I enlisted in the Marine Corps. I was trained as an 0311, Infantryman Rifleman. Thirteen months later I arrived in Vietnam. I was an 18-year-old corporal assigned to Hotel Company, 2nd Battalion of the 3rd Marines. We fought all over I Corps, in the Cong Mountains southwest of Danang, Khe Sanh, Hill 881 North, along the DMZ, on Mutters Ridge, and extensively in the Leatherneck Square. A typical battalion back then had about 800 men. In one year, including replacements, my battalion lost 174 men killed in action and 870 wounded.

Every day had its drama and excitement, but there are two days during my thirteen-month tour that I'll never forget. The first of these was May 3, 1967, during the "Hill Battles." About midnight, Echo Company on Hill 881 North, part of the outer defenses of Khe Sanh, began receiving incoming fire, followed by an NVA ground attack. The NVA had infiltrated their lines. Before Echo knew what was happening, the enemy had shot and killed 19 Marines. Then NVA put on Marine helmets and clothes and intermixed with the Marines in the dark just before daybreak. After the initial burst of gunfire, one hell of a battle erupted. During the struggle, "Corpsman, Corpsman up," was called out. The two Navy Corpsmen who answered the cry were killed. It was the NVA who called the unsuspecting Corpsmen and shot them as they came to give medical assistance to a fallen comrade. By daybreak, 30 Marines from Echo had died, 40 were wounded, five were missing, and Echo was still pinned down.

Lieutenant Colonel Delong, CO of 2nd Battalion, told us that Echo had been attacked by an NVA regiment at 0300. He was reinforcing Echo with elements of Fox Company and sending Hotel Company around the right flank of Hill 881 North to attack the NVA where they weren't expecting it. As we moved out, we had indirect covering fire from a supporting artillery battery and direct covering fire from a battery of 106-millimeter recoilless rifles located at the battalion CP. We made a long, hot march in a column of platoons, with my 1st Platoon in the lead and the company command group behind us. As we were leaving the perimeter, the supporting 106 Recoilless Rifle battery fired short, and we took some casualties in our platoon. We stopped and had to Medevac the wounded before we could resume our attack. It was a long delay.

The march route took us through tall, dense elephant grass, and we had to use machetes to cut our way through the thick tangle of foliage. It was a stifling-hot steam bath. For long periods we couldn't even see the sky. Thankfully, they let us abandon our heavy flak jackets. Even though we were hot and thirsty, Marines didn't have to be told to conserve their water. We knew there were no landing zones for resupply out there.

As we maneuvered around to the right of the NVA positions under cover of the 106-millimeter recoilless rifles, other unit commanders asked for the fire to be lifted as it was hitting very close to friendly lines; but knowing we needed covering fire to move in unobserved on the NVA, Captain Madonna, CO of Hotel, pointed out his own command group was closest to where our recoilless rifle shells were impacting. Not until 1st Platoon closed the gap with the enemy, did he call off the covering fire. That was when Captain Madonna ordered Lieutenant Elliott of 1st Platoon to have his Marines "fix bayonets." He did this for two reasons. First, for the morale boost a bayonet charge stirs up in a Marine. Second, with all the trouble we had been having with the M-16s, he wanted to ensure his Marines had the best fighting chance he could give them if the new rifles went sour again. But I remember the chill I got when Lieutenant Elliott passed the word for us to "Fix bayonets!"

The fighting became mean and dirty when the NVA discovered us at their back door. Our attack was successful with Sergeant Ransbottom leading his squad in taking out an

NVA bunker line that had Echo pinned down. We took six prisoners for which the battalion commander gave ten days leave in Bangkok to the Marines who caught them. We had two Marines killed; but 25 enemy KIA. The key to the attack was the stealth we were able to maintain flanking them, helped by the 106-millimeter recoilless rifle fire that kept the NVA's heads down.

At 1500 the bunker line was declared secure and we began to sweep the area. By 1600 the five missing Marines from Echo were found, dead, on the other side of the hill. The official body count of NVA dead in that battle was 137, but we stacked 236 weapons, including AK-47s, Russian assault machine guns, mortars, Russian sniper rifles and SKR carbines. Hotel established a position adjacent to Echo's perimeter, but Hill 881 North was again

occupied by Marines. However, the day was not over for us yet. As we were digging in, the NVA opened up with a mortar attack. We hunkered down in hastily scraped-out holes and shell craters, bracing for a follow-up infantry assault, but none came.

Before the battle for Hill 881 North, all of our firefights had been ambushes with intense small arms fire, lasting maybe 30 minutes to an hour. The ongoing Battle for Khe Sanh, of which Hill 881 North was but a small part, was continuous fighting against hard-core NVA who were determined to inflict as many casualties as possible on us. The US Marines were better, but the North Vietnam leaders later admitted that they were willing to lose ten of their men for each American they killed because of the effect that had on the US public back home.

There was more death over there than anyone should see. More than fifty years later I still have nightmares, in which I scream and fight for my life.

The second day I'll never forget came about a week later, on May 20, 1967, when we went into the DMZ as part of "Operation Hickory." My battalion was then the 7th Fleet's Strategic Reserve, Special Landing Force Bravo, or SLF Bravo on the USS *Princeton*. It was an old WW II aircraft carrier refitted into a Marine amphibious assault ship that floated off northern I Corps. That wasn't my favorite duty assignment. On May 20, CH-46A Sea Knight helicopters carried us into LZ Parrot in an "opposed air assault." We were hit with small arms fire and mortar rounds and the LZ was closed to further landings until we had it secured. Nothing makes a person feel more at home than having nice, friendly people shoot at you for a reception. It makes you feel important.

Most of the day was spent ferrying the battalion and supplies. This was the Marines' first incursion into the DMZ. It had been a safe haven for the NVA, and they were using it as a staging area for supplies and troops. Hotel then moved toward its initial objective, a village to the north-northwest. It was fortified and defended by what appeared to be a reinforced NVA platoon supported by mortars and artillery firing from within the DMZ. 1st Platoon of Hotel Company was told to go to an area where another platoon from the 9th Marines had been ambushed. Because this was the DMZ, we were instructed not to fire on the enemy, unless they fired first. Another stupid rule from the politicians stateside.

I had a bad feeling about this mission. It was the only time I felt like this in Vietnam. My fire team was point for the platoon, but we were short a man. Lance Corporal Mike Sevard was the point man, I was number two and Private First Class Mark Landers was third. As we moved down the trail to the ambush site, we came to a clearing next to a rice paddy, when we found our first dead Marine from the previous ambush.

We continued for about 100 yards across the clearing when all hell broke out. We found ourselves in a classic L-shaped ambush. That meant the long leg across the paddy from us was shooting all along our line of march, and they had a machine nest on the short leg, blocking us and shooting down our length. I jumped behind a bush, about three feet high and three feet around, and began firing my M-16 at the enemy across the paddy. The call for "Corpsman" was coming from everywhere behind me. I glanced forward to try to find Lance Corporal Sevard, but he was nowhere to be seen.

Continuing to fire, I glanced behind me and saw Private First Class Mark Landers lying dead in the open. I could hear our M-60 machine gun start and then stop. This happened several times and we were having trouble gaining fire superiority. I learned later that two machine gunners were killed by NVA snipers and two more gunners wounded. I know this, because I met the wounded gunner, Corporal Latcher, in Camp LeJeune in 1968. He had a scar starting at the top of his forehead across the bridge of his nose and continued across his cheek. It was an ugly, nasty-looking thing, but he had survived.

Realizing we were in trouble, I did what I never thought I would do, attempt a "John Wayne" action. By this time I'd seen the NVA machine nest across the rice paddy. I removed my LAW, a Light Anti-tank Weapon, from my left shoulder. It's a small rocket designed to take out tanks or bunkers. I pulled the retaining pins, the end caps opened, and I stretched the LAW to its full-open position. I needed to move out from behind the bush to get a clear shot; so I quickly put the LAW on my shoulder, sighted on the machine gun nest and pushed the firing trigger. DUD, NOTHING! At the same time, I was knocked backward onto the ground. I was hit!

I crawled back behind the bush and saw blood soaking the front of my shirt. I called for a Corpsman, and then realized that wasn't going to happen. I removed my pack and looked at my shirt, there were several holes in it, I thought from shrapnel. I removed my cartridge belt to get my battle dressings; but as I glanced at my pack on the ground, I noticed it had blood on it. There was a hole in it. Turning the pack over I saw a hole on the other side. I reached around to my back and found a hole and blood with my fingers. I pulled up the front of my shirt and saw a round hole in my side about half-way down. It was a bullet wound. I tied one battle dressing over the front bullet hole and the second over the rear exit wound. Only minutes had passed, but I heard calls that the platoon was falling back. I could envision F-4 fighters screaming in shortly, dropping napalm all over this whole area; so I needed to get the hell out of there. I looked back across the 100 yards of open ground and knew I would never make it across there alive.

About 20 yards behind me there was a small hill, completely covered with small bushes like the one in front of me. I decided I would travel light: twenty ammo magazines in my shirt side pockets, four hand grenades in my pant pockets, one canteen, my compass, and my rifle. I left my pack, my cartridge belt with all its junk, and my helmet. I took a compass reading back toward our LZ, and it was escape and evasion time. I scrambled across the twenty yards on my hands and knees. Once I got under the low bushes, I turned to the right for a short distance and then back up the hill, figuring if any NVA had seen my dash to the hill they wouldn't be able to target me. To this day I do not know if anyone saw or shot at me, but I crawled over the crest and part way down the far side before I sat down and rested for a few minutes.

I took out my compass and determined the direction to travel to the LZ. It was only half an hour away, but I had crouched down and stayed near bushes, tall weeds, and grass to hide my silhouette. After one and a half hours, I knew I was lost. I took out my compass again and plotted a course southeast, away from the DMZ and North Vietnam and east to Highway 1 and the South China Sea. I would find help in that direction, but I would have to remain concealed.

About two hours later I spotted what appeared to be a "292 antenna" on a hilltop. The Marines would set up 292s to boost radio range. Did the NVA have something similar? Not wanting to be captured or shot, I crept closer to see who they were. It took me 45 minutes crawling on my belly like a snake to get close enough to hear Marines talking in their fighting holes. I slowly stood up to let everyone see I was a US Marine, but I didn't need to worry. No one was paying any attention. I walked right through their perimeter and headed to their CP. Two Marines came walking toward me, one I recognized from Golf Company. I stopped in front of them and said, "Could you get me some help, I'm wounded." The Marine I knew just stared at me like I was an alien, but the second Marine turned and ran toward the CP calling "Corpsman, Corpsman!"

I sat down and waited. Very soon I was surrounded by a captain, a lieutenant, the other

Marine, and what I wanted, a Corpsman. The Corpsman started treating me immediately. The captain asked who I was and what unit I was from. I replied, "I am Corporal Bellis, 1st Platoon, Hotel Company and we were ambushed earlier." He said, "Don't worry you're okay and not going to die."

Die? What the hell, I hadn't thought about buying the farm since I was first hit. But maybe I was in worse shape than I thought. The captain must have seen something on my face, and he repeated: "Don't worry, you're okay. You're not going to die." Damn, I've been told twice in one minute that I was not going to die! This was not good for one's psychological well-being.

A Sea Knight Medevac helicopter was diverted, and I was put on board. The floor was already covered with Marines on stretchers; so, as a "walking wounded," I sat in one of the canvas seats and helped the Corpsman give water to the Marines he said could have some.

I held the canteen and slowly let them drink. The helicopter set down on the USS *Princeton*. Sailors rushed aboard, grabbed the stretchers, and took them to triage up on the flight deck. Doctors would then evaluate the wounds and send them to the proper location.

I walked from the helicopter last and was led to a doctor. He removed my shirt and bandages examined my wounds. I noticed sailors outside the triage area pointing at me. There I was, standing with a bullet hole through-and-through, front to back, with blood running down my sides. Well, I decided I'd show them how tough Marines are! When they said I'd be taken to X-ray, I straighten up, stood tall, and followed the sailor down the ladder (stairs to you landlubbers). I was surprised to see "Doc" Tom Monti, a Corpsman, working in X-ray. He motioned to a table and told me to sit up there while he set up the machine. I sat down, watched him for a few seconds, and then said, "Doc, come over here, I'm going to pass out."

The day's fatigue, stress, and loss of blood had finally caught up to me. The last thing I remember is falling forward. Doc must have caught me, because I awoke the next day in sick bay. The X-ray showed no broken ribs, front or back. The bullet had passed between them on both sides and left a neat bullet hole punched through my body. I remained on the USS *Princeton* for four weeks, including the trip she made to Subic Bay, Philippines for supplies, food, and ammunition.

During the time my 45-man platoon was part of Special Landing Force Bravo, from April to July 1967, we had 27 men killed in action, 17 wounded in action, and everyone else earned at least one Purple Heart. I received two Purple Hearts, the first was for that through-and-through bullet wound and the second was for shrapnel from a Chinese Claymore. Only one Marine in my platoon served his full 13 months without any wounds or injuries.

I finished my tour in Vietnam, was assigned to the Naval Hospital at Camp Lejeune, and discharged at the end of my enlistment in April 1969. The reason I left active duty — you never quit being a Marine — was the Vietnam War was being run by the politicians, not by the Military. The Marines offered to send me to OCS, but I could not in good conscience lead Marines UNLESS the country was fighting to win.

I went to College on the GI Bill and graduated first in my class in Mechanical Engineering. It was the Marine Corps that taught me discipline and responsibility. I was not smarter than the younger students; I just worked harder and longer. I was hired by Eastman Kodak, as a junior engineer. I worked for them for 33 years, becoming the Director of Engineering. Same story. I worked harder and longer.

Today I have a 50% disability from PTSD, a 50% disability from Agent Orange-related heart damage, 50% hearing loss, a 40% disability from muscle damage in my legs, 10% diminished eyesight, and diabetes.

The only military association I belong to is the VFW. I believe the Veterans of Foreign Wars represent past and current Veterans. The federal government uses Veterans when they need them and would like to forget them afterward. We have only to look at how the Veterans of Vietnam, the Persian Gulf War, and Iraq and Afghanistan have been treated.

Being a Marine, I am disciplined, loyal, and tireless in achieving my goals. I went from a 17-year-old farm boy to become the Director of Engineering for a multinational company. It was the Marine Corps with the G.I. Bill that made this happen.

NEVILLE "JACK" MADDEN'S WAR

Australian Army, Staff Sergeant, 32nd Small Ship Squadron, Royal Australian Engineers, East Coast of South Vietnam 1966–71

I grew up in Adelaide, the capital city of South Australia, an environment similar to Nevada. In the 1950s everything in Australia was still very British. My father joined the Army the first day of WW II. His younger brother did the same, and he was only 16. I joined the Royal Air Force Cadets when I was 14. The tradition of service was in our blood.

When I graduated from High School in 1955, only the rich went to University. I was lucky enough to get a job as a cadet surveyor for the Highway Department, working on a new road in western South Australia – hot, dry, dusty, and plenty of nothing. After five months in the "bush" with the flies and temperatures that often reached 120 F, I decided to try the Army. Recruit Training was sixteen weeks long and everything was British – British tactics, British .303 Lee-Enfield rifles, a 10-round magazine, WW I hand grenades, 18-inch bayonets, and WW II huts. When it was over, I qualified for the School of Military Engineering near Sydney.

The training was twelve weeks long, in demolition, equipment bridging, hydrology, field engineering, water supply, mine warfare, and field hygiene. At the end, I asked for a Construction Battalion, where I could finish my surveyor's certificate. Instead, I was sent to a supply unit, but I finished my certificate at night school. I went on to a school in the new science of soil mechanics, which was great, and worked on civil attachment at the Sydney Airport, post offices, government buildings and others, doing materials testing.

When that job was done, I volunteered to Papua, New Guinea, supervising works and maintaining roads, bridges, and airfields, much of which dated to WW II. The Army was transitioning to more modern personal equipment like the Belgian FN 7.62 rifle. It wasn't much good for jungle warfare, but it was an improvement.

After two years in the jungle, I was posted to the Army Water Transport Organization as a clerk, which I wasn't happy about. It was all very secret, but I ended up in the 32 Small Ship Squadron as the Squadron Quartermaster Sergeant, and two hours later was informed we were headed for Vietnam to transport men and stores. The Army had bought four US Landing Ships Medium, LSMs, and a 3,000-ton cargo ship, the *John Monash*, which had been built to Maritime standards, which meant sergeants and above had their own cabins. Not bad!

At the request of the US, Australia gradually sent more and more small units to Vietnam, from advisors in 1962 to several infantry companies, an artillery battery, medical units, engineers, and others. By 1966 that became a full Task Force, which was assigned its own province, Phouc Tuy, and was based at Vung Tau and later Nui Dat. To operate, they needed ships and logistical support, and that was us. In 1967, an Australian destroyer joined the US 7th Fleet, and Australian Canberra bombers were based at Phan Rang as part of the 35th Tactical Fighter Wing.

When we arrived, we knew very little about the country, its people, or the war situation. I'm sure we looked like a bunch of amateurs. Our job was to carry men and supplies wherever they were needed, and we frequently put in at Subic Bay in the Philippines, Singapore, Malaysia, and refitting in Australia. Increasingly, we provided shipping support to US troops and carried ammunition, artillery shells, and bombs, and made stops at Cam Ranh Bay, Vung Tau, and Phan Rang. The *John Marsh* worked right up to the end of the war, and its crew was arguably the last Australian combat troops in Vietnam, other than the Embassy guards.

My role as the ship's quartermaster was acquisition of the ship's rations, all aspects of accommodation, individual protective clothing, ammunition, weapons, the ship's stores, and consumables. Being a small country, we were frugal when it came to supplies and ammunition, so dealing with the US logistic system was interesting. One day, I ordered 5,000 rounds of .50-caliber machine gun ammunition. When the shipment arrived, they had sent 2,500 boxes, each with 200 rounds, or 500,000 rounds. I told them I only wanted 5,000 rounds and to take the rest back. No, they said. The replacement ammo was already in the supply stream and they would have nowhere to store it all. So, I gave some to the cavalry, and the rest to the British in Singapore.

We had a modified stun grenade we could use. It was quite effective when thrown overboard against swimmers, but they really pissed off any of the crew that were trying to sleep after their watch. Subic Bay, the home of the USN 7th Fleet, was a good port to obtain rations, because the food was much better than what we were supplied in Vietnam. I don't know how many tins of canned turkey, ham, and chicken the cooks threw overboard. The tinned bread mix was good, though.

Australia's commitment to Vietnam rapidly declined in the early 70s, and by January 1973 our involvement was formally ended. By then the LSMs were beat up. The cost of maintaining them was not worth it, so they were donated to the Philippine government, which soon sold them off. The unit was disbanded and there were many surplus NCOs  after Vietnam ended. I was posted to an Army Reserve Unit. I had been promoted to Staff Sergeant and I told my boss that I wouldn't mind being posted to Singapore. One day I got a phone call from Army Headquarters, "Do you still want to go to Singapore?" Naturally, I said yes. The Army put all our furniture into storage, at their expense, and we prepared to fly to Singapore.

On the Saturday before we departed there were federal elections and the Labor Party won. So, when my wife and two children boarded the civilian flight to Singapore on Monday, we didn't know if we would be there a day, a week or how long. The new Government was very anti-colonial and wanted to pull our troops out of Singapore. But the engineer unit was a tri-national one, with Australian, New Zealand, and United Kingdom Engineers, called the ANZUK Force. My role became closing the unit down and returning all the equipment to Australia, New Zealand, or the UK. It was a time-consuming job, but I was already used to dealing with multinational organizations.

The house we were given was fully furnished and rent was cheap. We were paid overseas allowances, heat money for the tropics, an education allowance for the children, a servant allowance, and finally a gardener allowance. The cost of living was half of Australia and the new Labor government had given the military a substantial pay increase. We lived like rajahs.

But all good things come to an end. The job was finished. I owned a beat-up Ford Falcon station wagon. The registration and gasoline prices were very high, no one wanted to buy it, and there was no place to abandon it. I used the unit's last bulldozer to dig a hole in the middle of our football field, drove the Falcon in, and then crushed it with the dozer and back filled the hole. I've been back to Singapore many times since, and have encountered no hassles with Singapore immigration; so it appears no one ever found it.

I was able to obtain another posting to a unit that trained public utilities personnel to be ready for an overseas deployment similar to the Seabees, and it included a promotion to Warrant Officer Class II. The downside was that I supervised soldiers learning how to use dynamite. My ears still have tinnitus or ringing from those days. From there I went to a regular Army Engineer Regiment in Brisbane, doing pre-exercise construction on roads and airfields and repairing private lands that were damaged during the exercises.

As the Army downsized further, I was actually promoted up to Warrant Officer Class I. My pay was now more than a major, and I was responsible for supervising many far-flung smaller units. They may have made the Army smaller, but it was far less efficient. Once again, in a cost-cutting measure, the Army consolidated three heavy construction units into one regiment which was to be available for natural disaster relief throughout the Western Pacific, as we did following a major hurricane in Tonga and for UN work in Namibia, flying for days in the back of a worn-out C-130. I talked my way into a civil aid project in the Fiji Islands to build prefabricated hurricane-proof storage sheds that could double as community shelters.

After several more assignments in several more rounds of government budget cuts and troop strength reductions, I had served 26 years and decided that the time had come to

retire. I was offered a commission, but my Warrant Officer pay was now equal to a major, the position would only be that of a captain, and I was a field man and it would be a desk job so, I said goodbye.

I went to college and received a Diploma of Information Technology, and then on to University for a Bachelor of Science in Geography and another science degree, majoring in Environment and Sustainability subjects, took other courses in GIS and GPS data and earned a Master of Science degree specializing in use of satellites to detect irrigation channel leaks. I have just finished my MSc, only to realize that the new Un-manned Aerial Systems, or "drones" have superseded the need to use expensive satellite imagery for that task. Futile? Perhaps. Expensive courses? Yes. But in Australia student loans only need to be repaid if your income exceeds $54,000, and my disability pension income is exempt. So I can study forever.

Now, I enjoy model railroading and go to US railway historical conventions. Fortunately, in Vietnam I had minimal exposure to Agent Orange and my health is still fair to good. I can no longer run after buses due to my breathing problems, but Australia has sold off its Veterans' hospitals and we can go to civilian hospitals and doctors for treatment.

So, the story goes on, and life is good.

HOWARD TOY'S WAR

**U.S. Army, Sergeant and Machine Gunner, Company B,
3rd Battalion, 7th Infantry, 199th Light Infantry Brigade,
Long An Province and the Mekong Delta, 1966–67**

Late on the afternoon of March 14, 1967, a large force of VC, estimated to be around 120 men, was spotted in our operating area in the rice paddies and jungle fifteen miles southwest of Saigon. Our company commander decided to send a 12-man squad, including me, on a night ambush patrol to see what we could find. I was a Spec-4 at the time and an assistant machine gunner.

Our ambush patrol was led by Staff Sergeant Leroy Guild. He briefed us at the old schoolhouse we used as a base camp and we headed out just before dark toward a specific location picked by Battalion. But before we got there, we were the ones who were ambushed by at least a platoon of VC who hit us with automatic weapons fire and grenades. Six men in the patrol were killed, including Staff Sergeant Guild, Ron Bass, George Cook, William Hogan, Angel Fragosa-Garcia, and Angel Sanchez. Two more guys were seriously wounded, including William Lane and myself. How I wasn't killed with the others that night, I will never know.

I grew up in LA, graduated from University High School, and was drafted in April 1966 while attending college. I completed Basic Training, Leadership School, and Advanced Infantry Training at Fort Ord. Ultimately, I trained as a 11B40, Light Weapons Infantry, which meant an M-60 machine gunner. By that December, eight months later, I was in Vietnam, assigned to the 199th Light Infantry Brigade. We were the "Fire Brigade," the mobile Reaction Force for the Saigon area.

Unfortunately, I don't remember every detail of that ambush patrol. That could be the result of the horrors of combat; but after the ambush, I remember much less. That's why I'm using the statements of other guys in the company, the Reaction Force, and the medic who came to rescue us, to fill in the gaps. To this day, I will always hold the highest respect for Sergeant Guild and his actions on that fateful night. He was an outstanding squad leader, who made the ultimate sacrifice as did the others killed that night.

As we headed to the ambush site, it was dark and very creepy. Normally, you saw candlelight inside the huts in the villages we passed. That night, it was "candle lights out." They hid as we approached, and everyone in the patrol had a very bad feeling that something was going to happen. First, one of the semi-demolished footbridges we came to was booby trapped. Sergeant Guild stopped the patrol and made sure that everyone was especially alert after that and designated a "fallback position" in the event that we were ambushed.

I recall Sergeant Guild radioing back to the Company CP requesting permission to stop and set up a night defensive position there; but the request was denied. Instead, we were ordered to proceed to the objective on a new trail. Shortly afterward, our point man, Ron Bass, got caught in a tripwire and the patrol came to a halt. It was just as Sergeant Guild managed to free Bass from the tripwire that all hell broke loose and the firefight started. George Cook was carrying our M-60. He and I were only inches apart when a grenade landed in our position. He was killed instantly. As the assistant gunner, I took over the M-60 and yelled for help feeding ammo belts into the gun. Angel Sanchez came crawling over and proceeded to hook up belts of ammo and feed them to me, when another grenade landed in our position and exploded. Angel died and I was wounded from the blast. I kept firing, over two hundred rounds; but that was when the M-60 became non-operational. Our firepower was dwindling quickly, and I could tell we were about to be overrun. All I could think of doing was to destroy the M-60, so I put a hand grenade under the feed tray cover.

During the firefight, I recall Sergeant Guild, who carried an M-79 grenade launcher, putting rounds wherever there was a muzzle flash. He never gave up!!! After destroying my M-60, I found an M-16 and continued firing until I ran out of ammunition. By then, I believe I was the last guy firing.

George Cook and I had been M-60 partners the entire three months I had been with the squad. We decided we wouldn't allow ourselves to be captured and taken prisoner. We each had a hand grenade specially marked to blow ourselves up if all else failed. As it turned out, during that firefight I expended everything I had, and had even tossed that last hand grenade which I had reserved for myself; so there was no way for me to take my own life.

When the firing stopped, the enemy came around policing up our equipment. I remember them shooting the guys that were wounded. As I lay in the mud in that rice paddy, bleeding and wounded, I thought I was about to kiss my ass good-bye. That was when I had another "flashback" and saw myself growing up as a child. I'm not sure if you have ever heard of this, but I had an image of myself as a child riding my favorite tricycle, I saw myself playing and growing up with my friends. And last but not least, I remember saying good-bye to my parents and family – thanking them for everything.

When the enemy finally got around to me, one of them kicked me in the side. He broke one of my ribs, but when I didn't move, he must have presumed I was already dead. Ultimately, he searched me and took my wristwatch along with my last cluster flare, but he didn't shoot me. I was extremely fortunate, and I guess the Man Upstairs was watching over me that night. At this time — a big THANK YOU to the Reaction Force!

After that, I was in and out of it, mostly out, and don't remember much before the

Dust-Off picked me up and I woke up on the cold slab of an operating table under the bright lights of an x-ray machine at the 24th Evacuation Hospital at Long Binh. I had facial, head, and body wounds from shrapnel, which they were trying to find. I remember a nurse cutting away my jungle fatigues, but I never wore any underwear out in the field. EMBARRASSING MOMENT! Oh well….

As I said, there are holes in my memories of that day. Fortunately Texas Tech University had a Vietnam History project in the works and Richard Hearell, one of the members from Bravo Company, compiled a lot of information that was submitted to their project. Excerpts from Richard's interviews and documentation substantiate that different people remember things differently, but taken together with mine, their stories form a clearer picture of what transpired.

Doug Allen Wrote: I was on the rescue team with Lieutenant Roberts, RTO Boyle, Burke, and someone else. As we left the schoolhouse, I remember seeing the tracers from machine gun fire against the evening sky. It was already dark, and I could tell we were already too late. We double-timed it from the schoolhouse, heading east toward the ambush site. First, we met up with Howard Toy, who was in bad shape. I couldn't shake the extreme guilt I felt that I couldn't run that mile faster. One of the guys, I'm not sure who, took Toy back to the schoolhouse. There was also a Vietnamese Popular Forces soldier behind Toy, who didn't look as upset as I would have expected him to look. I never did trust those guys.

The rest of us continued east to the ambush site. I had been through that area many times before, but this was definitely surreal! There were hand grenade craters all over the place. We found six guys down, several of them on the west side of the trail in the rice paddy lying beside the grey-colored craters. They were completely covered with mud from the grenade blasts and difficult to recognize. I think Hogan was up on the hooch-side of the trail. He had initially been wounded, and then shot in the head, as Toy said.

By then Lieutenant Roberts and Boyle had called in a Dust-Off chopper, which landed in the road. Burke, me, and another guy, maybe Barr, proceeded to get the dead guys to the chopper. Their bodies were very heavy and slippery from all the mud, so the three of us would switch off, with one playing guard while the other two carried someone to the chopper. We had aerial flares coming down lighting up the area, but it was very dark back where we were working. The whole time, the chopper pilot was asking us to hurry. The flares had them all lit up and they were sitting ducks on the road.

This was extremely stressful for all of us. By the time we got the sixth body out, we were covered with rice paddy mud and blood. My eyes were as big as saucers, and with my M16 slung on my shoulder, I must have looked like a zombie. The two guys in front of me were carrying the last body, and it was my turn to play guard. As I got closer to the flare light, Boyle and Lieutenant Roberts saw my appearance and were startled, thinking something had gone wrong. I think I heard Burke ask if I had a knife in my back or something. The Dust-Off left with the bodies, and we double-timed it back to the schoolhouse.

The next day, we had services for the six dead guys and gave them a six-gun salute. Our 2nd Platoon was assigned to bunker duty, while the ambush area was investigated by others. But things weren't the same for me after March 14. Reality had hit home, and this was a war where you could get killed.

Jim Barr added in a phone call: I was with the patrol that found Toy. I remember him coming down the road yelling, "Don't shoot!" After he calmed down, he told us all the others were dead. We knew where they had gone, so I sent him back with two other men. We went on into the ambush site, searched the bodies for booby traps. Mike Franklin and I carried George Cook out and loaded him on a helicopter.

Robyn Crombie Wrote: As for the sweep the next day, it was pretty much cut and dried. Third Platoon came over from our perimeter and I remember we walked down to the schoolhouse. We made the sweep with another platoon, but don't remember which one. I was carrying an M-60 machine gun and was walking up the trail until I reached the spot where the ambush patrol had been hit the night before. The site was trampled over pretty bad. The thing that really sticks in my mind was the large number of footprints we saw in the mud. We followed them back to the riverbank, where they vanished. They must have had sampans waiting there, because when we got to the river there was nothing.

John Shewmaker Wrote: I was a member of the Reaction Force that went out that night. My most vivid memory is loading the bodies onto a slick later that night. I also remember trying to assist the medic in patching up Howard Toy. He very nearly lost an eye as it was out of its socket. I was also an admirer of George Cook and I was devastated that he was one of the guys killed. On either Christmas Eve or maybe Christmas night 1966, three months earlier, he shot and killed a VC that I believe would have killed me a moment later. Two weeks earlier, I turned 19 years old. The only other friend I really remember, besides Howard Toy and George Cook, was Dan Coughran.

To get back to March 14, 1967, I was also in the squad that returned to the ambush site on the 15th, the day after. We were trying to determine exactly what happened. As I recall, we did, and the order it happened in. I ran into a survivor of that ambush in Panama sometime in the early 1980s, maybe 1982 or 1983. I believe his name was Ramirez but I'm not positive. I believe he was the RTO of the patrol that got ambushed, and it was his radio, the AN/PRC25, that had a bullet lodged in it. At the time, he was an instructor at the "Green Hell" jungle school down there and close to retirement. Other than that, my memory is vague.

John Shewmaker Also Wrote: I read the narratives from Howard Toy and the others, and was overwhelmed by a flood of long-forgotten memories. As I remember, we had been out on a day mission, perhaps an airmobile mission, and hadn't been back at the schoolhouse long. It was after dark, and I was still in my gear, talking with a member of our platoon. I think his name was Wermine. Suddenly, we heard the distinct sounds of a firefight out in the bush, and the sky lit up with explosions and red and green tracers. The CO came running out of the command bunker and hollered for an LT, probably Lieutenant Roberts, to round up as many men as quickly as he could, because one of our patrols had been hit by enemy fire.

Within two or three minutes he had eight or nine men, including a medic, and we departed by the east gate, double-timing it down the road. The LT put me on point. By this time, the gunfire had ceased. Two or three hundred meters outside the gate, I heard someone running down the road toward us. It was Howard Toy and someone chasing him. I took aim but that second guy was screaming "No fire! No fire!" with one hand raised in the air. It turned out he was a Vietnamese Popular Forces soldier.

Howard ran past me and right into the arms of the LT, who stopped him. The medic quickly came forward, laid Howard down on the road, and checked him out. Howard had an eye out of its socket and his face and neck were covered in blood. The medic gave him a morphine injection and proceeded to put his eye back in its socket and cover it. This all happened in a space of about two minutes.

The LT then ordered us on toward the ambush site. As we started to move again, I heard someone else running toward us. I stopped and raised my weapon. It was Sergeant Ramirez. When he saw us, he started screaming, "They're all dead! They're all dead!" He ran right up to me and stopped. The LT came over and started asking Ramirez questions. When the LT asked him if he was wounded, Ramirez replied something like, "I don't think so, but I did feel something hit my back." I looked and saw what appeared to be a bullet lodged into the back of the PRC25 radio he was carrying. After determining that Ramirez was okay, the LT ordered him back to the schoolhouse and we continued on toward the ambush site.

When we turned off of the road onto the trail where the ambush occurred, we quit double-timing and moved cautiously forward. Someone came up with a night vision scope and checked out the area up ahead. He saw no signs of movement. We proceeded forward again and soon found the first body on the hooch-side of the trail. There was another body two or three feet from the first body, and there were still tripwires laid across the trail.

On the rice paddy side of the trail, which had a berm that was about two feet above the rice paddy, there was a row of small banana trees. I went up the trail until I didn't see any more trip wires, but next to a banana tree was a body that turned out to be Sergeant Guild. There were no other bodies further up the trail. Someone else from our small Reaction Force discovered the last three bodies on the rice paddy side next to the banana trees. I didn't know who they were. I stood guard next to Sergeant Guild's body, watching the trail coming toward us. Others in the Reaction Force checked the hooches and the small wooded areas beside them.

I believe we were waiting for a slick to retrieve the bodies, but my memory of the timeline is dim. When the slick did come, there were four of us in two-man teams ordered to load the bodies. I know me and another guy loaded two or three of them onboard. The clearest memory I still have is the disgust I felt at the door gunner who was trying his very best not to touch the bodies, especially Sergeant Guild's. He gave us no assistance whatsoever. Meanwhile, the other door gunner was doing all he could to help, trying to carefully arrange the bodies, and not caring about the blood or mud that inevitably got on his own clothing. After the slick left, the LT collected us, and we withdrew carefully but quickly back to the schoolhouse.

My memories of the next day, March 15, are not as sharp. I remember going back to the ambush site again. I believe we went with two or three squads. As I recall, there were two or three hooches at the ambush site, and we relocated the occupants and all of their belongings to another small village four or five hundred meters down the road. We then conducted what I would now call a "forensic investigation" of the ambush site.

The VC ambush had been laid out very well. They placed four wires across the trail and lightly buried them. They were not tripwires but wires to be pulled. Further up the trail, they had placed three wires on top of the trail, very loosely. These also were not tripwires but wires that were placed so that the squad would discover them and stop in place. Every small banana tree along the trail had a NVA grenade attached to it and the wires were to pull the pins out of the grenades. The VC knew that when the firing started, our squad would take cover on the paddy side of the trail, since the low dike would provide protection from machine gun fire coming from the hooches and woods next to them. When the firing started and the squad reacted as expected, the VC began exploding the grenades attached to the trees. Only four of them actually detonated, one of which killed Sergeant Guild. Three of the grenades didn't, and we found them, still live, tied to the trees during our investigation.

You probably don't want to publish this, but two other things happened that day. The Brigade Commander visited. When he flew out, we had a new company commander. Also, after completing our investigation of the ambush site, we burned the now empty hooches, not as retaliation, but so they couldn't be used by the enemy for another ambush. That's about all I remember about the 15th unless someone releases some other long-buried memories in me.

Mike Franklin Wrote: I didn't go on the ambush patrol because I had an earache; but afterward, I went out to help. We found Howard Toy on the road coming back. He was pretty messed up. Nobody wanted to be the one who took him back, so I said I would. On the way, he told me George Cook had been killed. This hit me hard, because George Cook, Howard Toy, and myself had been like brothers over there. We still feel that way today. On the way back to base, I felt someone was behind us and turned around. I almost opened fire on a Vietnamese Ranger who was following us. I never reported this as I was still shook up over the losses we had that night.

Larry Nyland Wrote: I saw Howard Toy come back into the perimeter, covered with blood and yelling for another weapon to go help his friends. That night was a rude awakening for all of us in Bravo Company.

Howard Toy, Continuing: When I was finally released from the 24th EVAC at Long Binh and returned to my unit, I wasn't sent back to the field in the same capacity. They gave me a security clearance and put me to work in the Battalion S-2 Intelligence office for the rest of my tour. My new job involved going out in the field on occasion to help gather intelligence, but I no longer was required to go out on ambush. When I got home, I had five months left on my enlistment. I was an E-5 by then and they assigned me to be an instructor at the Fort Ord machine gun range.

In May 1967, two months after the ambush, Staff Sergeant Leroy Guild was awarded the Silver Star, posthumously. In part, the official citation reads:

"... Sergeant Guild was leading a patrol near the village of Binh Chanh when his men began to receive intense machine gun, small arms, and grenade launcher fire from a platoon size force of Viet Cong... Observing that his men were pinned down by the fierce enemy fire, he courageously moved into the line of fire in order to direct the patrol and administer first aid to the wounded. With complete disregard for his personal safety, Sergeant Guild exposed himself to the enemy while firing his grenade launcher at their positions in an attempt to cover the evacuation of the wounded. He continued his valiant efforts until he was mortally wounded by fragments of an enemy grenade."

In June, I was awarded the Bronze Star with "V" for Valor, which reads in part:

"... Specialist Toy was assisting the machine gunner. Although suffering from painful facial wounds, Specialist Toy, without regard for his own safety, immediately assumed the position of machine gunner and continued to place effective fire on the insurgents. After firing approximately two hundred rounds, the machine gun jammed... Using his M-16 rifle, he continued to resist the enemy until he ran out of ammunition. He then threw his last two grenades at the advancing Viet Cong..."

In addition to the Bronze Star with "V" and the other more routine Vietnam service ribbons, I received a Purple Heart, a Combat Infantryman's Badge, and Expert Badges for the M-14, M-16, and M-60. After I was discharged in April 1968, I returned to college and completed my BS Degree in Quantitative Analysis at Cal State Northridge and later my MBA at the University of Redlands, becoming a computer programmer and manager

at Rockwell International, Boeing, Pratt and Whitney, and United Technologies as my division was bought and sold by those aerospace firms.

Now, my wife and I enjoy travel, camping, cycling, and babysitting our grandson. I have also been involved in setting up four Bravo Company reunions for everyone who served in the unit from 1966 to 1970. Other than some shrapnel that was never removed, and some Agent Orange-related disease issues, I've been very fortunate to have survived since my Army service.

WALT BRINKER'S WAR

U.S. Army 1st Lt and Platoon Leader: A & B Companies, 2nd Battalion, 503rd Infantry 173rd Airborne Brigade, Dak To and Tuy Hoa, 1967; Captain, MACV Mobile Advisory Team IV-39 in Vinh Long Province, 1968–69; and Company Commander, C Company, 2nd Battalion, 7th Cavalry, 1st Cavalry Division, Tay Ninh, 1969

My father was a career Army officer, a member of the West Point class of 1939, and a WW II Veteran who commanded an 8-inch artillery battalion in the epic battle to seize the big Ludendorff Bridge over the Rhine at Remagen in March 1945. My boyhood heroes were my father and Audie Murphy. After the war, my family moved around to a lot of U.S. Army posts, from West Point, where Dad was a professor of economics, to Fort Leavenworth, Kansas; Paris, France; Carlisle Barracks, Pennsylvania; Fort Sill, Oklahoma; and Alexandria, Virginia, where he worked at the Pentagon. In 1962 I was admitted to West Point, graduated in the class of 1966, and was commissioned an infantry officer. After Airborne training and Ranger School, most of my class were assigned to troop duty where we learned how to work with NCOs and soldiers before being sent to Vietnam.

More than 100 in my West Point class were in Vietnam as platoon leaders within one year after graduation. I arrived in June 1967, assigned as a rifle platoon leader in A-Company, 2nd Battalion, 503rd Infantry, 173rd Airborne Brigade, the "Sky Soldiers." They were the first US combat brigade to arrive in-country. The brigade's combat battalions were up at Dak To in the Central Highlands, where the mountainous

terrain was covered with triple-canopy jungle infested with leeches, thick bamboo, very aggressive mosquitoes, and the North Vietnamese Army, the NVA. I had been in Vietnam a week, waiting to go through the unit's 5-day in-country orientation, when the company I was assigned to suffered heavy casualties in a battle with a larger NVA unit: 76 killed, including all the platoon leaders, two of whom were West Point classmates I had seen the week before. This confirmed that we were playing hardball, and I had better focus on being the best platoon leader possible.

Arriving at Dak To, I saw the burned, scarred side of the mountain where air strikes had tried in vain to help my company, survivors of which had since been withdrawn and were assigned as perimeter defense for the fire support base. It was monsoon season, and by the time I reported to my company commander that night in his small hex tent to be briefed on his SOPs, I was soaking wet and muddy from setting up my hooch in the driving rain. As I left that meeting and went back out into the darkness and driving rain, I recall telling myself, "This is going to be a long (bleeping) year."

A week or so later, my newly reconstituted company was sent out on a "shakedown operation." Jittery from the earlier catastrophe, the CO ordered us to form a perimeter on a ridgeline when the lead platoon encountered enemy. C-Company was also in contact a kilometer or so away, and 105-millimeter artillery was firing in support. One of its six howitzers fired two rounds by mistake right into my company's position. The first round came screeching toward my platoon and landed ten feet away, killing three of my men. Their squad leader and I heard it coming and we flopped safely to the ground just before it impacted. Seconds later the second round landed in the middle of the company perimeter killing and wounding several more and severely wounding the company commander. In spite of this incident, I later became a big fan of close-in artillery support and used it often.

My first big firefight occurred near Tuy Hoa, after being reassigned to B Company as part of a major reorganization, while on a platoon patrol in heavily vegetated high ground overlooking another fire support base. During that fight, which seemed to last forever, one of my squad leaders, right next to me, was shot between the eyes and killed. I killed the shooter with a couple of hand grenades. After the fight, my troops told me they approved of the way I had led the platoon; this was huge positive reinforcement.

My last big battle on that tour was on November 12, 1967, one of the early fights during the major, infamous "Battle of Dak To." My platoon position was coming under attack, but I couldn't determine whether my soldiers on a forward observation post (OP) had come back into our position. Since I didn't want my men to fire until I knew the OP was in, I scampered toward them to bring them back. My radio operator (RTO), Art Fleming, then shouted that the OP was in, but their radio had been shot out. He also told me that there were five NVA soldiers in a bomb crater just outside the perimeter ahead of me.

About that time, I saw those NVA raise their AK-47s above the edge of the crater and spray fire toward my platoon. My preferred solution was to have the squad leader closest to the crater handle the problem; however, the extreme and unprecedented din from all the gunfire and explosions didn't allow any voice communication. So, I figured it was going to be my "showtime" – the reason the Army paid me "the big bucks."

The bomb crater the NVA were hiding in was surrounded by scraggly bamboo and about twenty feet from me. I would have preferred to lob grenades over the bamboo at them. However, grazing incoming machine gun fire about a foot above the ground would have hit me, and throwing the grenades in low risked bouncing them off the bamboo. So, Plan B! I told two men to my left to cover me while I crawled closer to the crater and intended to flip grenades into the crater through the small gaps in the bamboo. I was about halfway there, when a mortar round, certainly NVA, landed two feet to my left, splattered my left side with shrapnel, and wounded the men who were there covering me.

My RTO, responding to a call from my company commander, told him I was seriously injured and needed a medic. Somehow my platoon suppressed the enemy fire and drove them off. Since my legs were OK, I was able, with help from the medic, to stumble back to cover behind a thick, felled teak tree.

A major artery on the left side of my neck had been severed. The medic saved me by clamping it. I later learned I had lost two quarts of blood and the plasma injected via IV tube prevented my going into shock. I also had a "sucking chest wound," treated by placing a piece of plastic sheet over the wound to seal off air loss, and by laying me on my left side to enable my right lung to function without also filling with blood. Heavy enemy fire prevented bringing in a Medevac helicopter for an hour, until Air Force fighter-bombers arrived and plastered the enemy positions.

Meanwhile, I stayed down behind the tree, as enemy bullets ground into it, and spoke with the company commander by radio. My main concern was that we would be overrun, and I would not be able to defend myself. Luckily that didn't happen. When the first evacuation helicopter arrived, several litter cases were loaded aboard behind the pilot and I was jammed into a tight space sitting next to the door gunner. As we lifted off, he was firing his M-60 machine gun, and green enemy tracer rounds zipped past us. It was quite a ride! A sad note: the medic who saved me was killed the next day.

At 71st Evac Hospital, the surgeon, Doctor Kurris, removed my spleen and one third of my pancreas, tied off my severed left neck artery, and left me with an impressive array of surgical scars on my neck, lower and left chest, shoulder, forearm, and buttock. The back of my left hand is still partially numb.

They made me stay in Vietnam until my fever went down. That was followed by two more weeks at the 249th General Hospital at Camp Drake in Japan before I was flown to Walter Reed Hospital in DC and allowed to go home on convalescent leave. Christmas 1967, with my family, was my best ever. I had survived and apparently would recover okay. But as I walked around shopping centers before Christmas, my mind remained on that battlefield. I couldn't comprehend the stark contrast between the mall and the jungle, and I remember thinking what boring lives all these folks led.

The Army had a policy to ban service in Vietnam for personnel without a spleen, which is a blood filter, because it makes one more susceptible to malaria. I was dejected about the policy and briefly considered a career as an FBI agent. My family lived in the DC area, so while on convalescent leave from Walter Reed in January 1968, I went to the FBI Building there and got a tour, followed by an interview, which told me that the facet of the Army I enjoyed most, leading others, would not be a big part of being an FBI agent. Luckily for me, the Army revoked this policy shortly afterward since too many were abusing it. I was thrilled, and the rest is history!

After a few months of reflection and recuperation as a general's aide in Hawaii, I volunteered to go back to Vietnam. I knew I had performed well under fire, but I had a nagging question about whether I had lost my nerve. I didn't think so, but I needed to see if I could still "ride the horse"; also, I had acquired a great set of combat skills and I wanted to continue to contribute and save lives. I did come down with malaria in Hawaii but recovered quickly. Thirteen months after being seriously wounded I was on my way to Vietnam for my second tour.

However, shortly before I returned, tragedy struck: my best friend, David Brown, was killed in Vietnam. We had been Ranger buddies and had known each other since taking the USMA entrance exams in high school. We became best of friends and were roommates for a semester. We stayed in excellent physical condition and knew we would be assets to each other if times got tough – especially in Ranger School, and they did. On one especially cold night in the mountains, we stopped and were allowed to rest for a couple of hours. We decided to snap our ponchos together and stay warm by wrapping them around both of us to help retain our combined body heat. Well, it was so dark, and we were so exhausted, hungry, wet, cold, and shivering, that we couldn't agree on how to snap the ponchos together, or even line up the snaps. We nearly came to blows over whose poncho was reversed and why the other was taking so long – before we finally succeeded and grabbed a few shivering winks. But we both earned our Ranger tabs.

Both Dave and I became infantry platoon leaders in the 173d. We feared no evil, "because we were the toughest 'muthas' in the valley" – just like the cartoon on our door at

West Point had said. In Vietnam we learned about our own mortality as we saw others around us killed. I lasted six months before that mortar round got me Medevaced from Dak To. Dave survived Dak To and extended his tour so he could command a rifle company in the 173rd. He was killed doing that job on September 7, 1968. News of any classmate's death was dreadful, but Dave's hit me hardest.

His funeral was held at West Point, and I attended. The viewing was at a funeral home in Highland Falls, NY, just outside the Academy. As I looked through my tears at his still, peaceful form in the casket, I noticed that something was wrong: his Army Green uniform included his medals – two Bronze Stars with "V" for valor, two more for service, two Purple Hearts, a CIB and jump wings, but there was no Ranger tab or 173rd patch. I asked his father whether he minded if I went to the PX or clothing sales store to get the missing insignia so I could pin them to Dave's uniform. His father did not object, so I went on post to find them, but could not because the facilities were closed for the day.

I had traveled to the funeral in my greens, since airlines let us fly at half fare if we were in uniform back then. The only convenient source of insignia for Dave's uniform was my own greens; so, I cut off my own Ranger tab and my 173rd patch with the Airborne tab, and gently pinned them to Dave's uniform in the casket. I said to myself, "I'll be damned if I'll let Dave rest in peace without a Ranger tab and 173rd patch on his uniform." Since my Ranger buddy Dave had played such a key role in my earning that coveted Ranger tab, I figured giving him mine was the least I could do!

After the funeral, I traveled back to Fort Lewis, the only time during the rest of my

career that I did not wear a Ranger tab while in uniform. I felt a little naked, but I didn't mind. And every time I visit Dave's grave, I get a special feeling, besides the sadness, since an important part of me will be with him always.

For my second tour, I was assigned to MACV Mobile Advisory Team IV-39 in Vinh Long Province in the center of the Mekong Delta in the far south of the country. The work there wasn't very exciting, and I was an advisor, not a commander – which I wanted to be, but I probably contributed more there to our national objective of empowering the South Vietnamese to defend themselves. Nevertheless, after six months, I transferred to the 1st Cavalry Division as commander of C Company, 2nd Battalion, 7th Cavalry in Tay Ninh Province north of Saigon toward the Cambodian Border. I had just turned 25, and I was the "Old Man." My radio call sign was "Pony Teams 6." Best job I have ever had.

After I had been there a month, with several tactical successes, my battalion commander made it a part of the orientation for all new company commanders to spend three days with me in the field. My job was to explain to them my thought processes every step of the way. Now, that's having your boss's confidence! My successor, who came from 1st Cavalry Division G-2, told me that they heard intercepts of NVA Radio traffic advising units to "Beware of Pony Teams," a sure sign that we were doing our job well.

After my second tour, I reflected on all this, and I felt like a king. I accomplished exactly what I wanted. For me, this was huge. I went on to have a fulfilling Army career while marrying and raising five great kids, retiring from the Army in 1990 as a lieutenant colonel. But nothing could match my time and experiences in Vietnam. Still can't. Awards from my Vietnam service include a Silver Star, two Bronze Stars with V, two more Bronze Stars for service, a Purple Heart, and the Combat Infantryman's Badge, the CIB.

Forty years after Vietnam, during a reunion of my 1st Cav company, two former privates walked up to me independently with their wives and said to me: "Captain Brinker, I just wanted to tell you that you were the reason I finished my tour." That's priceless!

West Point's class of 1966, and those just before and after, served in Vietnam as lieutenants and captains during the height of the war 1966-1970, and our classes suffered the most casualties. Thirty USMA '66 graduates were killed there. Many military combat Veterans, as well as civilian first responders, suffer from some sort of PTSD or depression. I'm no doctor, but I have a general antidote to PTSD and depression: Be a habitual giver; thus, have a purpose.

To make a difference and ward off PTSD and depression, I perform roadside assists free-of-charge as a hobby – well over 2,000 since I began doing this in 1980. I wrote a book, *Roadside Survival*, then set up a website to enable driver education teachers to train drivers to prevent and contend with breakdowns; also to train law enforcement officers to perform safe, quick, simple roadside assists to win hearts and minds of the public as they help themselves therapeutically deal with PTSD and depression.

I still have skin in the game. Three of my sons are US Army soldiers on active duty. All three were in special forces. Two still are; the third is now an Army aviator. All three served multiple combat tours in the Middle East. All of them told me that the reason they are in is because they were proud of me. They wanted to do something exciting and that made a difference. I would do it all again!

DENNIS GRIFFIN'S WAR

Royal New Zealand Infantry Regiment, Radio Operator, Victor 2 Company, Nui Dat and Phuoc Tuy Province 1967–68

There are two reasons I am alive today. One is the relationship I developed with my God and the other is my wife. Without her, I would have committed suicide many years ago due to PTSD, the physical effects of Agent Orange that I have suffered through, and the rejection by my country because I was a combat soldier in Vietnam. I realize that American and Australian soldiers also had problems after they came home, but not nearly as severe as we New Zealanders were subjected to. Memories remained bitter for decades, and our first semblance of a national reconciliation did not come until our Tribute Parade in 2008.

In May 1965, our government made the unpopular decision to send a small contingent of troops to Vietnam because of our mutual defense treaty with the US and Australia. That initial complement of troops was the 161 Artillery Battery, some engineers, and a medical unit. In 1966, that was followed up with one and then two infantry companies from our regiment based in Malaya, which had been fighting communist guerillas for years. I was part of "Victor 2," a 180-man rifle company, all professionals, all regular army volunteers, all well-trained in jungle warfare, which was deployed to Vietnam in May 1967. Our unit was ethnically and geographically diverse and included 35% native Maoris.

I spent two years in a technical high school and quit at the age of 16 to become a military cadet. After that, all recruits went through a 10-week Basic Course, after which we were selected for our branch. In my case, that was the infantry, which meant a second ten weeks of intense, specialized small-unit infantry training. Those who passed were assigned to a specific infantry company and to six more months of intense jungle warfare training in Borneo and Malaysia. Only then were we allowed to volunteer for Vietnam duty, and we went over as a well-drilled infantry unit, not as replacement soldiers.

When we arrived in Vietnam, our first base was the "Horseshoe," in the Phuoc Tuy Province of South Vietnam, southeast of Saigon near the coast. The base was called that because of its shape. I enjoyed the Horseshoe and felt safe there, but only five days later we received our first contact. There was a main road at the base of the hill leading to our camp from a village. During the day we manned a roadblock, controlling the traffic on the road; but at night, the Viet Cong ruled the area, murdering people at will. It was not uncommon to find the bodies of local villagers at the bottom of the hill, tied up with barbed wire. Over the next five years, more than 1600 New Zealand soldiers served in the nine rifle companies that rotated in and out of the country. We spent our time out in the bush, engaging in a constant round of jungle patrols, night ambushes, and cordon-and-search operations. Our days would begin before first light and end long after dark, often running 12 to 14 hours.

In early January 1968, we left the Horseshoe and moved to our new base at Nui Dat, which became the ANZAC headquarters for the remainder of the war. It was well-fortified, laid out with good accommodations and many comforts not present at the Horseshoe. From Nui Dat, our patrols were primarily long-range ones. We would be flown into the bush and left for three to four weeks at a time, setting ambushes on the main infiltration routes the enemy used throughout the Province. Then, we would return to Nui Dat for rest, resupply, and refitting until required again.

For me, my memories of Vietnam were of slowly walking through the jungle hour after hour with sweat pouring out of me, aching shoulders, and occasional contacts with the enemy. We were well-trained in water discipline, and I only drank on the hour. After my experience in Borneo I always carried an extra water bottle at the bottom of my pack, just in case. Others could choose to drink as they needed; but without regular supplies of water coming in by helicopter, they would have been in trouble.

I must admit that after 50 years, my recall of the events is sometimes confused. However, what I do vividly recall are the events that meant something to me.

On our first patrol from Nui Dat I learned God does answer prayers. We were making good progress when we received a message over the radio that we were in danger of being cut off by the enemy. We had to force-march to a pick-up point, so I whispered a quick prayer. I was amazed to feel my fear dissipate and a great sense of peace take its place. I don't remember being afraid again because I had no fear of dying. If I was killed, I would go to a God who loved me. And if I lived, He would stand by me throughout my life. I believe that being a Christian made me a better soldier, able to do my job without constantly being afraid of being killed, and that in turn made me a more efficient instrument of death. I did not hate my enemy, but I intended to kill him or her if I could. And after we heard how the Viet Cong women treated captives, if I was being attacked by a man and a woman, I would shoot the woman first. During my tour, I took part in the killing of 52 people and am not ashamed of it. I was a soldier and a soldier is trained to kill, if need be.

When it came to casualties, it was the Australians who did the most damage to my company with "friendly fire." On one patrol, we had been out for a week and stopped to make camp for the night. As usual, our artillery liaison would have the Australians fire-test their mortars. In that way, if we were attacked, they could use those settings as aiming points. Things were progressing normally that day until an Australian mortar round landed in the midst of us. That was followed by four more before they could be stopped. One round landed in front of a large tree I was lying behind. The blast picked me up and slammed me back on the ground. I shakily looked around and saw my corporal grab his arm and fall into a depression in the ground. I rolled in after him and saw he had shrapnel in his arm. That gave me a chance to practice my first aid skills, and I put a ring bandage on him. Still, the Australians put four of us out of action that day, more than the Viet Cong did during our tour.

On another night, we were camped beside a trail. Two of us were posted in front of the rest as a listening post or ambush, waiting for someone to come down the trail so we could blow them to bits. I raised my hand in front of my eyes but couldn't see a thing, except when the fireflies flashed in front of me. It was quite nerve-wracking. After thirty minutes, the soldier with me couldn't stand it anymore and scuttled back to the safety of the others, leaving me alone out there. He was never disciplined for this and I never trusted him again.

We had sporadic contact with the enemy on patrol. One time we were fired upon, and as we rushed toward the spot, I became tangled in vines and couldn't move. I was a sitting duck; but before the enemy could kill me, he was killed, and I knew God was protecting me.

Another time, an Australian unit had stumbled across a base camp full of NVA and had come under fire, suffering heavy casualties. We were sent in to relieve them and as we approached, at night, we could see fighter planes whooshing over our heads and firing rockets into the enemy camp. The Australians withdrew and we braced ourselves to attack, but for some reason it was called off until the morning. Only another soldier can understand how I felt, lying there, waiting for the sun to come up. We knew we were going to attack in the morning, and we might be killed. I don't know how others handled it, but it was time for me to reaffirm my faith in God and prepare myself to possibly die.

When the morning arrived, we lined up with about six feet between each man and walked slowly forward into their camp. I can still see myself moving forward, holding my rifle, ready to fire. We came to a suspicious-looking bush and threw two grenades into it. It was the first time I had thrown a grenade in combat and it went off with a dull sound, not at all like you heard in the movies. But we soon discovered that the enemy had pulled out during the night, leaving only a few wounded behind. They were in a bunker and I felt disgust as other soldiers threw in grenades and fired flares into their hiding place. That didn't stop until our officers came over and restored order. I can understand this release from tension, but I realized the veneer of civilization was very thin on all of us.

As we swept on through the NVA camp, I heard gunshots in front of us and saw an enemy soldier lying on the ground. It was standard policy to not approach a body until two more bullets had been put into it. The Americans lost men from VC fanatics pretending to be dead. This was done, but I was glad I wasn't the one who had to do it. The body was removed, and our perimeter was expanded, but I found myself positioned next to a pool of blood and gore which I continued to smell for many years afterward. We searched the camp; but before we left, someone hung two enemy bodies in a tree for the enemy to find. The war had become personal.

Another incident that stuck in my mind for many years was when a New Zealand soldier was killed. His body, along with the enemy who killed him, was waiting for a chopper to fly them back to base when we received word that the enemy's body was no longer needed. We buried it but didn't bury it deep enough, and by the next day it began to smell. This was another odor I found hard to forget: the sweet smell of decaying human flesh.

It was on our last patrol before going home that we saw most of our action. It was during the Tet Offensive in February 1968, and we were sent to block enemy reinforcements coming down the Ho Chi Minh Trail. This was tough, because I knew if I survived, I was headed home. Until then, I had not given much thought to surviving; but when we started on this operation, we all knew it would be our last.

We had been fired on during the afternoon, with a bullet going through the pack of our CO, Major Worsnop. Another round killed a young observer from the British Army who was serving with us. All in all, after many months in the bush, it was a tired group of soldiers who set up camp for the night. The area was rocky, making it impossible to dig in, so we built low walls of stone around us for protection. My partner was the same one who ran out on me while we were on sentry duty those months before. And since our wall had to be propped up with sticks, I looked around for better protection. Beside me was a large stone, so I decided if needed, I would go behind the stone rather than stay with my trusted mate. Today I know that wasn't right, but back then it seemed like the sensible thing to do.

We placed an anti-personnel mine in front of us, had laid the plunger between us, made our evening meal, and settled down for sleep. We always got up before dawn so as to be ready for an attack. That morning we heard noises coming toward us, and realized it was the enemy. We were surprised by all the noise they were making and found out later it was at least a company of North Vietnamese who had spotted us and were moving in. Their pathfinders had laid vines down on the ground along the trails leading to our positions, and their troops were following them in the darkness.

One of our officers came over and asked if we had the plunger ready. I had it in my hand and was surprised when he told me to press it. I must have looked stupid because he repeated the order, so I pressed the plunger and all hell let loose. The officer disappeared; I grabbed my gear and threw myself down behind my rock.

It is strange what you do in moments like that. I remember thinking to myself, "This is where you stand and fight." I felt no fear, took out my double-sided machete, plunged it into the ground at the ready, and fired my first shots as the enemy passed in front of me. The main enemy attack came where one of our machine guns was placed. The gunner swiveled it from side to side, keeping his head below ground level. He must have been placed at the right location, because most of the enemy casualties were killed there in front of him.

The whole action didn't last very long before we heard the enemy retreating. We found fourteen NVA bodies out there, but we knew they always carried most of their dead and wounded away with them. We advanced beyond the bodies and searched the area. I knelt beside a large, dead, well-built Vietnamese whose foot had been blown off by machine gun bullets. He looked fit, well-fed, and strong. My last memory was of stacking him with the other bodies in a heap, to be left there for the enemy. I found a blood-soaked neckcloth and notepaper with lists on it, which I kept for many years.

One day, after I returned to Nui Dat from Vung-Tau, I met my platoon returning from a patrol with silent voices and serious faces. I asked why, and they told me they had been on ambush duty and caught a group of villagers carrying supplies to the Viet Cong. The ambush had been set off and the villagers were decimated. What upset the guys most was when they heard female voices calling for mercy, but they knew they were still very danger-ous and had to fire another volley into them. I'm glad I wasn't on that patrol.

One very impressive experience I had was moving from one valley to the next because an American B-52 strike was expected there. We were on one side of a mountain range, could hear the bombs strike, see the pressure waves rise above the mountain, and imagine what it would have done to us if we had been caught in the middle of it. Another unforgettable experience was watching a napalm bomb explode, tumble, and cascade fire as it exploded over an enemy position.

I suppose it was experiences like these that increased my feeling of being different from most men in my generation. How many had seen bodies piled in a heap, been shot at, or been the hunter of men? These are unique experiences that only soldiers can relate to.

The debate over Agent Orange chemical poisoning has gone on for years in America and in New Zealand. I saw large planes slowly spraying the area around the Horseshoe, I waded through defoliated tidal swamps, and we had large blowers operating near our quarters spraying chemicals in to kill the bugs. The other danger of contamination came from helicopters that blew up large clouds of dust and debris from contaminated vegetation and soils. I was diagnosed with sarcoidosis, an inflammatory illness with no known cure. The latest evidence of a link to Agent Orange comes from an American decision to grant a War Pension to a sailor with sarcoidosis who experienced dust contamination while serving in the area.

During my tour in Vietnam I decided to stay on in the Army and submitted my papers. I didn't see those papers again until we got home, but by that time I had changed my mind. My faith in the Army had taken a severe battering during Vietnam.

The first episode was when I heard that a corporal at the edge of a rice paddy called to his men, "Follow me!" He was halfway across before he realized he was by himself. It may have been a silly decision on his part to try to cross an open field like that, but what upset me more was that his soldiers were never disciplined for disobeying his order.

The next episode was when we went to an artillery base, where we stayed for ten days. I looked around and saw my sergeant, who was forty years old and an experienced Veteran who could still run around with us with a pack on his back, was talking to a young officer who had just gotten off a chopper and looked to be only eighteen years of age. That was when I realized I wouldn't want to obey his orders.

It was a progression of events like that which made me realize it was time to get out. When I was handed back my papers to sign for another re-enlistment, I refused to sign them. That was the beginning of my problems with authority that have plagued my life ever since.

Six months after arriving in Vietnam we boarded a plane and I got my last view of the country as the sun descended behind the hills. It was not long before we arrived back at Terendak, our base in New Zealand, ready for some leave.

Was I right to go to Vietnam? I believed so then and I still do today. When we got home, like many Veterans I faced an ongoing, uphill fight to get the compensation and medical treatment I had earned from my service. On top of that, we were shown great disrespect from the government and many citizens for obeying orders and fighting in a war that they didn't like. The personal sense of betrayal which I have struggled with ever since comes from being rejected like that by my own country, and from the way the Americans and us betrayed the Vietnamese people and abandoned them to their fate. We should have won that war and blasted the Communists in North Vietnam off the face of the earth. I have believed for many years that the only good Communist is a dead one, referring to the card-carrying, dedicated Communists, not the people who lived under their system.

ED BURKE'S WAR

U.S. Marine Corps, Lance Corporal and Radio Operator, Golf Company, 12th Marines and Bravo Company, 4th Marines, 3rd Marine Division, Phu Bai, Camp Evans, and I Corps 1967

My Vietnam War lasted all of 17 days. It garnered me three serious bullet wounds, two Purple Hearts, eleven months in military hospitals, and one leg two inches shorter than the other; but despite all that, I grew up in the Marine Corps. My family had moved around a lot. By the time I was seventeen years old, I had only finished eighth grade and was jobless. I decided to follow a friend into the Marines, but my parents insisted I join the Air Force, where they thought I could learn a trade. So that's where I went. Even today I'm ashamed to say that I washed out of Air Force Basic as "Unable to adjust to military life," and found myself back home.

For the next few years I worked as a roofer in Miami, restaurant worker in New Orleans, and tree trimmer in Houston, until I finally got my act together. I passed a high school equivalency correspondence course and GED test. But by 1966 the Vietnam War was heating up and I felt guilt-ridden by my Air Force failure. I went to see an Army Recruiter and was told the only way I could enlist was to petition the Draft Board to change my Draft status to 1-A. I wanted to go into the Army for Airborne and Medic training or into the Marines for two or three years. All those quotas were filled, but the Marine recruiter said if I signed up for four years I could be on the bus in a couple of days, so that's what I did.

In the LA recruiting office, the senior Marine gunnery sergeant grilled me. If I couldn't make it through Air Force Basic, how did I think I could make it through Marine

Corps boot camp? I told him I was a changed man and wanted to make up for my Air Force failure by becoming a Marine. In the end, he said the Marines would take a chance on me.

I asked for the infantry but was trained to be a field radio operator instead. In October 1967 I arrived at Phu Bai and reported to Golf Company, 3rd Battalion, 12th Marines, 3rd Marine Division. When they outfitted me, there were no M-16s available. Being the "new guy" they gave me the choice of an M-14 or a .45-caliber pistol. Not being too bright, I opted for the 14-pound rifle with its extra bandolier of six magazines. The very next day Lt. John Dawson came to the communications tent and asked if I wanted to replace the radio operator on his Forward Observer team. I jumped at it, and that afternoon we headed north to an ARVN Artillery Base near Dong Ha to coordinate artillery as part of Operation Fremont. The next day we went to Phu Bai, assigned to Bravo Company, 1st Battalion, 4th Marines. We moved to their base at Camp Evans (but not before I unloaded the M14 for a

.45-caliber pistol) and spent the next couple of days humping on company-sized sweeps.

After a week with no contact, on October 25 the Marines launched Operation Granite, which was "search and destroy" sweeps of Hills 674 and 300 in Thua Thien Province west of Hue. It was known to be the Regimental HQ of the 6th NVA Division and the 800th NVA Battalion. Hill 674 had been bombarded with artillery and naval gunfire several days before we began our ascent. That operation resulted in 25 Marines Killed in Action and 110 wounded, 88 of whom had to be Medevaced. On October 27 alone, the second day of the battle, 13 Marines were killed, including Lieutenant Dawson, and 31 men were wounded, including me.

I wanted to reconstruct that day and clear my fading memory, so I turned to the Command Chronology of the battalion, testimonies of the men who were there, and three Silver Star Citations earned during the battle.

Here is how it unfolded. Three companies were sweeping, and Alpha Company was blocking, with the objective of driving the NVA into a vice. Our Forward Observer Team was attached to Bravo Company, and we were climbing up the left side of Hill 674. At 11:36 a.m., an estimated 6 to 10 NVA ambushed us. We only had one man wounded and called in an artillery strike without any results. We regrouped and continued our climb until we were ambushed again three hours later. We called in another artillery strike and killed one NVA. Someone tied a rope to his body and rolled him over, in case he was booby trapped, but nothing happened. The CO then ordered him tied to a tree with a "Compliments of

Bravo 1/4" sign pinned to his chest. I remember standing there looking up the hill into the jungle, thinking if someone was watching, they weren't going to like it. It was a premonition of bad things to come.

The trail was narrow and steep, and we were strung out in single file as we continued the climb. Up to that point, our FO Team had traveled with the command group in the middle of the company; however, because of the hit and run pattern of the ambushes, Lieutenant Dawson decided to move us forward on the next contact, so we would be in a better position to spot targets. Big mistake! We were ambushed again 20 minutes later. This ambush was three-sided, across the ravine separating Hill 300 from Hill 674, above us and in front down the trail. It began with small-arms fire to our front that took down our point man, PFC Verne Johnson III. Lieutenant Dawson and I ran forward to about 15 meters from the point and took cover behind a rock outcropping as the firing increased.

An NVA machine gun that was located on the trail ahead opened up on us, and more rounds came flying in from across the ravine from Hill 300 to our left. One of our fire teams rushed forward toward the machinegun. Their lead man made it abreast of me before taking a round in the gut. He landed next to me and a second man fell near my legs. Our Corpsman, Kenny Stommes ran out, dropped to his knees next to him, and was reaching for a dressing when I saw him blown backward by another enemy machinegun burst. We couldn't call in artillery because we had helicopters in the vicinity. I had abandoned the M-14 by this time, so I did what I could with my .45-caliber pistol, emptying it until it jammed. I had the Lieutenant give me his while he handled the radio, but his .45 also jammed – a useless weapon in that situation anyway – leaving me with nothing but a couple of smoke grenades.

The Marine who had fallen next to me was still alive and writhing in pain. I reached for his M-16 and took a round through my left hand, from the base of the thumb through the center of the palm and shattering the M-16. My hand was completely numb and the hole in my palm looked as if it had been made with a spike. I tucked my hand in my armpit to stop the bleeding and tried to calm the guy lying next to me. All of a sudden, he screamed, "I can't take it anymore," and rolled away. I never knew whether he made it or not, but when I turned back toward Lieutenant Dawson, he was gone too. I later learned that he crawled back to confer with the CO, but the enemy gunfire was too heavy for me to follow him.

It was very difficult for me to piece together everything that happened that day, but I think I've got it.

Sergeant Tom Jacobs, who led one of our Bravo Company fire teams that day, later told me, "I lost two men in my four-man team running up the trail to get the machine gun, plus my best friend, our Corpsman Kenny Stommes, Second Lieutenant McClavey, who was shot in his left side, and another Marine who was shot in the head. The NVA across the ravine missed me but hit a nearby Marine numerous times in the lower torso."

As we lay on the trail, another friend, Vince Matthews from White Plains, N.Y. ran past us and fired three LAWS – anti-tank rockets – into an enemy bunker that lay beyond the dogleg to the right of the trail.

Three of our men were awarded Silver Stars for that day's fighting. The Citation for Lance Corporal Hackett read, "...in the initial moments of the attack, the platoon sustained several casualties and was temporarily pinned down. Although painfully wounded himself, Lance Corporal Hackett unhesitatingly directed a heavy volume of assistance for the wounded men who were lying in an area dangerously exposed to enemy fire. Leading several Marine companions and a corpsman to where the injured lay... he rendered medical aid to one Marine and then courageously assisted him to a covered position. Fearlessly returning to the hazardous, fire-swept area... Lance Corporal Hackett continued to fire his weapon and succeeded in killing several enemy soldiers before he was mortally wounded by enemy fire."

The Citation for Lance Corporal Vince Mathews read:

"In the initial moments of the firefight, the company sustained several casualties and was pinned down. Realizing the seriousness of the situation, Lance Corporal Mathews unhesitatingly ran forward, ignoring the enemy rounds impacting around him, and accurately fired his light antitank assault weapons into the enemy positions. Observing an enemy machine gun that had pinned down several of his comrades, he fearlessly maneuvered across the fire-swept terrain and fired another anti-tank round into the bunker, killing the enemy soldiers and destroying the emplacement. Having expended his supply of ammunition, Lance Corporal Mathews returned to his unit's position, obtained additional light anti-tank assault weapons from his wounded comrades and repeatedly ran forward to deliver accurate suppressive fire upon the hostile forces. On one occasion, he was attacked by a group of enemy soldiers. Steadfastly maintaining his position, he calmly fired his weapon, killing one enemy soldier and forcing the others to flee. When his company began to withdraw to a more defensible position, Lance Corporal Mathews, fearlessly exposed himself to the intense hostile fire, seized a machine gun and skillfully utilized it to cover the movement, delivering accurate protective fire."

I was wounded a second time late in the afternoon when I caught shrapnel or a ricochet in my right forearm. Sometime around dusk, I was wounded for a third time when I took a bullet through my right mid-thigh, shattering the bone and taking bone and tissue out through a 12-inch exit wound. As luck would have it, the round only nicked the femoral artery, otherwise I would have quickly bled to death. I didn't call for a Corpsman since I realized if they tried to reach me, they would probably be killed like Stommes had been. So, I lay there going in and out of consciousness and shaking violently from shock and loss of blood. My hand was mostly numb, but every muscle twitch in my leg brought on spasms of excruciating pain. I remember thinking I was going to die. I also remember a sense of panic when I realized my only weapon was a smoke grenade.

I recall feeling some rocks land on my leg and hearing a voice say they were pulling back. That was when I yelled, "Hey, I'm still alive out here! Can someone help?" With that, two guys ran to me. "Give me your hands," someone said. The next thing I remember is being surrounded by faces as a corpsman splinted my leg with a sapling hacked from a nearby tree. I was repeatedly dropped and dragged as they carried me down to the LZ, and I later woke up on a pitch black LZ.

Another Bravo man I just heard from, Mike Thompson, told me, "I was the Senior Line Corpsman with four other aids. Kenneth Stommes was the only corpsman KIA that day. You were in bad shape when I reached you. You had been pinned down for about six hours, being one of the first ones hit. I reached you about two hours after Lieutenant Dawson was calling for air support. He got hit, and then Captain Ross was hit in the back, leaving him paralyzed. I ran out of morphine on you, after having given you four shots in two hours."

Years later, I also got an e-mail from Bob Lascher, who told me, "I was one of the guys who helped carry you and Lieutenant Dawson down the Hill after the ambush during Operation Granite. You, my friend, were not very happy with the clumsy Marines who tried to carry you down that slippery trail. I knew you were hit bad in the leg. You grabbed me by the throat, and later apologized, but I remember telling you, 'It's okay, we're going to get you out of here.' That was a tough day for all of us."

I remember being put on the Medevac chopper and then being pulled out and rolled under bright lights before I lost consciousness again. I woke up in the hospital ward in Phu Bai, or maybe it was Danang, in a whole-body cast from high on my chest down to my toes, with a cast on my left hand up to the elbow, and with bandages on my right forearm. My CO, Captain Ross, was in the next bed. He told me Lieutenant Dawson covered him with his body. In doing so, Lieutenant Dawson took a round in the shoulder and died on that hill from loss of blood. Lieutenant Dawson was later awarded the Navy Cross for his action that day.

For me, the ordeal was just starting. I was asked where I lived so they could send me back to CONUS to a Navy Hospital nearest my home, which was San Diego or Long Beach. Instead, they sent me to the Naval Hospital in Oakland. When I asked if there was a hospital closer to my home, I was told, "Oak Knoll Naval Hospital is the amputee center for west of the Mississippi, and that was the closest they could get with my leg wound."

The telegram to my parents said my "condition and prognosis were good," but it was delivered by a Marine Casualty Officer the same day I arrived at Oak Knoll Naval Hospital, on November 7, ten days after being wounded. I have little recollection of those days except being in constant pain and being awake only briefly between morphine shots. I don't know why they delayed my family notification. Maybe they were waiting for my condition to stabilize. It never did. In the hospital, I developed a rampant leg infection, barely survived pneumonia, and had a blood clot in my lung on Christmas day. Another embolism from my infected leg a month later set me back again. Oak Knoll was laid out with a series of long, barracks-like buildings on a hill, connected to one another by an outside walkway. You knew you were getting better when they moved you down the ramp to a lower barracks. And you knew you were getting worse if they moved you back up the line. In the first months, I ping-ponged up and down the ramp a few times. It took a dozen or more surgeries to save my leg, but I wasn't planning on being a long-distance runner anyway. After ten months of multiple leg and hand surgeries, I finally walked out of Oak Knoll on two legs, aided by a cane.

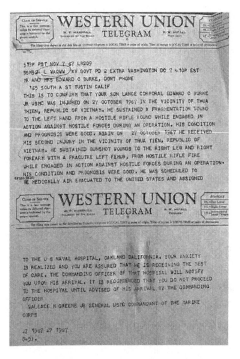

I lost some of the use of my left hand, and my right leg was two inches shorter than it had been, with extensive muscle loss and circulatory issues. I have a prosthetic knee and a dropped foot to top it off. Inevitably, the tilt of the skeletal structure to one side as a result of the shorter leg creates havoc in the back leading to spinal deformities. Overuse of my right hand causes problems with that hand and shoulder as well. After 51 years, my left hand is still frequently ornamental rather than functional and I have trouble standing or walking for any length of time. On a lighter note, while in the hospital recovering, I had a surprise visit by the Everly Brothers singers and a couple of Playboy bunnies. Governor

Ronald Reagan and his wife Nancy also came by and signed my scrapbook. Unfortunately, I was in surgery at the time.

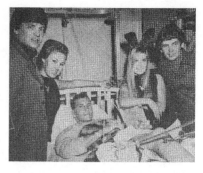

Looking back on it, some of my proudest achievements were finishing Marine boot camp after washing out of the Air Force and being awarded two Purple Hearts and a Combat Action Ribbon (CAR) on the same day, 27 October 1967. The Purple Hearts made me a second-generation combat-wounded and disabled Veteran after my paratrooper father at the Battle of the Bulge.

While recovering in Oak Knoll, the VA administered a battery of tests that suggested that I would be an A student if I pursued a college degree under the Disabled Veterans Vocational Rehabilitation Program. That came as a surprise, since I only had an eighth grade education and a Florida State GED. That September I was Medically Retired from the Marine Corps and discharged from the hospital. I immediately began taking classes at the local community college before transferring as a junior to the University of California, Riverside for a BA and MA, and went to Princeton University for a Master of Public Affairs. My job focus became working with the disabled or with Veterans.

In 1974, out of grad school, I went to work for the Washington State Vocational Rehabilitation Department. Six months later I was appointed to be the State Director of Veterans Affairs, the youngest in the country at that time, and probably the first who was a Vietnam Veteran. After that, I held multiple finance positions with hospitals and health systems in New York City, California, Louisiana, and New Jersey, co-founded a telecommunications

start-up in Alaska, was CFO of a Medical Center in Scotland, GM of a computer system start-up in Japan, worked for the Koch administration in NYC, and for a multinational foundation in London.

Surviving combat and its aftereffects required self-discipline, persistence, and the determination to overcome, which the Marine Corps taught me. I was "Gung Ho" and carried that spirit to do well into college and then on to my jobs. I still spit-shine my shoes. As Director of Veterans Affairs in Washington State, when Vietnam fell in 1975, I was appointed co-director of the state Vietnamese refugee resettlement program. We resettled more than 1500 refugees in Washington, and I personally supervised the selection of those we resettled from Camp Pendleton in 1975. My interpreter was an ARVN Master Sergeant named Binh Doung, who earned a US Bronze Star in the Chu Hoi program and was wounded three times. My wife and I became sponsors of his family of six. He continued working as an interpreter for the Washington State Social Service Department until he retired a decade or so ago.

My second wife, Judy, is a Vietnam Gold Star widow, whom I married in the chapel at Camp Pendleton in 1994. Her first husband, Petty Officer Third Class John Gilliland, was a Seabee who was killed in a C130 crash near Danang in October 1967, the same month I was wounded. John is interred at Arlington near the Tomb of the Unknown. He was attached to the 3rd Medical Battalion at Khe Sanh and was on his way home on a flight from Danang to Saigon after an 18-month tour. Judy and I toured Vietnam in 1994 on our honeymoon. Neither she nor I had any PTSD ghosts to excise on that trip, just a curiosity about a place where a life was lost and another saved. We were treated with smiles in the South and stares in the North. Not many Americans had visited there at that point in time. The Citadel in Hue was a definite trip highlight along with Ha Long Bay in North Vietnam. The Citadel still bore all the bullet holes and scars from Tet that were soon to be repaired by a UN grant.

The VA has treated me very well. They gave me 48 months of cost-free education and increased my disability rating as my combat-related injuries worsened. Starting at 60%, I rose to 80% in the in the 90s to 100% in 2009 when because of frequent outpatient care, I couldn't hold down a full-time job. All in all, aside from orthopedics, I am in pretty good health and enjoying my retirement in New Mexico.

CHARLES "DOC" PICKARD'S WAR

U.S. Navy, Hospital Corpsman Second Class and Senior Corpsman, M Company, 3rd Battalion, 4th Marines, 3rd Marine Division, "Leatherneck Square," Con Thien, and Cam Lo, I Corps, 1967–68

I grew up in Billings, Montana, and attended Eastern Montana College from 1962 to 1964, and the University of Montana from 1965 to 1966. In July 1966, I decided I didn't like my major and ran out of money. I knew if I dropped out of college I'd get drafted into the Army, but I didn't want to go through six years of reserve meetings; so I enlisted into the Navy to get into medical training and to qualify for the G.I. Bill so I could finish college when I got out. There was a doctor in my family, so I thought I'd try medical training. I knew that the Navy provided the Corpsmen, or combat medics for the Marine Corps. So, after I finished Hospital Corpsman training, I figured that was where I'd probably be assigned, because of the high casualty rate they were having. No surprise, after I finished Corpsmen "A School," which was like Army AIT, my orders came down and I was assigned to Mike Company of the 3rd Battalion of the 4th Marines.

I arrived in Vietnam in December 1967 and spent the next twelve months, basically all of 1968 as a front-line platoon combat medic in "Leatherneck Square" just south of the DMZ up in I Corps. That included places like Mike's Hill, Khe Sanh, Hills 552, 689, 471, 542, and many more that a lot of Marines will remember, because we were up against hard-core NVA regulars and we experienced some of the heaviest fighting of the entire war. The battle at Mike's Hill, where we lost many Marines, was actually the kick-off of the Tet Offensive of 1968. From March 1967, before I arrived, to February 1969, just after I left, the Marines lost 1,419 men killed and 7,563 wounded.

Many of the Marines and Corpsmen who I got to be friends with ended up killed or wounded; and every one of them was significant to me. Some I could help, but others I couldn't. Some of their wounds were so bad that they were beyond any medical help. That was a life-changing experience for me, to be sure!

On January 18, 1968, my Mike Company was acting as a blocking force during a sweep in the "Marketplace" area near Con Thien. We were told to get online and assault a bunker complex, but the NVA opened up on us with small arms and mortars. The mortars were coming in, hitting everywhere among Mike Company's line, and I found myself crawling from one Marine to another treating each wound as quickly as I could. A squad radioman near me took a direct hit with a mortar round that peppered him with shrapnel. As I was running to him, another mortar round hit four feet to the side of me just as I was diving on the ground, and I was wounded by the explosion. I got up and another Marine and I tried to help a wounded Marine to a bomb crater when an AK-47 round hit my helpmate in the leg. All three of us ended up on the ground, wounded, and we had to belly-crawl the rest of the way to the bomb crater. After treating all the wounded, I looked down and saw I had been hit in the hand and right leg with shrapnel. I pulled the piece of shrapnel out of my hand myself, but I had to have help to treat the leg.

On January 27, the battle of "Mike's Hill" kicked off the Tet Offensive in 1968 in our area. I had been there a little over a month when the NVA attacked our company at 0530 with a reinforced battalion. We were set up in our usual "night defensive positions" and fought them from daylight to dark. A 105mm howitzer air burst flattened about ten of us against the side of the hill, and we lost Second Lieutenant Burns and one Marine who was hurt very badly. He had lost a lot of blood, and I stayed up throughout the night pumping IVs and morphine into him until we could get him out in the morning.

There were only two Corpsmen from 1st Platoon on top of the hill that day, Hospitalman Cruz and I, and we were overwhelmed with casualties from the get-go. The first group of four I got to were US Marine scouts who were attached to our unit. All of them had bullet wounds. When I finished with them, I slid down the hill to help a sergeant with a sucking chest wound. He was lying in a small fighting hole and the NVA had us zeroed in. They continued to fire at us as I was trying to move him to cover on the back side of the hill. That was when an "ammo humper" saw my problem and came over to help. As soon as he arrived, he was hit in the leg with a bullet. He and I continued working up the hill from wounded man to wounded man, under fire, until he was hit in the back with yet another bullet. I began treating both of his wounds, until he saw his gunner get hit, ignored his own wounds, returned to his machine gun, and opened up on the NVA with the M-60.

I returned to the sergeant and managed to carry him about half-way up the hill, when four Marines with a poncho came scrambling down the hill to help. We put the sergeant in the poncho and started back up the hill, when one of my new helpers was shot in the butt and two others were hit in the arms. That only left a lance corporal and me who had not been hit, but we did manage to make it to the top with the wounded.

The next guy I reached was a first lieutenant who had been badly mauled in the groin. I was trying to pump an IV into another man at about that time when the bottle was hit by a bullet, and other men were now being brought to me with multiple wounds. After I did what I could for that group, I came upon Hospitalman Dale Cruz, who had been hit in the back of the neck and leg with bullets. He was in bad shape. I knew he needed an immediate emergency Medevac out, so I put him on my back and carried him to the LZ.

Returning to the back side of the hill, I ran into a Marine major, who took me into 3rd Platoon's lines to tend to guys who had been hit at 0530. We worked there all day, until about 1700, when we began putting the bodies of Marines who had been killed on 6x6 trucks heading for Camp Carroll. As we then moved into our night defensive position, the 105 airbursts hit us. I carried a small notebook, and wrote down everyone I knew that had been hit, by name, service number, rank, etc. I think I wrote down 31 names for the 27th of January.

Corpsmen are a close-knit brotherhood and some of the Corpsmen who impacted me the most that year included:

Hospitalman Cecil Belt, who was killed on his first combat patrol. He was a nice guy and recently married. He was writing a journal and wrote to his wife all the time. When I learned of his death with Lima Company, I almost lost it. All his hopes and dreams were gone. What a tragedy.

Hospitalman Third Class Larry Wells was killed by artillery. I had thought we were going to be good friends, but after the explosion I couldn't even recognize him. By the time I got to him and began working on him he was already dead. All I could do was move on to the next wounded Marine.

Hospitalman Dale Cruz was another Corpsmen who was wounded on Mike's Hill from gunshot wounds to the back of his neck and his leg. I was able to stop the bleeding and carried him down Mike's Hill to a CH-46 helicopter for a Medevac.

The 3rd Platoon Corpsman – I didn't know his name – was wounded in the leg on Mike's Hill. He lay there untreated all morning until I was able to get to him in the afternoon.

Hospitalman Roderick was wounded at Cam Vu from a shrapnel wound to his head. I dressed it and put him on a tank headed back to Cam Lo Bridge. On the way back, the tank hit a large mine and blew all the wounded off the tank onto the ground.

We were at Dai Do when we were air lifted into the battle to help the 2nd of the 4th Marines and the 1st of the 3rd. I saw a shirtless disoriented troop crawling out of the bush. I went to his aid and found he was out of his mind. I checked his dog tag and discovered he was a Corpsman from the 1st Battalion of the 3rd Marines. We could not get a Medevac flight in to pick him up because all Marine resources were maxed out. After three pleas, an Army gunship answered but said he could only pick-up one man. They landed and I belted the Corpsman to the machine gun and the bulkhead so they could take off. I never knew his name or what happened to him afterward.

Hospitalman James Cruse and I were getting to be good buddies until he was killed from a gunshot wound to the head by a sniper. He was dead when I got to him.

Hospitalman Second Class Mercer was another Corpsman with whom I saw a lot of combat until he was also killed from a gunshot wound to the head by a sniper. He was dead when I got to him.

Hospitalman Third Class Don "Doc" Ballard and I had been in heavy fighting all morning. The battle kept changing and we had lots of wounded Marines to take care of. Don and I met up trying to save the life of Corporal Planchon. As we worked on him, an NVA grenade landed at the feet of the corporal. Planchon's feet took most of the blast, but that saved Don and me. When we finished with him, we moved back to our fighting hole. We were only there a short time when we heard the "Corpsmen Up" call again. This time, it was Doc Cruse and I who ran down the hill. We began treating a new Marine, until Doc Cruse was shot by a sniper and killed. When I finished with my guy, I climbed back up to the fighting hole.

Doc Ballard was there, and shortly after I returned, the "Corpsman Up" call came again. Now it was his turn to go and he ran down the hill into the brush. It wasn't very long before I looked out and spotted him, but he was moving very strangely from side to side. I ran down the hill and could immediately see he was in trouble. I found him in shock, with blood coming out of his ears, internal injuries, and shock from the blast from an NVA Chi-Com grenade. I stripped him naked, checked him out, treated him for shock, and started an IV. I even had to use his own medical supplies because I was totally out. As I was gathering his gear, I discovered a large piece of grenade shrapnel had torn into his Unit One Corpsman's bag. After I had done all I could, I carried him up a very steep ravine and another steep hill to get as close as I could to the LZ, where I was able to get him on a Ch-46 helicopter before I returned to my fighting hole.

I never found out what happened to Don until I met up with him at a 3rd Battalion of the 4th Marines Reunion in Seattle in 2001, over thirty years later, and learned he received the Congressional Medal of Honor for his actions that day, May 16th of 1968. His Citation reads:

For conspicuous gallantry and intrepidity at the risk of his life and beyond the call of duty while serving as an Hospitalman Third Class with Company M in connection with operations against enemy aggressor forces. During the afternoon hours, Company M was moving to join the remainder of the 3rd Battalion in Quang Tri Province. After treating and evacuating two heat casualties, Hospitalman Third Class Ballard was returning to his platoon from the evacuation landing zone when the company was ambushed by a North Vietnamese Army unit employing automatic weapons and mortars and sustained numerous casualties. Observing a wounded Marine, Hospitalman Third Class Ballard unhesitatingly moved across the fire-swept terrain to the injured man and swiftly rendered medical assistance to his comrade. Hospitalman Third Class Ballard then directed four Marines to carry the casualty to a position of relative safety. As the four men prepared to move the wounded Marine, an enemy soldier suddenly left his concealed position and, after hurling a hand grenade which landed near the casualty, commenced firing upon the small group of men. Instantly shouting a warning to the Marines, Hospitalman Third Class Ballard fearlessly threw himself upon the lethal explosive device to protect his comrades from the deadly blast. When the grenade failed to detonate, he calmly arose from his dangerous position and resolutely continued his determined efforts in treating other Marine casualties. Hospitalman Third Class Ballard's heroic actions and selfless concern for the welfare of his companions served to inspire all who observed him and prevented possible injury or death to his fellow Marines. His courage, daring initiative, and unwavering devotion to duty in the face of extreme personal danger sustain and enhance the finest traditions of the U.S. Naval Service.

Of course, not everything that happened to us over there was life-and-death serious. Humor had its place, and funny events helped us keep our sanity.

Corpsmen were in charge of field sanitation, which meant we had to supervise "burning the shitters." Those were the half-barrels that sat under the latrines to collect waste. They were to be pulled out and burned every day. That job was usually given to the "FNGs," or new guys. One day, all the guys assigned showed up except one PFC, who was a "no-show." I called down to his squad leader, and then to his platoon sergeant to get this PFC to report for his assigned detail. Finally, he trudged up the hill wearing his gas mask. He never said anything to anyone; he just took his E-tool, opened the back of the "shitter," and pulled out the half-barrel. He dumped fuel on the contents, lit it, then stood back, still not talking. When the detail was completed, he walked down the hill, still wearing his gas mask, until he got down to the bottom. Finally, he took his mask off and walked away. From beginning to end, he never said one word. I guess he didn't care for his assignment.

And not everything we did was treating war casualties. At Cam Lo Bridge we were allowed to run clinics and perform civic affairs humanitarian work for the locals. They would bring their sick and injured children and babies to the gate for Corpsmen to treat. I would bring bar soap to the children. That would often clear up many of their skin infections.

Of the medals I was awarded, I am proudest of the Vietnam Cross of Gallantry with Bronze Star, because I was recommended for it by my squad leaders for a string of firefights we survived. We had a lot of KIAs and many, many WIAs. I also received the Navy and Marine Corps Achievement Medal with Combat "V." This was what we called an "end-of-tour medal" for my performance during all of 1968 with 3rd Battalion of the 4th Marines. The problem we all had up there in I Corps with medals was that we could never keep a platoon leader alive long enough to write up the guys who deserved them. Even if they did, the papers had to be signed and pushed up the chain of command by someone, usually the company clerks, and there were too many deserving Marines and not enough clerks to get it all done and push it. I also received a Marine Corps Medal for saving the life of my Mike Company Commander.

After Vietnam, I was assigned to the Sere school on Whidbey Island, Washington,  for one and one half years as a survival instructor. As my enlistment was coming to an end, the Navy was offering a three-month "early out" for Vietnam Vets. I jumped on it. I was happy to get out, but the Marines forced me to grow up. It taught me how to adapt and improvise throughout my life both in business and personally, but I had other things I wanted to do with the rest of my life. I moved back to Montana, resumed college, and finished my degree. I decided not to go on to Medical Service School and rejected an offer to work for Air America as a Survival Instructor. There was talk about a Physician Assistant program that was being started at the University of Washington, which people said I should look into, but I enrolled at the University of Montana instead, finished my degree, and graduated with a BA. I accepted a job with 3M Company. I worked for them in Montana,

Tennessee, and Oregon before I retired at age 57 in 2001. I moved back to Montana and now spend my time with family, church, hunting, fishing, and the Marine Corps League.

Author's Note: if there was ever a story about the inconsistency of the way medals and decorations were given out in Vietnam, perhaps in any war, this is it. The guys who really deserved them and were in the worst fighting, were rarely in units where anyone had the time to write them up or push them through the bureaucracy. Clearly, Charles "Doc" Pickard, like so many other Corpsmen, Combat Medics, and Medevac pilots, is one of them. He deserved a whole lot more honors than he received for the many lives he saved in those battles at great personal risk.

JOE WRIGHT'S WAR

**U.S. Marine Corps, Sergeant E-5, Field Radio Operator and
Forward Observer, C Battery, 1st Battalion, 11th Marines, and
Battalion Landing Team (SLF/BLT), 3rd Battalion 1st Marines, Quang Tri,
Dong Ha, Qua Viet River, Camp Carroll and Danang, 1967-1969**

I graduated from high school in Overland Park, Kansas, in 1965 and enlisted in the Marine Corps the next year, in August 1966. My family made me go to college, which I tried for a year, but to no one's surprise, that did not work out. I had barely graduated from high school, so college wasn't going to work. I'm not sure why I picked the Marines. My mom begged me to go in the Air Force, but I couldn't because of my vision. Over the years I have been asked many times why the Marines. My normal wise guy answer was "to beat the draft." My father was in WW II and my grandfather was in WW I. Both served in the Army.

I went to boot camp in San Diego and graduated in October 1966. I was assigned my M.O.S, 2531, Field Radio Operator, completed ITR, and then went off to radio school. After completing radio school, I was assigned to Marine Corps Air Station Beaufort, South Carolina. While there, I attended several more schools on the AN/TSC-15 truck mounted radio and on GMST, both at Camp Lejeune.

In July 1967, three of my buddies and I volunteered to go to Vietnam. In September we went back to Camp Pendleton for Advanced Infantry Training, ITR. On October 10, 1967, we arrived at Danang in South Vietnam. We didn't have specific assignments when we landed. We had hoped to stay together, but that was not to be. We were each assigned to different units. Mine was 1st Battalion 11th Marines, an artillery unit. I rode in the back of a six-by-six 5-ton truck

from Danang to Quang Tri, just north of Hue, and was placed with Charlie Battery. My main job was to communicate with the Forward Observer radio operators in the field and coordinate info between them and our guns so they would have accurate artillery support. When not on radio duty I helped load and fire the artillery. I also at times went out on patrol of our perimeter.

On November 19, one day after my 19th birthday, I volunteered to be transferred to the Special Landing Forces, or SLF. I was chosen partially because I had been trained to call in naval gunfire support. I volunteered because I had been communicating with Forward Observers and radio operators in the field for a while and it seemed like something I should be doing instead of being back at the artillery battery. Around Thanksgiving, we were sent to Subic Bay in the Philippines for additional field training. Upon my return to Vietnam, I was assigned to SLF Battalion Landing Team, BLT, in I or India Company, 3rd Battalion, 1st Marines. We were placed on the USS *Valley Forge*, a Landing Platform Helicopters, or LPH, a converted aircraft carrier.

Our first mission, Operation Fortress Ridge, was scheduled for December 21, 1967. I was assigned a Navy lieutenant as my forward observer. Early on, my radio was a PRC-10 but I soon carried a PRC-25. The weapon issued to me was an M-16. The early M-16s had a tendency to jam due to the sandy conditions. Later and for most of my tour, I carried a .45-caliber pistol. In addition to the radio, I carried an extra battery, a couple of mortar rounds, a poncho, up to a three-day supply of C-rations and five or so canteens of water.

We took CH 46 Helicopters from the ship to a landing zone on a beach about 100 meters or so from the edge of the jungle's tree line. We jumped a small distance from the chopper to the beach with the intention of getting to the tree line as soon as possible. What we didn't know at first was that we were under heavy fire, both from small arms and mortars. We couldn't hear anything because of the noise from the chopper's engines. Within seconds we knew we were in trouble. Guys were getting hit and mortars were going off all around us. We were crawling in the sand trying to get to the tree line when the guy in front of me took a direct hit from a mortar. Welcome to Vietnam. For the next four days we were in combat. I did my job, calling in artillery, air and naval gunfire support. We returned to the ship on December 24, 1967, after losing men: nine killed and seventeen wounded, including my Lieutenant.

The unit was scheduled to go back to the field on Operation Badger Catch on December 26, 1967. The day before, on Christmas Day, I came down sick. I was diagnosed with malaria and transported by helicopter and ship to the hospital at Cam Ranh Bay, an Air Force base. On January 18, 1968, I was released from the hospital 20 pounds lighter and sent back to the USS *Valley Forge*. I was sent back out to the field with India Company, joining them on "Operation Badger Catch" and then "Saline." Tet, Chinese New Year, was about to start. We were told that several regiments of NVA regulars were coming down from the north to overrun the south. Our job along with others was to stop them. We spent the bulk of our time along the Cua Viet River, a major supply route for the NVA. We were in the field for thirty-seven days straight with no change of clothes and no showers, nothing but C-rations and water. Hardly a day went by that we weren't hit by rockets and ground assaults.

The weather was also a big enemy. In early March, we went to Camp Carol, a base camp, near the river and had our first hot meal. While there we helped provide artillery support for Khe Sanh. We were only there a short time before the camp came under attack by rockets. We pulled out while the attack was taking place and returned to the field and back along the Cua Viet River.

In mid-April, we were at Ca Lu, which was located somewhere between Camp Carol and Khe Sanh near LZ Stud. This was beyond naval gunfire range from the US ships in the South China Sea. The fighting really picked up, but we were getting a lot of replacements. On one of the operations, we were so far north that we were hit with NVA artillery. We had taken a village and it was late at night when we finally settled in. We were tired and we made the mistake of not digging fox holes. At sunrise the NVA artillery attack began. Three of us took cover in a dried-up rice paddy, up against the dike. We were lying head to toe and staying as low as we could. I was on one end of the trench when an artillery round exploded about ten feet from my feet. The concussion was huge. I was knocked unconscious; and when I woke up, my legs were burning like hell. I was sure I had been wounded. As it turned out my physical injuries were minimal, but the other two guys in the ditch were injured and Medevaced out. The barrage continued until our air support arrived. Our CO later told us it was the first time the NVA had been able to reach us with their artillery.

Toward the end of May, I found out I was eligible for R&R. We had now spent over 100 days straight in the field and found out our unit was not returning to the ship. Our gear was sent back to Danang. I did go back to the ship for transportation to R&R in Okinawa. At that time I got my shot card up to date for cholera, typhus, typhoid, and TB.

When I returned from R&R, I learned my unit had been reassigned to the Danang area and was no longer in the Battalion Landing Team Special Landing Force. I was assigned to Lima Company. No more calling in naval gunfire. Those of us who had survived the patrols along the northern DMZ found ourselves in a very different kind of war. We were assigned to a hill about five miles west of Danang overlooking Elephant Valley. We would go out on platoon-sized patrols lasting up to a week, searching supposedly civilian villages for Viet Cong, ammunition, etc. We would find things like that on a regular basis and would then burn down the village and take prisoners. Booby traps were commonplace and awful; and the enemy was everywhere and not in uniform. You could trust no one, women and children included, and the Viet Cong were a fierce and dedicated enemy.

We lost almost half our unit one day to one booby trap. We were later told it was one of our own 500-pound bombs that the enemy had buried. We were on patrol, walking behind a tank. A friend of mine and another guy who had survived all of our battles along the DMZ stepped on it and were killed. We were supposed to walk in the tank's tracks to avoid buried booby traps like that, figuring that if the tank hadn't triggered it, the area must be safe. Turns out I had walked right past it, as did other guys, but my friend must have stepped outside the tracks. I stayed with the battalion on multiple search and destroy operations like that until August 1968, and then requested to return to the artillery battery I was originally assigned to. At first, my request was denied. Then I said I would agree to extend my tour in Vietnam for six more months if I could return to the battery. They agreed to that.

A Marine Corps tour of duty in Vietnam lasted thirteen months. If you extended, that second tour was for six months. My logic was twofold. First, I could get out of the field and go back to the Artillery unit; and second, after nineteen months in-country, when I finally got home, I would not have enough time left on my enlistment to get sent back for another thirteen months. So, that's what I did.

I went home on 30 days "free" leave and returned to 1st Battalion 11th Marines, or "1/11," around September 1968. When I returned, I was told that the radio operator who took my place with 3rd Battalion 1st Marines had been killed by a booby trap.

I was with 1/11 for the rest of my tour. My time there was pretty quiet when compared to my time with the 3rd of the 1st. I even went on another R&R, this time to Hong Kong. At our base, we would regularly get hit by rocket attacks, but it was pretty secure and safe. The bunkers were well-designed and well-built and there were several rows of concertina wire around our perimeter, which did a good job of protecting us during those attacks. Just days before my tour was over, the Viet Cong tried to overrun our base. The battle started after dark and lasted until morning. We were hit with rockets, mortars, and small-arms fire.

When the sun came up there were many Viet Cong dead inside our perimeter and many more trapped in the wire. Our own casualties were minimal.

I went home on June 11, 1969, after spending nineteen months and five days in-country. I went over a Private First Class E-2 and came home a Corporal E-4. My physical injuries were minimal, although I contracted malaria, had been bitten by a dog and had to take rabies shots in the field, and had multiple small injuries; nothing major, however.

In July 1969 I returned to Camp Pendleton, assigned to 1st Battalion, 13th Marines, 5th Marine Division, as a Field Radio Operator. I was promoted to Sergeant E-5 on September 8, 1969, made new friends, and reconnected with some old ones while in California. Unfortunately, since then, I have only remained connected to one. I went home on leave in December and married a girl I went to high school with. We moved back to Oceanside, California, and lived there until I was released from active duty on March 8, 1970. I was honorably discharged on June 8, 1972.

My first few years of civilian life were not easy. We moved back to Lawrence, Kansas, so my wife could finish her last two years of college at the University of Kansas. As we all know, Veterans were not well-received back then, especially not at universities. I struggled with getting along with people. You couldn't talk about the military or Vietnam without being harassed or worse. I was hired by Southwestern Bell Telephone Company and allowed to work part time as a Supply Attendant while I attended KU myself. I went to school for several years using the GI bill, which back them paid $205 per month. Finally, I dropped out and worked full time. I stayed with Southwestern Bell starting out as Installer/Repairman and as a Cable Splicer. I transferred and we moved to Springfield, Missouri, in 1978. I was later promoted to management and remained with them until I took a management buyout in 1992. I continued in the telecommunications business working in sales for a company named RepCom International (RCI) until my retirement in 2017.

My first wife and I divorced but not before we had two great kids. A son and daughter. I am remarried and have been for 20 years. My life is very good.

I have had very good experiences with the VA in Springfield. I was diagnosed with PTSD many years ago and they provide me with good counseling and medications. They also provided me with hearing aids.

In 2015 my mother passed away. I knew that she had saved every letter I sent home from Vietnam. Some of them I remember writing on a C-ration box. After I retired, I took the time to read each one. That was tough. But it helped me put together the things I have written here. I am proud of my time in the Marine Corps. I am very proud of all the men and women who served. I have no regrets.

JOE ABODEELY'S WAR

U.S. Army 1st Lieutenant and Platoon Leader, D Company, 2nd Battalion, 7th Cav, 3rd Brigade, 1st Cavalry Division, An Khe, Phan Thiet, Bon Son, Khe Sanh, A Shau Valley, and I Corps, 1968–69

I was born in Tucson, Arizona, on July 14, 1943, Bastille Day, and graduated from Rincon High School. I went on to receive my undergraduate degree in 1965 from the University of Arizona and was a Distinguished Military Graduate from their ROTC program, being commissioned a Second Lieutenant in the Infantry in 1965. Instead of going right into the Army, I went to law school for a year, winning 1st place in the Fegtly Moot Court competition. I then spent a semester in business graduate school, and finally went on active duty in 1967. It was a somewhat unusual background for an infantry lieutenant. I later wrote a book titled *Dear Mom and Dad, Love from Vietnam,* which earned three Global E book Awards, and the stories below are excerpts from that book.

After the Combat Platoon Leader's Course at Fort Benning, I arrived in Vietnam six months later, in January 1968, just as the big Tet Offensive began. I was assigned to D Company, 2nd of the 7th, 3rd Brigade, 1st Air Cavalry Division as a combat infantry platoon leader. The year 1968 was the bloodiest year of the war. Think *Apocalypse Now* or *We Were Soldiers*, Air Cavalry helicopters, and combat air assaults. President Johnson and his advisors were terrified for weeks that the Siege of Khe Sanh by the NVA would be like General Giap's 1954 Viet Minh attack and victory over the French at a similar base at Dien Bien Phu.

As soon as I arrived, we began relocating from An Khe to Camp Evans further north. That became our primary HQ to operate out of. We were "The Cav" and highly mobile. We didn't have a "base camp" with barracks or even tents to come back to.

Even when we did go back to Camp Evans to resupply and get new men, we slept on the ground with our poncho liners. The vast majority of my "base camps" were wherever I set up my platoon's perimeter defense, in the boonies or on the sands along the South China Sea.

When the Tet Offensive began, the Special Forces Camp at Lang Vei was quickly overrun by the NVA and the Khe Sanh Combat Base was cut off and endangered by intense shelling that began January 21. This photograph shows Khe Sanh from the air. It was an

airstrip cut across a red dirt plateau, surrounded by low mountains, with 5,000 Marines trying to hold it. With the base constantly under fire, the Air Force was forced to devise new methods of resupply. Instead of using parachute drops, they pushed pallets loaded with supplies out the rear ramp of cargo aircraft as they skimmed down the runway without landing. It was called LAPE – Low Altitude Parachute Extraction. It kept the base supplied and operational and was safer and more efficient.

General John J. Tolson, commander of the 1st Air Cav Division developed a three-fold plan for the relief of Khe Sanh, called Operation Pegasus. First, we were to relieve the Khe Sanh Combat Base itself. Second, we were to re-open Highway 9 from Ca Lu to Khe Sanh. And third, we were to destroy the enemy forces within our area of operations. The 1st Air Cav Division, augmented by non-divisional units of U.S. Marines and the Army of the Republic of Vietnam, was perfectly suited to accomplish that mission. Linkup of everyone at Khe Sanh was planned at the end of seven days.

On April 3, my company, with four platoons, moved through dense jungle in a column formation like a large winding snake. I was leading 2nd Platoon, and 3rd Platoon was the point platoon as the company moved out. We heard semi- and fully-automatic weapons fire and explosions up ahead, announcing a firefight was in progress and that 3rd Platoon had made contact. These were hard-core, main force NVA regiments we were up against. The vegetation was thick and rich, and the upturned dirt was soft from the many bomb explosions we came across. They made gigantic craters and were "great, pre-dug foxholes." In a fire fight, you did not see a person shooting at you. In a firefight, it was the bushes that shot at you. And the NVA had a special knack for immediately dragging away their casualties. As soon as we reached their location, even though you knew you hit someone, they had disappeared. It was as though the NVA were ghosts.

A 3rd Platoon NCO was killed when he went to retrieve an enemy RPD light machine gun. The Battalion S-3, the Operations Officer, brought him back and placed him on the ground near me. Before the S-3 set the dead soldier down, the body started regurgitating — the involuntary action of the body after death, which I had never seen happen before. That taught me there is nothing as permanent as death. I often had bouts with internal terror, but I couldn't show fear because I was leading a platoon of about 40 men, trying to keep them alive, and trying to accomplish whatever mission we were given.

Late that afternoon we moved to Hill 242 near Route 9 and set up a company-sized perimeter. We wanted to get resupplied from helicopters; so we began clearing a Landing Zone, an LZ, by wrapping detonation cord, "det cord," around the smaller trees to blow their trunks in two and cut them down. Unfortunately, there were too many trees and we couldn't make an LZ.

As we worked, the NVA moved in and surrounded us in the jungle. Apparently, they did not have the numbers or the will to attack us directly. One of the other units took a "mule," a small, flatbed utility vehicle, to bring our supplies down the road. Unfortunately, they were ambushed, with some KIA; so we didn't get any food or water except for the rainwater we were able to catch on our ponchos, which we tied to trees like funnels. We were mortared that day, and 10 or 11 of my men received minor shrapnel wounds. They were extracted from our perimeter by a jungle penetrator – like a heavy plumb bob dropped down through jungle canopy so a person could sit on it and be lifted to the helicopter. The rest of us made fortifications with some overhead cover.

My Platoon Sergeant and I checked the perimeter, and we heard the distinctive "clank" of the bolt of an AK-47 being pulled back in the jungle outside our perimeter. I yelled, "Get down," and we both pancaked to the ground as the automatic weapons fire chopped the leaves from the trees, which fell down on us. Before we began our push on to Khe Sanh, my platoon had received two new M-60 machine guns. When that AK-47 opened-up, one of my gunners kept spewing automatic weapon's fire from his M-60, which never jammed once. He probably saved my life. Two of my RTOs, my radio operators, were always nearby for commo. That night, I heard the company commander on the radio saying it appeared NVA artillery rounds had landed inside our perimeter but did not explode. He thought they were "duds" or chemical agents; so I lay awake all night thinking I was going to die from a nerve agent.

On April 4, we moved back to where an LZ had been cleared so that 105-millimeter howitzers and our supplies could be brought in by Chinook helicopters. On the way, we picked up the dead and wounded from the "mule" who tried to bring us supplies the day before. We manned the company perimeter and saw more dead and wounded. One Medevac chopper had been shot up, and the platoon leader of Second Platoon in C Company had been killed. I identified with him because I was the platoon leader of Second Platoon in D Company. When I saw the other lieutenant dead, I really personalized it. The NVA were dangerous. In my view, if anyone has been in real combat and said he was never scared — he's simply a liar.

On April 5, I was told that our battalion would make the walk to Khe Sanh the next day. From what I had heard about Khe Sanh and what I had seen, I thought this could be disastrous. The 5,000 Marines there had been continuously shelled and surrounded by superior NVA forces, three divisions' worth with over 20,000 men, who continued to hold on and continued to control the area. We already had a lot of dead and wounded, and I personally had a lot of close calls. As we dug in for the night, we heard jets and helicopter gunships circling the hill we occupied, and artillery pounding the surrounding areas.

On April 6, we tried to walk from this LZ to Khe Sanh, but we had to come back when the two forward companies received effective fire. Our company was supposed to be flown in by air assault to a position 500 meters east of the Khe Sanh Combat Base. I thought going in by foot was a "glory push" to see who could be the first to walk into Khe Sanh, but I hoped we would make it because we had a lot of reporters with us. Some 1st Cavalry Division troops were airlifted to Hill 471, relieving the Marines at this position. Two 1st Cav companies remained on that hill while two other companies attacked to the south toward the Khe Sanh hamlet. The 1st Cavalry forces on landing zone Snapper were attacked by an enemy force, but it was a disaster for the enemy.

Route 9 was still a problem and still had to be cleared to the base. It was the major east-west highway that ran parallel to the DMZ and the 17th Parallel from Dong Ha on Route

1 near the coast all the way west to Khe Sanh through Lang Vei to the Laotian border. My platoon was designated to be the tip of the spear to move up Route 9. We thought we had caught a break by not being point, but the two forward companies were already in firefights with the NVA. We were ordered to go to the road to be picked up by chopper, make an air assault, leapfrog over the other two companies that were already in contact, and continue the mission to clear Route 9. My platoon was on point, again.

On April 7, they landed us near the top of a strategic mountain. As we moved toward the crest, I heard bullets whistle overhead and noticed that the ground we were on offered no cover. It seemed to be solid rock and was too hard to dig into. My point squad radioed that they saw bunkers up ahead and were cautiously approaching them. I got the rest of my platoon in an "on-line" formation, with all of our firepower to the front, expecting a firefight any minute. When we reached the NVA bunkers, we found they were part of a deserted, regimental-size NVA complex with all kinds of Soviet-made weapons, including nasty 4-barreled ZPU-4 anti-aircraft guns, AK-47s, SKS carbines, RPD belt-fed machine-guns, RPK light machineguns, mortars, RPG rocket-propelled grenade launchers, ammo, and commo wire linking the bunkers in the whole area. We also found dead NVA soldiers in bunkers with blood coming out of their ears, the telltale sign of heavy bombing. Still, it was most unusual for the North Vietnamese to leave their dead behind, much less all those weapons and ammunition. It showed how quickly they had chosen to abandon the position.

One of my guys nicknamed "Turtle" found an old French bugle in a trench and tied a parachute cord on it to make a tassel. While putting the cord on it, a cobra snake rose up next to him, and puffed out. He shot it with his personal, unauthorized, .38-caliber, snub-nosed pistol. It came in handy that day. Turtle brought the cobra to show us, stuck on an SKS rifle bayonet. It was a beautiful bluish and sil-ver-colored creature, but pretty much shot up. He must have put all six rounds in the snake. He gave me the bu-gle, which also came in handy later. The area around the bunkers was pockmarked with bomb craters courtesy of U.S. Air Force B-52 "Arc Light" strikes. The jet jocks can brag about how sexy their "fighters" are, but I loved those B-52s.

The hill we were on was about two miles outside of Khe Sanh, and although this NVA bunker complex was abandoned, Route 9 to Khe Sanh still had to be cleared. My platoon was tasked to lead the clearing action and to be the point platoon for the division on the march on to Khe Sanh. I was concerned about ambushes, because the Marines had not been able to move up and down Route 9 for over two months. If the NVA had really left the area, all they had to do was slip over the Laotian border and cross back whenever they chose to attack us. When Lang Vei Special Forces camp was attacked by NVA with tanks in February, the Marine contingency plan to bring a relief force down Route 9 could not be implemented, because the NVA controlled the area.

Now, the 1st Cav was told to open Route 9. As we started down the road, we knew we had to avoid "toe poppers," small, anti-personnel bomblets dropped by the Air Force, and other booby traps planted by the enemy. So, we proceeded cautiously, because we still did not know the real status of the NVA. I had some of my men out 30 to 40 meters on each side to provide flank security, and I kept my RTOs, my radio operators, nearby so I could communicate with whomever I needed to, especially my squads. Our weapons were "at the ready" for the unexpected. We soon discovered that the NVA had strategically built bunkers along the road all the way to the perimeter wire at Khe Sanh, ready to ambush anyone attempting to travel down the road. Inside the bunkers we found NVA backpacks, opium, weapons, and everything else; but the NVA troops had vanished.

The next day, on April 8, my platoon was the first American troops to walk into the Khe Sanh Combat Base in months. We were the 1st Air Cavalry Division relief force, and as we entered the perimeter wire single file, we probably made quite a sight. I was at the head of the column with all my equipment, an M-16 and an AK-47, blowing the cavalry "charge" on a bugle. Once inside, a Marine captain directed where my platoon should set up to provide security along the length of the airstrip. As the *Los Angeles Herald Examiner* reporter wrote on April 8:

"A two-mile victorious march by the Army's 1st Air Cavalry Division formally ended the 78-day Communist siege of the fort that Hanoi vowed it would take and American generals pledged would never be lost. The siege was over but the battle for control of South Vietnam's Communist-infested northern frontier roared on… At Khe Sanh, where round-the-clock Communist artillery fire had driven 6,000 Marine defenders underground, the Leathernecks Sunday whooped it up as Army 1st Lieutenant Joe Abodeely's unit walked the last two miles into the camp. Abodeely, 24, of Tucson, Arizona, and his platoon formed the 1st Air Cavalry spearhead of the 20,000-man Operation Pegasus drive that broke the Communist grip around Khe Sanh in a week-long drive that covered 12 miles of jungle, hills and minefields…"

And General Tolson wrote "… it became increasingly evident, through lack of contact and the large amounts of new equipment being found indiscriminately abandoned on the battlefield, that the enemy had fled the area rather than face certain defeat. He was totally confused by the swift, bold, many-pronged attacks."

On April 8, at 0800, the relief of Khe Sanh was "mission accomplished," and the 1st Cavalry Division became the new landlord. We all knew this was a big deal at the time, because Khe Sanh was all over the press in 1968. The Marines held the "fort" until "the cavalry" got there and ended the siege.

I came back "to the world" in January 1969 after my one-year tour was over. I was awarded a Combat Infantryman's Badge, a Legion of Merit, a Bronze Star, Air Medal, Vietnamese Cross of Gallantry with Palm, and others, and later developed Agent Orange-related prostate cancer and a 50% disability from PTSD. Still, I am most proud of having left Vietnam without losing a man during my entire year's tour.

I returned to the University of Arizona Law School in Tucson in February 1969 and graduated in 1971. The law and the military have been intertwined for most of my life ever since. After law school, I moved to Phoenix and immediately went to work as a Maricopa County Deputy County Attorney, where I worked for a decade and a half while serving in the Arizona National Guard as a Military Police Company Commander and later a JAG officer, eventually rising to the rank of Colonel in the Army Reserves. I found I was suited for an organizational structure having been in the Army, but I loathed politics. I tried cases or obtained pleas involving murder, rape, robbery, assault, child molesting, drugs, conspiracies, RICO, and organized crime, etc. I also learned various skills and became a very competent trial attorney – reading reports, interviewing witnesses, preparing motions and responses, arguing motions, and dealing with judges and juries. I even prepared some of my own appeals to the appellate courts.

I have had the pleasure of serving as the CEO of the Arizona Military Museum since 1980. The museum portrays the military history of Arizona from the Conquistadors to the present and has won numerous awards. The Governor appointed me to the Board of Directors of the Arizona Historical Society, and I continue to spend time advocating for and promoting the exemplary service of our Vietnam Veterans. Many people do not know that two thirds of the troops who served in Vietnam were patriotic volunteers – NOT draftees, and that the U.S. forces won all the major battles. The U.S. withdrew because our Congress refused to resupply South Vietnam as we had promised. The Communists renewed their attacks and invaded Saigon in 1975 – two years after U.S. combat troops left.

The U.S. defense of South Vietnam was reported by biased journalists, not historians; and the media, Congress, academia, and the anti-war protesters misrepresented Vietnam Veterans' service to justify their antiwar views. Five years ago, I wrote my story of my tour in Vietnam, which is available on Kindle.

The year 2018 marked the 50th anniversary of the Tet Offensive when so many young Americans risked or gave their lives, and nobody truly honors all those who served. As a lawyer and a soldier, I know we cannot have laws unless we defend them and the "defenders" of our Constitution and our nation. Remember and honor Vietnam Veterans, before they fade away. Telling the truth about their service would be a good start.

RICH JONES'S WAR

U.S. Army, Captain and Battery Commander, Battery C, 2nd of the 40th Field Artillery, Firebase Nancy, 1969–70

December 24, 1969. Firebase Nancy, just west of Dinh Quan, South Vietnam, was a small village surrounded by stacked boulders the size of houses, and home to Battery C, 2nd of the 40th Field Artillery, a 105-millimeter howitzer battery under my command.

The Christmas ceasefire had started at 6:00 p.m. By 9:00 p.m., without much to do that night except wish that they were home for Christmas Eve, a great depression had set in over my troops. For the first time in many weeks I had all six guns on station. Usually my battery was split into two firing elements of three guns each, many miles apart. I think having all six in one place actually made the depression deeper and darker.

One of the beauties of command is that sometimes you can do screwy things and get away with them. I had been browsing in Matthew's account of the wise men and the Christmas star. On an impulse, I called my officers and gun chiefs together and told them, "Let's shoot up a 5-pointed Christmas star at midnight tonight." The only things we had going against this idea were:

1. There was a theater-wide joint ceasefire in place.

2. A five-pointed star would require ten corners, five on the outside and five on the inside, but we only had six guns.

3. The star would be best with illumination rounds, for which firing tables were scanty, at best. There were no firing tables at all for high-angle illumination because nobody ever fired it that way.

And so we got to work. First, we planned the firing sequence for the six guns. Four would first fire a high-angle illumination round, and then quickly wind down the tubes to join the other two guns with six more illumination rounds fired low-angle. The target would be about five miles out over War Zone D, which supposedly was uninhabited. The target size and altitude were such that the star would be seen at several other US firebases, as well as our battalion and brigade headquarters 15-20 miles to our south. The face plane of the star was designed to face that headquarters to give them the best possible chance of seeing it.

There were no firing tables to establish the time of flight for the high-angle illumination rounds. We had to factor between low-angle illumination and low-angle high explosive tables, and then apply the factor to high-angle high explosive tables. This was really just a shot in the dark, but Colonel Nicholas, head of the Math Department at West Point, who wrote his own textbooks on differential and integral calculus, would have been proud!

These planning requirements made each of the ten rounds have a unique time of firing, as well as unique angles of fire. The whole firing schedule was based on a common "time on target" so that, if things went well, all the rounds would burst at the same time and War Zone D would be resplendent in Christmas joy!!

We rehearsed the firing sequence a couple of times. It was a tight go for the high angle guns, but doable. It was time to let Battalion know what I was going to do.

It pays in life to have an extremely excellent battalion commander. It probably also paid that the brass had been celebrating Christmas Eve their own way in their officers' club before I called.

Rather than discussing the ceasefire, I invited the battalion commander to go outside and watch the show at midnight. He should take his fellow colonels to see the show, I said. Without ever actually giving permission, he ended the call with the unspoken attitude that the show could go on. That was enough.

As midnight approached, ten illumination rounds were set up, all with different time settings on the fuse. Six guns were laid in and aimed in what amounted to six different directions, four of them at high angle. My battery executive officer, a former guidance counselor from inner-city Detroit, was set to count down the time-on-target. Each gun chief knew the sequence for his own gun.

At midnight gun number five roared as the first high-angle illumination round flew skyward. Within fifteen seconds all four high-angle guns had fired and were quickly dropping their tubes for their second rounds. Within thirty seconds, with ten rounds flying over War Zone D, all guns had fallen silent, and once again the joint theater cease fire took control.

The battery exec announced, "Splash!" which meant five seconds to detonation. Five seconds later the most perfect five-pointed star ever drawn appeared in the night sky: large, highly visible, perfectly proportioned, and a complete delight to the artillerymen of Battery C; possibly the best reminder of Christmas ever to emerge from the muzzles of an artillery battery.

For the rest of the night the depression that had prevailed before the star was no more. The troops celebrated and sang well into the night. As the gospel writer Matthew stated, "When they saw the star they rejoiced with exceeding great joy!"

To me, Matthew's story has always been not about the wise men or the gifts, but about the star. Perhaps my attitude is influenced just a bit by the events of Christmas Eve, 1969.

Author's Note: Rich Jones was from Pennsylvania, a 1967 graduate of West Point, and a captain in the Field Artillery. After service in Germany and Vietnam, and an assignment teaching thermodynamics at West Point, in Korea he was diagnosed with advanced Agent Orange-related Hodgkin's Disease. It prematurely ended his military career but led to a 30-year career as a CPA in Oklahoma. Rich wrote this story about Christmas in Vietnam as a part of a collection of stories from the class of 1967 put together by Freed Lowrey. Unfortunately, Rich passed away weeks before that collection was published, so Freed generously agreed to share it in this collection in memory of Rich and the other members of the class who died in Vietnam.

JOHN RUSS'S WAR

U.S. Marine Corps, Sergeant, Aircraft Structural Mechanic, VM02 and HMM163, Quang Tri and Phu Bai, 1968–69

I was born and raised in Huntsville, Alabama, home of the Army's Redstone Arsenal. When I was 18 years old, I graduated from high school in June and got my draft notice that summer. My only job experience prior to joining the military was being a bag boy at our local supermarket. I didn't have much going, but nothing about the Army appealed to me. That draft notice said I was to report on September 7, 1966, so I beat the draft by joining the Marine Corps on Sept 1st.

The day I left for boot camp my parents dropped me off at our local airport at my request. We were a close family and had already said all of our goodbyes. I just couldn't bear any more of my mom's tears. As I sat on a bench outside the gate entrance, one of the girls I had gone to high school with showed up. She had just bid goodbye to a relative and saw me sitting on the bench. This girl was a knockout and I was uncomfortable and nervous when she sat down next to me. As we chatted, she took

my hand and told me how brave she thought I was enlisting in the Marines like that. I remember that part, but with her hand in mine I was so flustered I couldn't think straight. When the loudspeaker announced my boarding call, she leaned over and kissed me! Not a big old wet kiss, just a little one, but warm enough to take an 18-year-old's breath away. Then she smiled and walked away. I never saw or heard from her again but what she did that day gave a young, scared, and insecure future Marine a lot of sweet dreams and he felt braver somehow.

My training began the minute the bus stopped at the USMC Training Depot at Parris Island, South Carolina. We were yelled at, cursed at, pushed off the bus, and told to put our feet on the painted footprints on the asphalt parking lot. I had never encountered such harsh treatment from anyone, and I was VERY intimidated, not to mention scared as hell.

Fast forward eight weeks. I was off to Camp Lejeune, South Carolina, for ITR, Individual Training Regiment as the Marines called it. It was like Army AIT. Then they sent me to Beaufort, South Carolina, for Aircraft Structural Mechanic training, as well as being assigned as a structural mechanic there at Beaufort. I was taught how to rivet, cut, fold, and repair most any type of metal used on aircraft, especially on helicopters. We were taught fiberglass repair also, which became extremely useful later during my service in Vietnam.

One of the corporals in my shop got his orders for Nam in March of 1968 but seeing as how he was an only son and his wife was very pregnant, he was deferred. Somehow, I was chosen to take his place. Our MOS was the same, I believe, so it was an easy choice for the Marine Corps. I had absolutely no desire to go to war, and to be honest, I was pissed about becoming someone's replacement.

I boarded the commercial flight to Vietnam on April 17, 1968, as a 20-year-old E-2 Private First Class. My birthday was the 18th. We crossed the International Date Line and it became April 19, which was when I realized I'd been 21 years old for a whole day and didn't even know it. To this day I brag I never turned 21, since I never lived through that birthday.

After several days in Da Nang waiting for a unit assignment, I was put on a troop truck headed north to the Quang Tri air base and assigned to VMO2, a Marine Huey Helicopter unit, where I met some of the best brothers I had ever known.

Unlike the grunts who patrolled the hills around our tiny base, I pretty much just reported each day to the tent that was our metal shop to patch up and repair bullet and/or shrapnel holes in our Hueys. Helicopter blades were always an issue and difficult to obtain. Without replacements, the birds would be grounded, so it didn't take long for us to figure out a way to repair them. This was supposed to be a big "no-no" at the time. Blades were simply too critical to the helicopter's stability to attempt to patch. That was the thought, anyway; but I always had a very sensitive touch and it fell to me to fill, patch and sand bullet holes in the blades so they looked brand-new.

My final inspection was simple. I closed my eyes and gently rubbed my fingers over the repaired section. If I felt the slightest bump or dimple, I kept sanding. Each repair had to be perfectly invisible to work aeronautically when the blades began rotating at high speed. If they didn't, it would be like a tire on a car that needs balancing; but with a helicopter blade, it could tear itself apart and the helicopter would crash. I'm proud to say we never had any of our blade repairs fail and even made a couple of spares should the need arise.

At Quang Tri, we had a mess hall that stayed open when we worked overtime. We lived in wood-framed "hooches." They had wooden walls up about four feet and screens above with a tent top. One nice feature was that the lower wall was a hinged "kick out" panel. We could shove it outward and roll right into the bunker if we got a rocket or mortar attack. Up at Phu Bai, the hooches weren't built that way with a hinged panel and when the siren went off or we heard the first rocket explode, there would be a mad scramble, and you'd better be fast if you didn't want to be beat up or run over.

We had a really crazy crew chief on one of our helicopters named Ralph. We called him "the Crew Chief from Hell." He was just plain mean. One day, we were having chow and a sniper took a shot at him from across the river. The bullet missed him but hit his food tray and blew mashed potatoes all over him. He got so angry that he got a pilot to take him up and he made a gun run over there. He shot up the bushes and finally came back, sat down, and finished his chow like nothing happened.

One day I was bored and volunteered to fill in as a door gunner on a Medevac helicopter that was short a man. We took no gunfire going out. It was nice and cool, and I enjoyed the view from up there. But we sure got shot at coming back. I almost peed my pants. I kept firing the M-60 at anything I thought looked suspicious. I got no confirmed kills, and I have no idea if I hit anything.

I made a best buddy over there pretty quickly and we hung out together as often as possible. His name was "Butch." He was a Huey helicopter crew chief and a real tough Marine, who loved flying and fighting. Butch was from Chicago, married, and I believe he had a toddler-aged daughter. We had many talks about everything. He was against his daughter marrying my son – if I were to ever have one – because I was white, and he was black. In the end, we just agreed to let them meet and make up their own minds. He and I were that close. There was no doubt that Butch and I would be neighbors when we got home.

One rarely quiet evening, after chow and quite a few "borrowed" beers, Butch and I made a pact. If one of us didn't make it home, the other would sit at a table each Memorial Day with 2 beers. We vowed to remember each other once a year and celebrate our friendship, toasting and sipping a cold beer for each of us.

I had just finished working on a shot-up Huey on the flight line, when I heard Butch's Huey coming in to land. After a while, you could tell the difference between the engine sounds of each of our various helicopters. It was close to lunchtime and unless he was out somewhere flying, Butch and I always had chow together. I was starting to gather up my tools when I heard them: two loud explosions that caused me to look up just in time to see two Hueys banging into each other at about five hundred feet over the flight line. The fireball explosion of their collision made me blink, and in that brief amount of time, I knew my best friend was gone. I ducked behind the Huey I was working on, but the noise was horrendous.

Debris from the two helicopters came down all over the flight line, and I heard a gut-wrenching scream as if it was from far away. It was mine. We searched for hours, but the only part of Butch we found was his boot, which we sent home to his bride and daughter.

It's been 50 years now. On each of the last 50 Memorial Days, I have found a quiet place to sit somewhere with two beers and a little statue I bought years ago and talk with my brother Butch. I still remember his goofy laugh, his dark brown eyes, and I hope that somehow, he knows how special he still is to me. This world is a better place because Butch was here once. So Semper Fi, My Brother.

I served thirteen months in Nam, all on Hueys or on CH34 helicopters. Three of those months were with Marine Medium Helicopter Squadron 362, the "Ugly Angels" on the USS Okinawa, an assault helicopter aircraft carrier. Our insignia was a circle with the face

of a really ugly angel inside it. Some of our guys got together and decided to paint our insignia on the fantail of the ship. Under cover of night and with flashlights, two guys were lowered by ropes tied to their legs and with stencils and spray paint, created a huge "Ugly Angel" right where they planned it. Naturally, the Okinawa's captain was extremely pissed but never found the culprits. He had to order his own sailors lowered over the fantail and to spray an even uglier gray blotch, which was still there when we moved out.

When my tour was over and I rotated back to the States, I had a little over a year left on my enlistment. When we landed back in "The World" we learned firsthand just how unpopular this war had become. We had to walk from the plane, along a roped-off area leading into the terminal. A crowd of civilians lined the ropes, leering, spitting at us, and calling us horrible names. I looked into the eyes of an old gray-haired lady and saw what hate looks like. We had been told to ignore them and keep moving, which is what we did.

Somewhere along the way, my stateside orders were lost, and I was told to report to the Admin Office at the Marine Corps Air Station at Santa Ana. During this visit, I thoroughly pissed-off a young desk jockey who simply didn't like his job or any "salty-ass Flyboys" as he put it. We had words. He disappeared for about half an hour and came back with my orders. I was officially assigned to be the Supervisor of the Mess Hall at the last of the "red line" brigs, which were the jails at Camp Pendleton, CA. No early out, no slack for me. These orders were for the remaining time of my enlistment, until September 1, 1970. The lesson here is never piss off the administration guys. The only good thing to come out of all this was my promotion to E-5 Sergeant in December 1969. And my assignment to the brig wasn't too bad. I supervised inmates as they did the nasty-ass mess hall jobs that were assigned to them. Most of these weren't bad kids, most had been imprisoned for excessive AWOL, Absent Without Official Leave, or desertion.

One young man I met there was called "Pappy" Rimmer. He was from Tennessee, had been in the Corps for all of 2 years, but had accrued only 45 days of "good time," which means he left and went AWOL every time he was released from the brig. In those days, any time you spent incarcerated or being AWOL didn't count as time served in the military. Pappy had a baby daughter and a young wife back in Tennessee that he dearly loved. This was his only crime. Each time he was released from the brig, he simply bought a plane ticket or hitchhiked back home until they picked him up again. I felt bad for him and we talked quite a bit about his attitude and his love for his Tennessee home.

With six months remaining on my enlistment, my First Sergeant spoke with me about re-enlistment. We had a good laugh and I went back to work. Gradually the bad feelings I had about the Corps have gone away, replaced by the pride of knowing that I was and am part of an elite fighting family filled with brothers and sisters.

I was discharged on September 1, 1970 and am very proud of my Vietnam service and the various campaign medals and the Republic of Vietnam Cross of Gallantry with Palm and Frame which I received. I also received a good dose of PTSD and tinnitus, a hearing disability. I attended Valley Community College for two years, worked at AlliedSignal now part of Honeywell, in Sylmar California, and finally retired from Lowe's Hardware in 2009.

Today I am happily married, and we live in a rural town in north Alabama with our goats, chickens and two miniature horses. Life is wonderful. Semper Fi.

DONALD "MAC" MACPHERSON'S WAR

**U.S. Army, Lieutenant and Captain, Airborne Infantry Platoon Leader
and Company Commander, C Company, 3rd Battalion of
the 503rd Airborne Infantry, 173rd Airborne Brigade,
Bong Son, Bao Loc, De Linh, Da Lat, and Phan Thiet, 1968–69**

My father attended Admiral Farragut Academy. He wanted to go on to Annapolis but was medically disqualified, so during WW II he promoted U.S. Savings Bonds. He died when I was only two. When I was six years old, I put on my first military uniform as a cadet at St. Aloysius Military Academy in Fayetteville, Ohio, a Catholic boarding school. The nuns would lead us in prayer for our soldiers fighting in Korea, which left a lasting impression on me. *There are no atheists in foxholes.* After my second grade, the Catholic school closed, and for two years I attended Millersburg Military Institute in Kentucky. From first grade on, my objective was to attend a service academy. Sixteen years later, in 1967, I graduated from West Point, where I swam and played water polo. I volunteered twice to go to Vietnam, "marching to the sound of the guns," as West Point taught us, serving eighteen months as infantry platoon leader and company commander.

From my first West Point reveille run, my branch choice was infantry. We would chant "All the way! Up the hill! Airborne! Ranger! Infantry!" as we ran. Upon completion of those three post-graduate qualification schools, I became a weapons platoon leader in the 82nd Airborne, and hand-carried to the Pentagon my request for assignment to the 101st Airborne in Vietnam. I arrived in-country in May '68, eleven months after graduation from West Point, as an infantry platoon leader in the 173rd Airborne Brigade (Separate), the "Herd," a ready reaction force with vast helicopter resources.

My tour began on the coast at Bong Son in II Corps. On my first patrol, I discovered the fortuity of war. My platoon sergeant was well below ground, in a foxhole we were digging. I stood next to the foxhole, pick in hand, ready to dig some more. Shrapnel from a mortar round ricocheted across the rice paddy, hit him – not me – in the shoulder, and he was evacuated. *Quirk of fate.* Soon afterward, we choppered into the Central Highlands, where we aggressively patrolled the triple canopy, Agent Orange-laced mountains near Bao Loc, Di Linh, and Da Lat. I completed fifty CAs, or combat assaults, in a Huey "slick."

On final approach to the LZ, six of us would get out and "ride the skids," standing so that we could quickly "un-ass" the chopper, with heavy rucksacks on our backs and M-16s "locked and loaded." The door gunner and crew chief would "recon by fire" with their M-60 machine guns, shooting up the LZ and adjacent wood lines. After eight months, and against my will, headquarters forced me to leave the platoon and serve in Da Lat with operations for the experimental Task Force South. It consisted of our battalion of the 173rd, a battalion from the 101st, and two ARVN airborne battalions. I had the midnight to noon shift and monitored the battalion radio networks as OIC, or officer in charge, of our tactical operations center located inside a city center French chateau. It was a good target for the enemy and proved very vulnerable to attack, a bad combination. One night our cook shot and killed several VC coming over the wall.

With my 12-month tour coming to an end, I received orders for Hawaii and was due for promotion to captain. Instead of leaving Vietnam, I extended six months, was promoted, and returned to my company as commander. I was 24 years old. My West Point roommate, Dean Kunihiro, was our intelligence officer; and, when I exchanged our area of operations with a mechanized infantry company, I coordinated with its commander, another classmate, Pete Hagen, who introduced me to Barbara in '64, whom I married in '70. *Small war.*

It took me only one week in-country to conclude that the war was not winnable; it was a political nightmare and a total waste. General Westmoreland was delusional and/ or a liar, and he and the other West Pointers in charge misled Congress and the President. Ken Burns's PBS series says it all. Although no longer believing in the war, I felt compelled – duty bound – to serve my country, and the war changed my life in ways I did not anticipate. For me the movie *Platoon* best illustrates my experience: a relentless search for the enemy; burning villages; restraining atrocities; avoiding booby-traps, punji-pits, snipers, and ambushes; and fear of being overrun by an NVA battalion in pith helmets. One of my sergeants was killed by an artillery-round booby trap. Another of my men – with only one week in-country – was killed by a Claymore mine. As I manned the tactical operations center in Da Lat one night, a Bravo Company platoon was overrun, with eleven US paratroopers and forty VC killed.

I was lucky – *Very lucky* – due in large part to our Central Highland location and timing. For me the war, often called "a platoon leaders' war," was akin to "Indian Fighting." We had many skirmishes, not battles; but I had gunships and air strikes upon which I could call. Like Daniel Boone, I had independence of thought and action. We were always on the move, never remaining overnight in the same location. In the wake of the '68 Tet offensive, we would build bunkers every night as a company, and one platoon would be put out on ambush. Headquarters feared an assault by NVA battalions, but I felt much safer out on ambush – "by stealth and under cover of darkness." Later, as company commander, we often operated in four man "Hawk" teams at night, taking from the enemy any surprise advantage.

One day up in the mountains, I was sitting on a large boulder, eating a can of peaches when the VC opened fire on me, the obvious leader. I dove for the ground and scrambled, seeing AK-47 rounds hit all around me. A paratrooper next to me was hit but survived. A week later, after my men ambushed some VC on a trail, I sat on a dead VC, eating my peaches. *Don't get even; get uneven. It was a crazy war and we were crazy. War is our business, and business is good.* Because the VC were superstitious, we put in the mouth of their dead a Herd patch – our calling card – or we would stamp airborne wings into the forehead. We did refrain from one Herd habit: cutting off and wearing enemy ears.

One night, as we were setting up trip-flares and Claymore mines as it grew dark, an eight-year-old girl walked into our perimeter. She had survived our bombing, which obliterated her village. Five minutes later, and she would have hit a trip flare wire and been obliterated by a Claymore mine.

My men ambushed and killed several VC one day, to discover that one was a paymaster, with lots of cash. "What should we do with the cash?" my platoon leader asked. "What cash?" I answered.

An NVA lurking in mangroves shot one of my men in the stomach and ran straight toward me and my RTO, "Professor." We were both down on one knee and the NVA soldier had his rifle raised, firing rounds that passed just over our heads. While I continued talking to battalion on the radio, Professor coolly fired one shot, hitting the NVA in the head. He fell at our feet, dead. Setting the Ranger example, sometimes I walked point. In a vegetated stream bed I snuck up on several VC. I was about to blow one away when he turned, and I saw he looked to be about twelve years old. Long ago, I concluded that for not firing I was blessed by God with three sons.

We lived in the jungle. We were rarely in fire support bases, and we never saw a USO show. Living on C-rations, we were resupplied once a week and slept under "hooches" we made from our ponchos, slung low to the ground. Our gourmet foods were hot chocolate and peaches. During the monsoon season we were soaked 24/7, except for the few hours each day that our clothes dried by body heat, thanks to the poncho liner over our heads while we slept. During dry season, from repeated sweating our worn fatigues had the stench of vinegar. It was body acid; a comforting smell. Rats ran down our bodies; leeches covered our lower legs. Deer ran through our position, and large monkeys climbed the trees around us. I once came across a spider in a web that stretched across a trail. Its body was as big as my fist. One of my men killed a 15-foot-long king cobra snake. Walking the ridge lines we always sought the high ground and could hear tigers at night below us. I am sure we covered some territory never walked by man. We were one with the boonies. *Boonie rats*. Once, I quietly approached a figure that had the backside and legs of a bent-over VC. I fired at him, but too high. Turned out it was a deer. My men laughed but were disappointed that they didn't get any venison.

In a platoon night ambush, we heard movement 360 degrees around us. Very close. I called in artillery, but too close, hearing the shrapnel "zings" passing by just over our heads and also into the large deadfall of trees, which protected us as we hugged the ground. At daybreak we found beaucoup trails leading away from our position. The artillery had saved us from a major VC attack.

During my last months in-country we returned to the coastal plain as "Vietnamization" began. My command post and one platoon were adjacent to a village, while my other three platoons were scattered nearby. A Navy barge with 3,000 Claymore mines had washed ashore. After that, the VC had the advantage: the mines, sand, and hedgerows, which we could not go around. We had to walk the sandy trails through them. I lost over forty men wounded and one killed from the Claymore-mine booby-traps.

My refuge was the *23rd Psalm*. It mattered not what your position was in the patrol; it only mattered who stepped on exactly the wrong spot. One of my platoon leaders, Lieutenant Frank Audrain, West Point '68, survived a Claymore that had been placed backwards; the VC could not read "FRONT TOWARD

ENEMY." *Fortuity of war.* There was a sniper – who almost hit me but instead hit one of my men down range – who we named "Six O'clock Charlie." He was always on time, until I requested a .50-caliber machine gun one day and returned fire, leveling the pagoda behind which he hid. There was no body or blood trail, but we never heard from him again. Or her.

I witnessed "waterboarding" of VC suspects by ARVN officers who used soapy water, which resulted in the victim vomiting and drowning at the same time. Headquarters ordered that I do nada, and I obeyed; but I ignored the new political order: we were not to return fire until clearance was received from the ARVN. *Fat chance, that.* Army rules were absurd, Westmoreland, hoping to win the war by body count, was making it a non-sequitur war of attrition. But the enemy had far more men. And women. Once, I called in an enemy leg as "VC KIA," but headquarters wouldn't count it. I needed a complete body.

I would have extended another six months, but my mother, who was dying of cancer, learned I was in Vietnam. I had told her my APO address was Okinawa. Receiving orders to train Rangers, I requested "compassionate reassignment" and taught ROTC at the University of Cincinnati. I coached the rifle team and served as a Survivor Assistance Officer, an SAO, as in the movie *The Messenger*, responsible for notifying the next of kin of the loss in Vietnam of their husband or son, plus arranging wakes, funerals, and posthumous award ceremonies. I concluded I would resign from active duty. Having commanded a company of over one hundred men in combat, I did not care to "command a desk" for ten years, awaiting battalion command.

In '71, I attended graduate school at Utah State University, obtained a master's degree in agricultural economics, and quickly – but only partially – satisfied my persistent need for "living on the edge" by joining the 19th Special Forces National Guard as an A-Team commander. I completed Jump Master school and we made a mountain night jump onto a 10,000-foot elevation drop zone. Later, as a major in the Special Forces Reserves, I trained officers, using my oldest son, age ten, as an "indigenous person."

After working for Virginia Tech, at age thirty I attended law school in Oklahoma, wanting to open my own business, to be the company "commander," and be independent. Without funds, the Arizona *Storefront Lawyer* was my solution. As an attorney "in search of a practice," I represented those whom other lawyers avoided: "tax protestors," who, for reasons of principle, based on legal conclusions, or in political protest, did not file returns or pay taxes. Federal judges regarded them with disdain. I became a "constitutionalist," with "the temerity to raise novel issues," many of which I won. This, coupled with flying my 1963 single engine Cessna 205, over mountains, at night, provided my "Highway to the danger zone." I was relentless defending clients. Courtroom Commando. One judge threw a pencil at me in front of the jury, so exasperated with my stubborn nature, my refusal to back off. *What could he do, send me back to Vietnam?* More recently two Tax Court judges sanctioned me $27,000 for "raising nothing but frivolous arguments for the sole purpose of delay." *Again I was walking point. Clients are my troops. I am not in court. I am in Vietnam.*

The VA shrink got it right. She said I need an enemy, a VC substitute. The IRS, as an institution, and some IRS criminal investigators and prosecutors, fit the mold. In over forty years of legal practice, I tried fifty-five criminal tax cases in federal court in twenty-five states, winning many. In a Bismarck trial, I won acquittals  for all five of my clients, "the Fargo Five." Aside from the tax protestors, my former clients: two governors; three state senators; two Hollywood stars; a major U.S. airline; and CIA operatives, including one involved with Colonel North's "Iran-Contra Affair." I wrote and self-published three books. In *Tax Fraud and Evasion: The War Stories*, I relate some Vietnam and SAO vignettes, providing some catharsis. I recently reduced my caseload and now mainly serve as a consultant to my two attorney sons, Scott and Nathan. *See* www.Beat-IRS.com. My third son, Ryan, is a professor at Bethany Lutheran College.

I have been married to my wife Barbara, from Philadelphia, for 49 years, whom I met in '64 because I swam in an Army-Villanova meet. We live in Encinitas, California, and have twelve grandchildren, ages 2 to 23, and two golden retrievers. My interests now are playing football, baseball, basketball, and soccer with our grandchildren; swimming; biking; and walking the dogs.

I had prostate cancer and have coronary heart disease – three stents in the "widow maker" – and I have major hearing loss. In Vietnam I hitched a chopper ride to Nha Trang to see my high school buddy, David Koffler, who was a Swift Boat skipper. I spent several days with him patrolling the coast, taking fire from shoreline VC, and killing several. David became a Navy Captain, a dentist, and while on carriers he wore a baseball cap with "Top Gum," written across the top, typical of his sense of humor. I refused to file a VA claim, but David persisted in assisting me. Nathan and I attended David's San Diego funeral in 2011. He died of cancer, which started with the prostate and spread to his brain. Survivor's guilt. "There, but for the grace of God, go I." Two-hundred-and-seventy-three West Point graduates were killed in Vietnam. My class of '67 and the class of '66 share the record with 29 each. Thirty years of government lies, and 58,000 Americans killed, and for what? Absolutely nothing! A total waste. Horribly tragic. But the word "tragic" is far too inadequate.

ALAN REED'S WAR

Royal Australian Air Force, Squadron Leader (Major), RF-4C Pilot, US 12th Tactical Reconnaissance Squadron, Tan Son Nhut, 1968

I grew up in Fremantle on the southwest coast of Australia. We had a draft back then. After graduating from Fremantle Boys High School, I was called into the Royal Australian Air Force for six months in 1952. I liked it and was accepted for pilot training in 1953, becoming a Sergeant Pilot in 1954 at the age of 20. I flew as a Second Pilot in the Lincoln heavy bomber in maritime reconnaissance and was commissioned as a Pilot Officer (a second lieutenant), in 1956. Converting to jets, I flew the Vampire and Canberra, and was selected to be a flight commander for the F-111C due in October 1968.

However, in 1967, now as a squadron leader (a major), I was told I had been selected for an exchange posting with the USAF to be trained as an IP (instructor pilot) on the RF-4C: the specially-equipped reconnaissance version of the powerful new Phantom. After training on that marvelous aircraft, I reported for duty in Vietnam.

I was well aware that the exchange posting was going to be a challenge. The job had previously gone to fighter pilots with instructor experience and I was surprised and delighted to be selected. The only jet aircraft flying I had experience in was the obsolescent Canberra medium bomber which dated to the late 1940s, and I was about to climb into the cockpit of a US F-4 Phantom, the hottest military aircraft in the world. It held fifteen speed, altitude, and time to climb records, so it was quite a machine. Had I known the extent of the job planned for me, I would have been much more apprehensive than I was. In my case, ignorance was bliss.

I was sent to Shaw AFB in Columbia, South Carolina, to

train on the RF-4C. Shaw is not a big base by USAF standards but compared to the RAAF, it was huge. The RF-4C was the reconnaissance model of the Phantom, loaded with film and infrared cameras of various types. After six months at Shaw, graduates would be sent to either the 12th or 16th Squadrons at Tan Son Nhut near Saigon in Vietnam or the 11th or 14th Squadrons in Udorn, Thailand. The Udorn squadrons covered the hot spots in North Vietnam around Hanoi and Haiphong and suffered a much higher loss rate than we did, as those areas were protected by the most effective air defense systems ever established with the latest Russian-supplied ground-to-air missiles and radar-guided anti-aircraft guns. The 12th and 16th Squadrons operated mostly within South Vietnam with some sorties into the North and into Laos, but the air defenses there were more benign.

The flying phase of the course began in mid-October 1967 and boy, was I impressed. The F-4 was a magnificent machine in every way. There was so much power, I just loved it. But there was also so much to learn. I went "solo" with an instructor-navigator after five sorties and then began the interesting reconnaissance exercises using the various sensors we carried. The wonders of in-flight refueling were also introduced, and how to rendezvous with a gas station in the sky. It was magical and awesome to me.

My assignment to Vietnam came through in May 1968 with an effective date of June. It was an interesting set of orders. As I was not a member of the USAF, they could not officially "order" me to do anything. Instead they issued me "Invitational Orders" for a 179-day "temporary duty" (TDY) in Viet-  nam. I believe I am one of the very few people in the world ever to have been invited to participate in a war. I was assigned to the 12th Tactical Reconnaissance Squadron, "The Blackbirds," at Tan Son Nhut in Vietnam. It was the busiest airfield in the world with a great mixture of fixed and rotary wing aircraft.

I arrived with several other new pilots and navigators, shown to our "hooches," and issued a flak jacket, rifle, and helmet. Memories of the Tet offensive were still very strong. Until Tet, the squadron had been housed in hotel type accommodations in Saigon, but one aircrew member had been killed and another wounded in the fierce fighting in the city. Consequently, all aircrew were moved onto the base after things settled down.

As the new guy, I had the top bunk "to catch any incoming." On my first night, a rocket arrived at around 4 a.m. and landed on the tarmac about four hundred yards away with an awful Crrrump! Another half dozen arrived with the mournful notes of the warning siren, which we didn't really need by then. The only real damage was to a C-130 which had been hit on the ramp, and a navigator, who arrived on my flight, fell off his top bunk, and fractured his wrist.

As I was processed-in the next day, like the US aircrew I was issued a "blood chit,"  printed on silk, showing a US flag and stating in several languages: "I am a citizen of the United States of America. I do not speak your language. Misfortune forces me to seek your assistance in obtaining food, shelter and protection. Please take me to someone who will provide for my safety and see that I am returned to my people. My Government will reward you." The RAAF hadn't issued me anything like that, so I decided it was better to carry it than not. Fortunately, it was not needed. Hand and fingerprints were also taken, and I was asked to remove my flying boots so that footprints could be taken as well. Intrigued, I naively asked why they needed footprints. I was told if you crash in one of these aircraft, often the only parts remaining for identification were the feet in their protective boots. I wished I hadn't asked!

Lastly, I was taken to the life support section and issued my personal equipment: a G suit, a new personally molded and fitted helmet, a harness, a life preserver, and a jacket fully equipped with survival rations, two radios, other means of making my presence very obvious on the ground or in the water if I really needed to, a tree escape device, and a trusty Smith and Wesson .38 revolver. I was at last ready to meet the enemy.

The two RF-4 squadrons at Tan Son Nhut alternated day and night missions with a change-over on the first of each month. Unlike the fighter and tactical strike squadrons, our planes always operated alone and our motto of "Alone Unarmed and Unafraid" had a certain irony to it. We had twenty-two aircraft in our squadron. The day roster began with take-offs from 0600 to 1800 hours and the night roster from 1800 to 0600 hours, thus providing 24-hour coverage. Day missions were normally flown using our wide range of cameras, while the night missions were usually covering areas of eight by six miles using our very sophisticated infrared detection camera. The amount of film both RF-4 squadrons plus the RF-101 squadron produced was mind-blowing, something like half a million feet a month, which kept our analysts extremely busy.

For my introductory missions I was crewed with Captain Don Verhees. Don had been shot down just a few weeks before I arrived. He ejected first and landed on one side of a hill and was quickly rescued. He had seen his pilot's chute deploy and expected they would soon be reunited. However, this was not to be. The pilot landed on the other side of the hill and was not seen again. He had been captured and was one of the early prisoners released after spending several years in the Hanoi Hilton. That was how it worked in the Vietnam War. You were lucky or you could be very unlucky.

On my first night mission, as I returned to base, I turned on my navigation lights and was shot at from downtown Saigon. The long arc of 12.5 mm tracers followed me around, so I quickly turned off my lights and told the tower about it. It was a crazy war where there was no safe place at all, not even in your own home base circuit.

Because there were so many bad guys so close to us, the night sky was something to behold. There were often AC-47 "Puff the Magic Dragon" gunships airborne and they would spit a barrage of tracers at any likely target as well as flares to illuminate the ground. On many nights, the display was better than New Year's Eve on Sydney Harbor.

The CO of the squadron permitted crews to name their assigned aircraft. In our case it was an almost-brand-new aircraft, #67-448. My navigator from North Carolina and I named it *Carolina Kangaroo* with "Have Camera Will Travel" as our motto. The plane actually survived the war to rest in storage at Davis Monthan Air Force Base in the Arizona desert.

Our normal routine was to arrive for briefing three hours before planned take-off time. We would be assigned three targets and told the desired results with recommendations of sensors to be used. The Meteorological Officer would brief us on expected weather, which was fairly accurate, while the Intelligence Officer would brief on known enemy surface-to-air missile (SAM) and anti-aircraft artillery (AAA) sites, and friendly forces in the area. Friendly artillery was supposed to be shut down where we were working, but sometimes that didn't happen. I was happily flying a low-level photographic strip when the whole hillside only a few hundred yards away erupted in a massive artillery friendly-fire barrage. It would not have been friendly to be hit by one of those shells; so we quickly exited the area, complaining loudly.

On "out-country" missions into North Vietnam, we invariably refueled prior to entry and usually topped up after the mission was completed. The whole system of control and support of operations into the North was amazing. A command-and-control C-130 with the call-sign "Crown" was the controlling authority for all aircraft entering the North. There were always two KC-135 tankers orbiting off the coast and Crown would tell us the vector to find it for refueling. In the event an aircraft was shot down, and many were, the whole rescue system would go into full forward gear. There were always flights of A-1 ground attack aircraft with the call-sign "Sandy," either airborne or on short-time alert, to suppress ground fire and support any downed aircrew until a big Sikorsky Jolly Green Giant helicopter could come in and attempt a rescue.

Most of my ten "out country" missions were flown in the area just north of the DMZ, but on one occasion I did a road reconnaissance further north where a suspected SAM site was being built. That mission contributed to one of my two Distinguished Flying Crosses awarded by the USAF. On another, I located the crash site of a downed F-4 which had been shot down a day or two before and the crew not heard from. The aircraft had hit the ground very hard. Most of the missions into the north were into reasonably well-defended areas and the technique was to fly at six hundred and fifty knots, with all cameras running, at an altitude between 4,500 feet, which was just above light ground fire, and 7,500 feet which was the altitude at which a SAM-3 missile became effective. At that speed, we had to use afterburner and fuel disappeared at an alarming rate. Once off target, we would get over water as soon as possible and check in with Crown, who would direct us to the KC-135 gas station in the sky for a big suck of fuel to get us safely back to Tan Son Nhut. This mission contributed to the second US Forces Distinguished Flying Cross that I was awarded.

When we rotated to night missions, the routine was much the same with briefings three hours before take-off. However, most night missions were infrared "area covers" where we attempted to locate enemy campfires or vehicle activity. We had a fairly primitive terrain-following radar on the RF-4 and we had to hand-fly to maintain a constant altitude of two thousand feet above the terrain. To cover the area, we would normally fly along seven or eight parallel lines less than one mile apart over the designated area. Doing this at night in mountainous terrain was fairly interesting and by the end of the night flying month, we were pretty good at instrument flying.

During a mission early in my time I stayed in an interesting area longer than I should. The mission was near Khe Sanh, close to the DMZ, which had been under siege from the North Vietnamese. Russian tanks had been reported nearby. I left the area with about a thousand pounds of fuel less than I should have and headed for Tan Son Nhut only to be told that a thunderstorm was over the base and a ground-controlled radar approach would be necessary. I decided I'd make one approach before diverting to Bien Hoa. As I taxied in, the storm hit, and I shut down with my tanks almost dry. That taught me a good lesson.

Five aircraft from the 460th Wing were lost while I was there, including two from my squadron. One crew bailed out successfully, with both the pilot and GIBS, the "Guy in the Back Seat." quickly recovered. They were back in the club that night to tell us their story. The other loss, which created a major issue in the USAF, was not so fortunate. Major

General Bob Worley was the Vice Commander of the 7th Air Force, which controlled all air assets and operations in Vietnam. He flew quite frequently in the front seat with our squadron IP. On a day mission in the DMZ, they took a hit in the nose of the aircraft, causing a small fire in the film. Detecting smoke, they assumed that they had been hit, and headed for the coast. The rear seater ejected first, into the sea, and was quickly picked up. Unfortunately, the rear canopy departing caused a massive draft, engulfing the front seat in flames and incapacitating General Worley. He was not able to eject, and the aircraft crashed on the beach. Worley was the only USAF general officer killed on operations in Vietnam, and that was the last combat mission undertaken by a general for the remainder of the war, and possibly for any future war.

On a few occasions while flying, I saw some "Ranch Hand" C-123 aircraft flying three abreast spraying the jungle with their evil load of Agent Orange poison. It was easy to see where they had been as the whole area beneath their previous flight paths was totally barren.

When a flight of three B52 bombers would each unleash a load of about 120 five-hundred-pound bombs, often very close to Saigon, the buildings would rumble as if an earthquake was occurring. Later, I learned that they were trying to collapse the tunnel systems which the Viet Cong had constructed almost up to Saigon itself. On a visit to Vietnam in 2007, I learned that while they caused some disruption to the tunnels of Cu Chi, even these B52 raids were not very effective against VC ingenuity and persistence.

We had a pretty good war compared to the troops out in the field and I used to think if one had to go to war, this was the way to do it. After about three months in our old hooches, our brand-new quarters were ready, and we happily moved into our individual air-conditioned rooms. Most people, me included, had acquired a TV set, a tape recorder, and a small refrigerator for our rooms, so life was pretty good. However, time passed slowly, and I was looking forward to the end of my 179 days and returning to my family I had left in a foreign land. Again, I was lucky as my colleagues had to spend a full year to complete a tour.

My personal target was a hundred missions, so I could qualify for the "100 mission" patch for my uniform. When it was completed, I was hosed down on landing and given the traditional bottle of bubbly by the CO. It was then time to go home.

Looking back on Vietnam, I view it as a very sad experience. At the time, I felt I was doing what I had been trained for years to do and was pleased about that. But I realized the war was not being run properly. The US had sufficient air and military power to win the war; yet for political reasons, F-105s and F-4s armed with only one or two bombs (much less than their capacity) were being sent into the hotbed of Hanoi and Haiphong where they were engaged by the most effective system of air defense ever developed. The Russians used the war to test their latest ground to air missiles, anti-aircraft guns and radar systems.

The SAMs 2 and 3 were very effective downing tactical aircraft as well as the heavy B-52s sent to the north during the Rolling Thunder operations and the very slippery SAM-6 was the latest to be deployed. Even so, the radar-directed anti-aircraft weapons took the biggest toll of aircraft. Shipping in Haiphong harbor was off limits to strike aircraft, so Russian and sometimes British ships, as well as those from many other countries, delivered supplies to our enemy with absolute impunity. Much mission planning was taken away from the operational commanders in the field and we learned that targets were actually being selected during discussions between Secretary of Defense McNamara and President Johnson. This was no way to conduct a war if actually winning was considered important.

We had a mini cease-fire while I was there, and the North was put off limits to our aircraft while the protagonists argued in Paris over the design of the negotiating table. Jane Fonda was sucking up to the North Vietnamese and tattling on her countrymen POWs who tried to get her to deliver messages to their loved ones. Martin Luther King had been assassinated shortly before I arrived in Vietnam and Bobby Kennedy just after, and there was an air of uncertainty enveloping the whole American society. Anti-war protests were gaining strength in America as well as in Australia and race riots over school busing policies were taking place in the US southern states and in other parts of the country. Our squadron people were beginning to ask what they were doing in Vietnam and why they were there. Most people were prepared to risk their life for a genuine cause, but that cause was appearing less and less worthwhile when we were not permitted to do what we saw as necessary to win the war. The first principle of war, "Selection and Maintenance of the Aim" had been totally ignored.

Later in Washington when I walked along the Vietnam Wall and saw that black marble edifice with fifty-eight thousand names on it including a couple I had known; I saw it as a national disgrace. We achieved nothing and killed many servicemen who were prepared to fight a good fight but were betrayed and only brought death and destruction to a nation of people who wanted nothing more than to decide their own destiny and bring up their children in a safe environment in their own country. The domino theory with which we had been brainwashed was a farce.

I was surprised to later learn that more than 750 Phantoms from the Air Force, Navy and Marine Corps were lost in the Vietnam War. Combined losses of all US aircraft and helicopters exceeded 10,000, while the South Vietnamese forces lost a further 2,500. In addition to the 58,000 American names on that somber black Vietnam Memorial wall, Australia lost more than 500 service personnel with over 3,600 physically wounded, and many more from both countries have emotional scars. How many Vietnamese died is not known. What a waste of assets and loss of lives in this pointless episode in military history.

With some reservations, I visited Vietnam in 2007. My negative views of the war and its outcome were only reinforced. While the Hanoi Hilton was obscene and it was quite off-putting to think about the people of my era who spent time in that awful place, I found ordinary people in the country who were genuinely friendly with nothing more on their mind than making a living and taking care of their family. I did not feel proud of my contribution to their oppression in the name of anti-communism.

Subsequently, I learned the extent of the involvement of China in the Vietnam War and the influence that had on the politics of the era. At one stage the Chinese had over 170,000 troops in Vietnam, mostly managing and training North Vietnamese on the very effective AAA weapons that they and the Russians had provided. China had also provided MIG aircraft and major logistic support for the  North Vietnamese who could not have coped without their assistance. Clearly, China and Russia would have intervened on a massive scale had the US and South Vietnamese attempted an invasion of the North and this could have led to a major nuclear war. The US authorities were well aware of this likelihood, and wisely I think, folded on what was a seriously poor hand. It would have been much better had they not joined the game at all after the so-called Tonkin Gulf incident which is now seen to have been at least partly faked.

However, Monday morning quarterbacking is much easier than being there at the time.

When my exchange tour as an IP with the American Air Force was over, I returned to various duty assignments with the Royal Australian Air Force. In 1971, I was promoted to Wing Commander (a lieutenant colonel) and commanded an F4-E Squadron. After that I completed the Joint Services Staff College and served on the faculty, becoming a Group Captain (a colonel) in 1977 and group commander of the major RAAF Base at Amberley. I completed conversion to the F-111C, flew the Canberra again as well as Huey and Chinook helicopters. I was then promoted to Air Commodore (a brigadier general) and assigned as commandant of the RAAF Academy. I went on to serve as Air Attaché in our embassy in Washington and finally as Air Vice Marshal (a major general) Commander of Support

Command, responsible for training, logistic, and maintenance support for the operational element of the Air Force. I retired in 1990 after 37 years' service.

On retirement, I continued to remain active as a consultant. During my career, in addition to the two US Distinguished Flying Crosses, I am pleased to have been appointed as an officer in the Australian Veterans' group, "Order of Australia." I am less pleased about the COPD and chronic leukemia, possibly Agent Orange-induced from my tour in Vietnam. I am now 85 years of age, reside in Melbourne, on the southeast coast of Australia, and enjoy playing golf, bridge and flying my de Havilland "Tiger Moth" 1930s biplane, the type I initially trained on all those years ago.

JOHN HART'S WAR

U.S. Army Artillery Liaison Officer; and Battery Platoon Leader, XO, and CO, 1st Squadron, 4th Cavalry; 8th Battalion, 6th Field Artillery; and Division Artillery, 1st Infantry Division, Phu Loi and region north of Saigon, 1968-1970

I grew up in Homewood, Illinois, a south suburb of Chicago, west of Halsted Street and south of the I-294 beltway. It was best-known by frazzled commuters on the Illinois Central for the busy commuter railroad station at 183rd Street and Dixie Highway. I graduated from Homewood Flossmoor High School in 1961 before securing an appointment to the US Military Academy at West Point in 1963. H-F is a large school in a large suburb and has always been a Chicago-area academic and athletic powerhouse. Four years after entering the USMA, I graduated with the class of 1967 on 7 June – sworn in as a second lieutenant.

My branch choice was Field Artillery, and after Ranger School, which had become mandatory for West Point graduates after 1966, I went on to the Field Artillery Officer Orientation Course at Fort Sill, Oklahoma, which had the necessary "wide open spaces" that allowed young lieutenants to fire every howitzer in the Army arsenal and not worry about hitting the wrong thing. By 1968, with more and more troops being sent to Vietnam, training classes were being shortened across the board, as was the normal "get your feet wet as a platoon leader" in Germany or at a stateside post. Instead, in the summer of 1968, thirteen months after I graduated from West Point, I landed in The Republic of South Vietnam, assigned to the

1st Infantry Division, where I would spend the next 18 months in a succession of increasingly responsible artillery officer slots in combat.

My first assignment was as a field artillery liaison officer, an LNO, for the division's cavalry squadron, the 1st Squadron of the 4th Cav, headquartered in Phu Loi, about 15 miles north of Saigon. The Cav squadron was all about the new airmobile warfare and movement, and its commander had a Huey for command and control (C&C) available to him full time in order for him to supervise and coordinate his troops and platoons in the field. When he needed artillery support or nighttime illumination, he would turn to his artillery LNO, which was me, so I accompanied him whenever he went up in his C&C bird, which was virtually every day. I also got to know the C&C pilot, a highly experienced, professional, and cool-as-a-cucumber chief warrant officer (CWO) named Dominguez.

One day in September we were airborne at 1200 feet, circling over a ground operation, when there was a sudden, alarming jolt and hideous shriek in the chopper. Prior to that moment Dominguez had always been unfailingly unflappable, but at that moment he reacted with patent alarm. Most of us presumed we'd been hit by ground fire of some sort, but not Dominguez. He knew the problem was with the *tail rotor*. Apparently, its gear had partially stripped, probably due to age and to wear and tear on the machinery. We were flying a third-string chopper that day because the first- and second-string C&Cs were both undergoing required maintenance.

I wore a customized aircraft helmet with two audio cables coming out of *each* earpiece. These connected me to a bank of radios that enabled me to monitor both the artillery communication frequencies and the cavalry command channels. Prior to losing radio contact, the last thing I remember hearing through my complicated headset was Dominguez's "Mayday" call, requesting an emergency "running" landing at our base at Phu Loi. All aircraft approaching the Phu Loi airstrip immediately veered away clearing the runway for us. Instead of coming down vertically, which was the norm for a helicopter, or trying an emergency "auto-rotation" to land, Dominguez decided to bring the Huey in horizontally, as a fixed-wing aircraft would do: landing on its skids and sliding to a halt rather than trying to hover vertically. He knew the tail rotor couldn't take strain like that and we would crash.

Dominguez thrust his control stick forward and put us quickly into a really steep dive! There aren't words to describe the feeling – plummeting downward as if in virtual freefall. Unsettling — to put it mildly. When we were somewhere around 100 to 200 feet of altitude, Dominguez pulled out of our "dive" and leveled off. What he had done was engage gravity to help accelerate (maximize) our forward velocity so that aerodynamics could stabilize the fuselage in flight – in case the tail rotor was kaput. Of course, none of us non-aviators understood this aerial maneuver at the time. It did, however, instantly capture our undivided attention.

En route to the landing strip, Dominguez tested the chopper tail rotor gently, and everything seemed to function normally. Apparently, there were enough threads left on the gear to withstand minor torque, so Dominguez informed the tower that he would make a "normal" landing — set down from a hover at his usual landing pad. That decision, however, proved to be nearly catastrophic: a calamity in the offing! As soon as we began to hover — thereby intensifying tail rotor torque — the damaged gear failed completely and the ship began tossing, flipping, and spinning uncontrollably. The C&C was about 25 feet above ground when the fuselage began countering (unopposed) the gyrating force of the rotating "wing," the main rotor. Dominguez wrestled with his flight stick, trying to control the overwhelmingly intractable aircraft. One moment I could see the horizon, then the sky, then tarmac, on and on. Disturbingly alarming! However, thanks to his superlative skill, Dominguez somehow managed to get the chopper down on the ground — landing it jarringly hard, but at least intact.

Well… almost intact.

The Huey was canted noticeably to the left: the left skid had collapsed on impact. That was very unusual for a Huey, because their skids were designed to withstand significant impacts when landing, in order to protect the fuel tanks situated beneath the passenger compartments. For a second or two we all just looked around in outright relief and utter astonishment that we had survived. I closed my eyes in a moment of silent prayer when cool, calm, and collected CWO Dominguez suddenly screamed at us at the top of his lungs, "Everybody *OUT!*"

He'd checked his controls and immediately discovered we had a large JP-4 fuel leak under the helicopter. A fuel tank had ruptured on impact where the skid collapsed. Also, while the chopper was tossing around like an erratic gyroscope prior to landing, an unsecured smoke grenade had rolled out of the C&C and landed on the tarmac right beneath the fated skid. By incredible coincidence, the skid hit the grenade on impact and activated it, suddenly generating intense heat and flames — more than sufficient to ignite the leaking aviation fuel. Although JP4 is not explosive the way gasoline is, once it ignites, no one should tarry nearby.

With Dominguez's agitated exclamation, all seven of us got out as fast as we could. It seemed like one audible click as everyone unlocked their safety harness latches at the same time and turned toward the closest exit. The squadron's S-3 Operations Officer, a major, who was seated on the left side of the Huey, naturally exited to the left. As soon as his feet hit the ground he began running away from the helicopter, oblivious to the fact that the chopper's big main rotor was still turning. Until it slowed down, it gyrated at such high revolutions per minute that it was virtually invisible. Worse, with the collapsed skid, the whole airframe was tilted *down* and to the left; so the blades were almost but not quite touching the ground as they swept past; and the major was about to run right into it. If he went one step further, in a fraction of a second, he likely would have been decapitated were it not for the timely, aggressive, and positive initiative of the left-side door gunner. Realizing what was about to happen, he sprang from his M-60 machine gun and tackled the major at the knees. That brought the S-3 down abruptly, roughly, and "discourteously"... but it prevented the S-3's decapitation.

It's funny how strange things can suddenly invade your thoughts at the oddest times. I had jumped out the other door and was running away from the Huey as fast as my feet would carry me, when I suddenly remembered I'd forgotten my area map. It was my most essential piece of "equipment." Without it, as LNO I'd have been completely useless if I was called upon to direct artillery fire (solicit, spot, and adjust rounds). So, I turned around and ran back into the burning Huey to retrieve my "invaluable" map. Later, of course, I realized the map really wasn't indispensable, and could easily have been replaced. A quarter of a million dollars' worth of avionics was going up in flames, and I risked my life salvaging an intrinsically worthless piece of paper. Fortunately, speed won out and I didn't get hurt.

I took cover behind a berm and watched as the Huey was consumed by flames. That was when I noticed that I was still wearing my special flight helmet: the one with four electrical cables to connect to the C&C's bank of radios. I was unaware that during my frenzied exodus from the chopper crash I'd snapped the cables. Now, all that remained were four dangling shoulder-length pieces of wire. Theoretically, those cables should have tethered me securely to the C&C radio bank... or, more likely, ripped the helmet off my head.

Five minutes later, the C&C chopper was little more than a pile of white ash. Critically damaged at 1200 feet, the helicopter ended up incinerated on the ground. Fortunately, all seven occupants had successfully evacuated unharmed. Not a bad finale to a terrifying nightmare.

As for CWO Dominguez, he got well-deserved pats on the back for his superbly executed emergency landing that saved the lives of all on board.

Another brief but unusual incident over there in 1969 remains to this day a vivid memory of my war experience. My days as a LNO were over. I was still assigned to the 1st Infantry Division but had been promoted to captain and commanded a battery of 155-millimeter, split-trail howitzers operating north of Saigon in III Corps. Officially labelled the

M-114, it was a big, powerful gun, much bigger than its small, much more common cousin, the 105-millimeter howitzer that you usually see in photos and movies about the war. It fired a 100-pound shell that was over six inches in diameter up to nine miles that made a very large, effective, and intimidating hole in the ground. A battery had six guns, which were normally located at the same place for effect. If you needed a 155-millimeter howitzer, more was usually better. My battery had three howitzers located at a base camp in Lai Khe. The other three were in a night defensive position or NDP, a term originated when tactical units would consolidate overnight and redeploy at first light the next day. However, NDPs, often became semi-permanent tactical encampments existing for months at a time. I shuttled back and forth between my two half-batteries by hitching helicopter rides.

One morning, I landed at the NDP for a routine visit. My three howitzers were interspersed among other units there including an infantry battalion headquarters. The howitzers were well dug in, each surrounded by a stout parapet protecting gun and crew from ground fire and providing sheltered storage for supplies and ammunition. The infantry battalion provided perimeter security for the whole NDP as well as a mess, or meal service facility, for all camp occupants—their own infantry grunts, the artillery "Redlegs," combat engineers, etc. The infantrymen who guarded the perimeter occupied two-man defensive positions, or "foxholes." At mealtime, one of the two guards would go to the mess, get chow for both of them, and bring it back to the perimeter position for them to eat it there.

About noon that day my battery received a routine "harassment and interdiction" or H&I fire mission. That involved shooting artillery rounds into hostile territory unoccupied by friendly forces. It was directed at arbitrarily selected coordinates and at randomly selected times, often at known trails and gathering points, and its very unpredictability was intended to keep the enemy on edge and deny him free movement. For field artillerymen H&I fire was never urgent, because it involved neither a real target nor critical timing. Standard procedure: prep the round, set the firing data, check the blast cone for vacancy, and then yank the lanyard. No big deal.

"What's a blast cone?" you may ask. The term refers to the area in front of and radiating out from the muzzle of the howitzer. It's where the concussive effect of the blast of a fired round can be acutely distressing to anyone positioned there. To the cannoneers behind the howitzer, the blast is shocking *figuratively*; however, to someone standing in front of the howitzer – IN the blast cone – the blast is shocking *literally*. It can actually be seen from aircraft flying nearby.

I relieved my executive officer so that he could go get lunch, while I conducted the H&I fire mission for him. Only one of the three howitzers was involved. The crew properly set the fuse, rammed the round, cut the powder, closed the breech, and oriented the tube in the direction of fire. The section chief read back the firing data for verification and awaited my command to fire. Everything was textbook, so I raised my arm, made one final visual safety check of the blast cone, and then ordered, "FIRE!"

Oops! At that very moment – too late for me to belay my fire command – from behind the parapet and right into the dreaded blast cone emerged one of the perimeter guards returning from the mess with lunch for himself and his fellow guard. His rifle was slung across his back and he balanced one of the large, compartmentalized mess trays filled with food in each hand. Lunch that day was A-rations, a prepared hot meal of meat, mashed potatoes, gravy, succotash, and cherry cobbler. Yum! Grunts out on patrol would gladly trade their containerized field rations for A-rats like that in a proverbial heartbeat.

The infantryman must have been "vertically challenged" and walking close to the outer edge of the parapet, because I couldn't see him even from my elevated position on the XO's post... until it was too late. Ultimately the net physical effect of the blast on the guard probably was no more than a temporary ringing in his ears, but the immediate effect appeared drastically worse. For a moment, he may have even thought that the muzzle blast from the 155 was the detonation of incoming enemy artillery.

In that instant, the poor grunt's reflexes took over. He winced, bellowed, dropped to his knees, and shielded both ears with his hands. Of course, he didn't stop to think that his hands weren't empty when he slammed them against the sides of his head. No, they held the two full trays of food he'd just gotten from the mess. He may not have immediately realized what he'd done, but he did notice the bright red cherry cobbler dripping down his front and felt warm mashed potatoes and gravy running down his neck. That caused a moment of instantaneous and utter horror as he must have thought his head had split open and his entrails had just become his "*ex*-trails." The shock staggered him, startled him, and must have scared the living daylights out of him. No doubt, he would have to change his complete uniform – "includin' his drawers."

In fairly short order, however, he would feel a wave of relief as he realized his predicament was nothing more than spilt lunch. But what he'd gotten *from the mess* had evolved into a radical *form of mess*.

When the proverbial dust settled, the grunt was so rattled and upset that he didn't know what to do. He milled around in place – moving forward, back, left, and right – but not really going anywhere. He didn't know whether to return to the perimeter without lunch, return to the mess for another lunch, or to dispense retribution toward those responsible for his frustrating predicament. Fortunately for us "Redlegs," the grunt forgot he had his rifle strapped to his back. Otherwise, he might have been seriously tempted to unsling it and take out a few obnoxious cannoneers in retaliation. Instead, he fired back with a profusion of profanity aimed at the field artillery. I considered going over and apologizing to calm him down, but it was obvious he was in no mood whatsoever to receive civilities of any kind from anyone. He was not a happy camper!

I really pitied that poor grunt. The "harassment" part of H&I fire was intended to distress an *enemy* at the *end* of the projectile's trajectory, not distress a *friend* at its *origin*. To this day I truly hope that the grunt made it home from Vietnam safe, sound, and unscathed … and hope that he doesn't still have some residual succotash lodged in his ear canals.

I remained in the Army until 1970, serving in various artillery units, as well as ROTC assignments and on the staff at West Point. I retired at the rank of Lieutenant Colonel and worked as an investment advisor, as the operations officer for a corporation, and on the staff of a local community college. During my military career, I was awarded the Legion of Merit, four Bronze Stars, two Meritorious Service Medals, an Air Medal, a Joint Service Commendation Medal, three Army Commendation Medals, one with V for Valor, a Vietnamese Cross of Gallantry with Bronze Star, three Overseas Bars, and others. Fortunately, I suffered no wounds, no PTSD, and no Agent Orange-related diseases. I have retired to Atlantic Beach, Florida, where I enjoy walking, writing, music, the arts, birds and animals, wood working, and food.

PAUL ROGGENKAMP'S WAR

**U.S. Army Captain and Commanding Officer, 1st Commando Company,
Project Sigma, 5th Special Forces Detachment 52, (MAC-V SOG),
II Corps, Ho Ngoc Tao and Ban Me Thuot, 1968–69**

I was born and raised in a small farming town of 1200 people, Eureka, South Dakota. It was a great place to grow up, although it was fairly isolated. My family did not have a significant military service history; however, I had an uncle, my mother's twin brother, who was in the Invasion of Normandy and fought in the Battle of the Bulge. My father served in the CCC, the Civilian Conservation Corps. As a young boy, I read a lot, particularly military history, books about the Revolutionary and Civil Wars, the development of the nation and frontier life.

When I was a junior in high school, an Army recruiter visited our high school looking for kids interested in applying to the Military Academy. Because of my interest in history, I understood the history, traditions and contributions of West Point to our nation. I wanted to be a West Point graduate. So I began the application process and as it turned out, it was the only college to which I applied. I sent a letter to Senator Karl Mundt and received his principle nomination. I had very good grades, passed the entrance exams, was appointed, and on July 2, 1962, I joined the West Point class of 1966.

After graduation and commissioning, I was eager to prove my skills and test myself. I attended and graduated from Airborne and Ranger School, and then deployed to my initial troop assignment in Korea as a platoon leader in A Company of the 1st Battalion, 23rd Infantry Regiment, of the 2nd Infantry Division on the DMZ, the Demilitarized Zone or border between North and South Korea. This was serious business back then. It had been 13 years since the end of open warfare and the DMZ had no fence, barriers, or watch towers. It was overgrown scrub land with nothing but rusty and ineffective concertina wire barrier separating us from North Korea. It wasn't until the next year that the first chain link fence was built. My unit was responsible for a one-mile sector, running patrols and manning defensive points. For my first six months, I was a platoon leader and after promotion to first lieutenant, I was assigned as the battalion operations office for about 4 months, and then as commander of B Company for the final 2. An important factor in those assignments was that the Viet Nam war was heating up and many captains and majors were ordered to that theater, leaving shortages in Korea.

At that time I was considering extending my tour of duty in Korea, I received orders to Fort Leonard Wood in Missouri. I knew then where I didn't want to go, so I volunteered for Vietnam, with additional training at Pathfinder and Special Forces schools. I arrived in Vietnam as a captain in August 1968. Despite all my troop experience and special ops training, I was only 24 years old. In the last hours of the long flight to Viet Nam, I asked myself, "Am I ready for this?" After reviewing all I had experienced, I was confident that I was.

I was assigned to the 5th Special Forces Group, which was headquartered in Nha Trang along with a number of the other special operations groups. By 1968, the Special Forces were no longer operating on the classic "A" team model, organizing the locals into militias, and conducting unconventional warfare. That is not what we did. Instead, I led small groups of largely foreign mercenaries on long-range recon patrols, "black ops," searching for enemy troop units to set them up for artillery or air strikes and engaging in counter-guerilla warfare. In assuming command of the company, I replaced a West Point captain, Jerry Ledzinski from the class of 1965, and we became life-long friends. Fortunately, he ensured that I received a great transition into my command role.

At West Point and in Korea, I had been trained and prepared to lead US soldiers; however, in Vietnam, I led soldiers of the CIDG, Civilian Irregular Defense Group. My company was comprised of me, as commander, a US Army first lieutenant as Executive Officer and a US first sergeant and two US sergeants plus a cadre of a Vietnamese company commander, Chinese first sergeant, and Vietnamese and Cambodian platoon leaders and platoon sergeants. The other enlisted men were from a wide variety of other Asian ethnic groups, including Vietnamese, Jah, Sedang, and Rhade Montagnards, Cham, Cambodians, Chinese Nung, and Hmong, who we used to wage counterinsurgency, black-ops, and para-military warfare against the VC and NVA on their

ground, mostly in the Central Highlands. They were an interesting group, some of whom were older and had fought with and against the Viet Minh, the Communists, the French, and the Japanese. The younger soldiers were not very well trained, but the older ones had been fighting for years.

The Sigma Group was comprised of Recon Companies and the Commando Company, which I commanded. When we went out on operations, we wore dark, camouflage fatigues, not American made, with no rank insignia or patches of any kind. Nor did we wear our "dog tags" or any other kind of ID whatsoever. We carried little American gear or food; our rations were mostly Japanese and Vietnamese combat rations. I carried a US M-16, as did the ARVN and many other national troops. I chose the M-16 because I was a very good shot with a rifle and had been since I was a boy in South Dakota because my father taught me very well to hunt and to use guns correctly. Sometimes, I also carried a .45-caliber automatic pistol. The helicopters which supported us were painted black. Like our fatigue uniforms, they bore no markings or insignia. While it would have been obvious eventually that we were Americans, had we been captured, the idea was to have no way to tie us and what we did to the USA. At times, our teams moved around through VC country posing as VC. We knew that if we were captured or killed, we would be on our own. No one would do anything about it, and no one would even know about it.

Many people think that the title "SOG" meant Special Operations Group, but that isn't correct. SOG stood for "Studies and Observations Group," which was a nondescript title for classified work that was undefined and meant nothing, for precisely that reason.

Two of my very good friends commanded recon companies in our organization. Both were wounded on insertions into the Parrot's Beak area along the Cambodian border. Fierce fighting began as soon as they landed. One was shot in the face and lost an eye. The other was shot in the arm, and the bullet traveled from his elbow to his wrist; following which the bullet struck a CS grenade hanging on his web belt; it went off, leaving him badly burned as well. The rescue and recovery operation was complicated and required all units' best efforts. I was fortunate to never be wounded, but truly empathized with my brothers in arms who were.

We were based at Ho Ngoc Tao between Saigon and Binh Hoa. Our missions were not like those used in conventional infantry units. We deployed in the jungles in groups of 15-25 men, a few with the entire company of 150, mostly in areas along the Cambodian border looking for enemy troop concentrations, communications centers, support bases and weapons caches. If we were spotted, we had to fight our way out or run like hell through the jungle, because we weren't a large enough force to fight it out against conventional units of enemy forces.

On one mission given to my company was to insert and advance into an enemy POW camp believed to contain US prisoners. We had three days of time to prepare and rehearse. The plan was to deploy the whole company of 150 men by Chinook helicopters at night to hit the POW camp and rescue and evacuate the prisoners. The entire area was to be gassed, and then we would be inserted with gas masks on. Only a few hours before we were scheduled to leave, the Air Force Recon unit flew another recon flight and discovered that the camp area was under four feet of water as a result of a monsoon flood. Because of this new information, the mission was cancelled. I was very thankful of that decision. Most of my men weren't much taller than that, and with all of their gear on, many of them would have drowned if we had gone into the target area.

When we went out on our operations, I do not believe we entered Cambodia. I always carried a topographic map of the area of operation and navigated so we knew where we were and where we were going, but never established the relationship between our area of operations and the entire country. I think I went on roughly twenty-five missions over seven months. They were usually ten to fifteen days long, some longer and some shorter. Rarely did we have a specific target. Usually, we were searching for enemy units, and sometimes had a rough idea of where they might be found or at least where they were last seen.

On one such operation, at the end of the second day we came upon a seemingly never-ending network of trenches and fortified positions, probably a base camp for a very large unit which had come over the Ho Chi Minh trail and would use the base to rest and prepare to move into the interior of Viet Nam. The base had tunnels with bunkers and cooking stations deep underground. It was all very complicated and sophisticated. One cooking station had an elaborate arrangement of tunnels where the smoke would be drawn and dissipate away, helping to camouflage the base camp from the air. It was getting dark, and we observed the first rule of special ops: "When it gets dark, go deep into the jungle and find a place to hide." When it is pitch-dark, you can't move in the jungle without making too much noise which would compromise our security. So we would form our defensive perimeter and we didn't move until we could see in the early morning.

During the night, my radio operator heard radio transmissions on our frequency in a strange language. Our Vietnamese and Cambodian interpreters didn't know what language it was, nor did any of the soldiers I checked with. My Chinese first sergeant wasn't sure, but he thought it was a Chinese dialect. Chinese soldiers? Or Chinese military advisors to an NVA unit moving close enough to allow the radio transmissions to be received by our radios? I knew we couldn't move without making noise because of extremely low visibility, so we remained on alert until the first light of dawn and moved out quickly and stealthily until we were out of the base area and into thicker jungle. I then called in air strikes on the base camp site.

We worked closely with the ARVN Special Forces and their 81st ARVN Airborne Ranger Battalion, two of the South Vietnamese elite units, and our air support came almost exclusively from the 281st Assault Helicopter Company, a unique special ops helicopter unit also based at Nha Trang.

The recon teams were often equipped with enemy uniforms, gear, and weapons, and were a primary source of intel for the 2nd Field Force and Corps. Our insertions were usually made at twilight using four Huey slicks and two UH-1C gunships. The aircraft flew in a Delta formation at a high altitude. The lead aircraft was the C&C ship. The slicks would descend to tree-top level and make a few false insertions before the teams rappelled down to the LZ. They'd check in at least three times a day via aerial radio relay. Other teams placed electronic surveillance devices, set mechanical ambushes and a host of electronic devices to hinder and harass the enemy along infiltration routes into South Vietnam.

The normal rotation for officers in Viet Nam was six months in the field followed by six months on a staff. For seven months, I commanded the Commando Company. After four and a half months, we were relocated to Ban Me Thuot in the Central Highlands. Same missions, different location. For my last five months, I worked on the staff of Project Sigma, reporting to the 2nd Field Force Commanding General, Lieutenant General Ewell, briefing him on our operations to ensure that there would be no interference of friendly forces in the areas of operation. That was not a job that I enjoyed; I would have preferred to remain in the field with my company.

While I was there, I met many great people and developed undying respect for our helicopter pilots. They were mostly young warrant officers and were fearless and dedicated to their mission in support of the ground troops. On insertions and air support missions, and especially when we were being pulled out at the end of operations they would fly anywhere, anytime to get us out safely no matter the conditions.

I thought I was well-prepared to lead men in combat when I went over, and I was. What I was not prepared for was the realization of how badly the war was being mishandled on so many levels, and how so many lives were needlessly squandered in fruitless battles retaking the same ground over and over again. My West Point class lost 30 classmates killed in action. Two of these were close friends and gymnastics teammates of mine.

After Vietnam, I remained in the Army, retiring as a Lieutenant Colonel after 22 years' service. My most rewarding assignment was teaching US Military history with the US Army ROTC unit at UCLA. I was the leader of a Ranger Club and trained cadets on field exercises, during which I was able to teach them about small unit combat tactics and

Ranger skills. I also coached and played with cadets in all intramural sports in which we competed. It was very rewarding, and I knew that the cadets would become fine officers. Following my UCLA assignment, I served as a commander of two different companies in the 101st Airborne Division (Air Assault) and graduated from the inaugural class of Air Assault School, then served as an Area Manager and Executive Officer of the US Army Recruiting Command in Seattle, in Korea as a training advisor to First ROK Army; reassigned to Ft Lewis, Washington, as adjutant of the 3rd Brigade, of the 9th Infantry Division, as operations officer of the 2/47 Infantry Battalion and commander of the Headquarters Company of the US Army Garrison; served as a training and leadership advisor to units of the Liberian Army in West Africa, and my final assignment as Headquarters Commandant of I Corps at Fort Lewis, Washington. I retire in September 1988. After all that adventure and moving around, I felt that my family deserved a stable home and I was ready to try a new civilian career.

I began a second career of 22 years in commercial property management in the Pacific Northwest. I began managing super-regional malls and then large portfolios of multiple large shopping centers and mixed-use properties in multiple states. In 2011 after I stopped active management, I started a third career teaching commercial property management at North Seattle College. In 2012, I also created a leadership development and team-building program titled "Lead With Courage," working with companies, businesses, sports teams, and individuals to increase their understanding and capabilities in leadership. I found that many corporate groups and managers may be well trained in their fields and in business analysis, but they often have little or no training or understanding of leading, organizing, or motivating their employees and staff, which I learned at the Military Academy and practiced throughout my Army and civilian careers.

My wife and I are now semi-retired in the Seattle area with a winter get-away in Palm Springs, California. In addition to teaching leadership, I enjoy training thoroughbred racehorses, traveling and "glamor camping" with my wife, playing sports, skiing, and spending time with my grandkids and great-grandkids. My passion was and remains to help others benefit from my experiences and give them life skills and capabilities that will serve them and all whom they touch for a lifetime.

DAVE NORTON'S WAR

U.S. Army Specialist 5, Huey Crew Chief, and Acting Platoon Sergeant, 118th Assault Helicopter Company, 145th Aviation Battalion, Bien Hoa, two tours, 1968–70

I grew up in Elma, Washington, west of Olympia and forty miles from the Pacific coast. I tried college but it didn't work for me. Rather than wait to be drafted, I enlisted in the Army in August 1967 to become an aircraft mechanic and work on airplanes. I did Basic at Fort Lewis, Washington followed by aircraft mechanics at Fort Rucker, Alabama. Unfortunately, there was a big need for helicopter mechanics back then; so, in Phase 2 of training they put me in Huey mechanic school. The good news was we were promoted very, very quickly, to E-3 and then E-4 right out of school, but it wasn't because we were great students. You were supposed to be E-5 to become a Huey crew chief, they needed Huey crew chiefs in Vietnam as quickly as possible, so we were promoted. I was assigned to Hunter Army airfield right out of school and my first sergeant wanted me to go on to the NCO academy, but I kept turning him down. To get away from him I volunteered for Vietnam, and they didn't waste time granting me my wish. After my leave, on July 31, 1968, I was in-country as an E-5 one year after I was sworn in, and that's where I stayed for the next 21 months.

We flew from Oakland to Cam Ranh Bay and then to the 90th Replacement at Long Binh near Saigon in the back of a C-130 with no seats. We sat on the bare aluminum floor facing forward, hanging onto cargo straps stretched across the floor. At Long Binh, I lucked out by being assigned to the 145th Aviation Battalion stationed on the Bien Hoa Air Force Base, not the Army side. Big difference! The Air Force had paved streets, nice barracks, real showers, flush toilets,

an air-conditioned EM club, and mama-sans to do our laundry. I was even able to buy a refrigerator and began selling cold pop to the guys.

For the first month, new guys had to do maintenance in the hangars before they could be assigned to a flight crew. After a physical and some check rides, on Sept. 4, 1968, I finally got to fly. The crew chief was responsible for the maintenance of the helicopter, but he also doubled as a door gunner with one of the M-60 machine guns. Our door gunner was as new as I was, and I had to show him how to put the barrel in his M-60. Unfortunately, he forgot to lock it in. We weren't very far from base when he noticed his looked funny. He looked at mine, which is when we realized his had no barrel. The vibration must have caused it to fall out after we left base. Our aircraft commander wasn't happy with us when he heard.

The countryside was beautiful, but with a lot of contrasts. There were lush green rice paddies and acre upon acre of rubber trees. The rivers were always a muddy brown. Out on the coast, the sand was snow white and the water was blue green. But almost everywhere the place smelled like an open sewer. It was definitely culture shock to a naïve country boy!

I got along well with my first aircraft commander, which we called the "AC." He was a very cautious flyer. When we flew near the Cambodian border, he'd be up at 4,000 or 5,000 feet and then quickly spiral straight down so as not to be a good target very long. He got good at this. Most guys thought dropping 2,500 to 3,000 feet per minute was fast, but my AC did 4,200 feet per minute almost every time. That's like falling 48 miles per hour straight down! What a rush!

Midday on Thanksgiving, we had a gunship shot down. They tried to take on a Chicom .51-caliber anti-aircraft gun. Not a good idea. They made a run straight at it and were shot down before they even got close. The opposing forces were NVA, disciplined and well trained. Battalion tried to get the ARVNs to get to the aircraft, but they were taking fire and wouldn't do it. The gunships swore they saw guys waving to them and tried to protect the crew, but they took a lot of fire. We did too and were ordered to leave. Eventually, our CO decided the crew was dead and called in an air strike to destroy the downed Huey, so the NVA couldn't get any guns or radios off it. When U.S. troops reached it in the morning, they found three dead crew, but not the gunner. Just before Christmas the Red Cross announced they had the gunner in Cambodia, and he would be released on Christmas as a good will gesture. He was in very bad condition and we all figured that may have been why the NVA let him go.

A couple of times while working for the Navy, we had to take some guys out to certain coordinates and drop them off. They were tough-looking characters with no identifying rank or name tags, not even matching uniforms, if you could call them uniforms. Some had bush-type hats, no hats, bandanas, and even blue jeans, long hair by military standards, beards, and mustaches. They didn't talk to us, and we didn't talk to them. We did what we were told and dropped them off. I thought they had to be CIA. Now, I'm sure they were SEALS, which I didn't even know existed until after I was long gone from Vietnam.

The transmission on my bird failed and the replacement ship was an older UH-1D that had been back to the States for rebuild and upgrade to the "H" model. The "D" only had 1,100 hp, underpowered in the hot climate of Vietnam, while the "H" model had 1,400 hp. That extra 300 hp made a huge difference in lift capability, and I was happy as a clam at high tide to be in it.

Post-flight inspections were required at the end of each day to find and repair anything that may have gone bad during the day. No one wanted a mechanical problem to pop up in the morning when we were headed out on a mission. Most guys took an hour to do one and

in maintenance school, they said to allow an hour and twenty minutes. I was pretty good at it and was usually done in twenty minutes.

When our company commander's command and control ship was down, he'd used mine as the C&C ship. One job I had then was to mark LZs with colored smoke grenades for the "slick" helicopters going in with troops. The CO had me doing it from 2,500 feet. 2,500! It's a wonder they didn't run out of smoke before they hit the ground! The CO would tell me when to drop them, and he would have been a great B-17 bombardier. He rarely missed.

April 20, 1969 is a day I haven't forgotten. It was hot and dry, and we were inserting ARVNs into the Mekong Delta. We had shut down for lunch at Duc Hoa and parked in our favorite place, right under the barrels of a 105-millimeter howitzer battery. As usual, they were firing over the top of us. Those things have a "Crack" that about blows out your eardrums, so I left my flight helmet on. Pretty soon, we got a call that a gunship was down in a rice paddy and we had to recover the crew, whether they were dead or alive. Talk about nerves. They could have been shot down and we were going to the same place to land and recover the crew.

When we got there, three other gunships were covering the area. They said there was no ground fire, so we went in. A guy from Guam was my gunner. On the ground, we jumped out and started looking for the crew. The site was a dry, burned-over rice paddy, and the helicopter looked like bent scrap metal with parts scattered all over. In a minute or so we located the co-pilot, who was dinged up, but not too bad. Next, we found the crew chief. His leg was broken in five places and he was hurting. He also had a broken hip, but we didn't learn that until later. We got him to the helicopter, but I'm certain he was in pain.

Because my Guam gunner wasn't taking this too well, I told him to stay at the helicopter with the guys we already brought in, while I went looking for the AC. I looked all around for him and was getting frustrated until I found him inside the fuselage strapped in his seat. His helmet was gone, his skin was gray, and he had a 50-cent-sized hole over his left eye. He was dead and I was sick about it, but I was getting out of there. Someone else could deal with his body.

As we headed for the Evac Hospital at Tan Son Nhut, 25 miles away, the gunship crew chief, who was lying on the floor, motioned me closer to tell me something. "Don't let my foot fall out!" he said. I looked down. It even hurts me to write this; but with all the breaks, his leg muscles were stretching. His broken leg was about two or three inches longer and his foot did appear to be falling out the door. I reached my foot over and pushed his foot back in.

When we returned to the crash site later, we gathered the radios and guns. Someone else had recovered the AC's remains, and I was glad it wasn't me. The door gunner had not been strapped in when they crashed, and he had been thrown clear of the wreckage. That was the only time not having a seat belt on was a good thing. The door gunner was squatting down behind the two front seats with a hand on each so he could get a good view through the front windshield of the impacts of the rockets and mini-gun, when they went in on that gun run.

They had just refueled and re-armed, and the aircraft was very heavy on a hot day. That wasn't a good combination. Hot air is thinner, making it harder to fly, and the gunner told me they had made a steep gun run at the tree line. The helicopter couldn't recover from the dive and mushed into the ground, skidding about 100 feet until it hit a paddy dike, which flipped it over, causing it to tear itself apart. The rotors ripped off the top of the cockpit. The hole in the AC's head was thought to be caused by his striking the gunsight. For my part in this crew recovery I was awarded a Bronze Star with "V" for Valor. It was not deserved, but I wasn't the one pushing for medals for our unit.

On July 30, 1969, President Nixon visited Vietnam and we carried the standby reaction force from the 9th Infantry Division. We landed on a road along the backside of a rifle range next to a military base. There we were, bored silly, looking at a twelve to fifteen foot high berm. We had different kinds of weapons, and we were like a bunch of thrill-seeking teenagers. What could possibly go wrong? Out came the M-16s, .38-caliber revolvers, .45s, Thompsons, grease guns, and M-60 door guns, and we began shooting. Eventually, we decided we needed better targets, so someone threw out a smoke grenade. That was pretty cool – shoot the fuse off and get lots of colored smoke. More of your tax dollars gone up in smoke! And lots of them.

At one point one of the gunners hooked up a 1,000-round belt of ammo to his door gun. We'd all heard that M-60 barrels can get red hot, or even white hot. It was 95 degree plus, with no breeze, and this kid starts shooting. He doesn't let go of the trigger till the whole 1,000 rounds are gone. Then, he hooked up another 1,000 rounds and did it again. It was hard to believe none of the officers made him stop. He shot off the second 1,000, but I never saw the barrel glow red. I don't know where that story came from.

Finally, we were scrambled and carried the grunts to check out some suspicious activity. After dropping them off in a swamp, we went back to continue wasting tax dollars. After a while the call came to retrieve the grunts, because they didn't find anything. After wading around in the swamp, they were wet up to their armpits. As soon as we landed, all those guys jumped out, threw down their gear, and stripped down to undershorts, or nothing. They looked over themselves and their buddies. I couldn't figure out why until the light came on. Leeches! I knew there was a reason I signed up for aircraft maintenance!

One day, we carried a load of ARVN into the jungle west of Katum. Normally they never went places like that, because there were lots of bad guys up there on the Cambodian border. The ARVN preferred to let the US troops do the fighting, while they walked around in places where there weren't any NVA. It was a beautifully clear day and we knew we were headed for trouble, but we were in a war, after all! The radios were quiet. I remembered a little ditty and began to sing. Not being a regular voice on the radio I knew I wouldn't be recognized, so I sang, "Oh what a beautiful morning. Oh what a beautiful day. I've got a funny feeling, everything's coming my way." By everything, I meant bullets. The CO came on, demanded the singer stop, and wanted to know who it was. No one answered and no one ratted on me, so nothing more was said about it.

The LZ had been prepped by artillery for 30 minutes. As we were getting close, the firing stopped and they brought in air strikes, which we could see coming in the distance. When the bombing stopped our gunships took over, and we went in using "full suppression." That meant all the "slick" crew chiefs and gunners fired their machine guns along with what the gunships were putting down along each side of our flight.

We got in and dropped off the ARVN without incident; but as we were flying away, we began taking fire and the AC's cyclic control froze. That was not good. The co-pilot had to grab it with him to help control the ship, but that was the end of our day. We flew back to Tay Ninh and the AC made a running landing. Later, we found out a bullet had hit and jammed in the bearing that allowed the cyclic to move.

I found out later that that ARVN unit we put in was wiped out. No one survived.

Nui Ba Den, or Black Virgin Mountain, was a tall, cone-shaped mountain in the middle of a flat area to the northwest of Saigon toward the Cambodian border. The U.S. owned the top, but the VC and NVA owned the sides. They had a lot of tunnels and they liked to shoot at helicopters. We made quick, descending approaches when we had to land up there, and then a high-speed dive over the side when we left. I wouldn't have liked being stationed there. It was a radio relay center, and the guys were either radio operators or grunt guards. They depended on helicopters for everything and had no place to go and nothing to do up there. Their tours must have seemed about ten or fifteen years long. Makes you wonder who's foot they stepped on to get picked to pull duty up there.

As I got "short," on my tour, I decided to "extend" by seven months. I liked my duty in the battalion and didn't want to go back to a stateside assignment for the rest of my enlistment. In return, I got a "reenlistment leave" back home, and a five-month "early out" discharge. After I returned, on October 9th we had to pick up some U.S. troops from an LZ in the jungle about 20 miles northeast of Bien Hoa. My ship was in for maintenance, so I was stuck with one of the two underpowered D-model Hueys, flown by my platoon leader, Captain Miller.

We were the lead ship. As we got to the LZ, I saw it was a small, bombed-out clearing surrounded by 120-foot-tall trees. The only way in was a "hover," where we'd drop straight down and then climb straight up when it was time to leave. The other option to get out was to climb up about 40 feet or so, go over some shorter trees, and drop down over a moderately large river, the Song Dong Nai. But a helicopter needs forward speed to get "transitional lift" if it is carrying more weight. Climbing straight up in a hover takes a lot of power.

I told the captain that once we were loaded and before we tried to go up, we should hover on the LZ to check the power on this gutless D-model. I was very insistent, and he agreed. We picked up the five U.S. grunts and their gear and went up to 50 feet to try to hover. Didn't work. Not enough power and back down we went. On the ground, I told one of the grunts to get out, and we tried it again. Nope, we went back down again. Another grunt got out. Finally, the helicopter would hover, so out over the river we went, knowing we had enough power to accomplish the mission.

I told Captain Miller to tell the second D-model to do a hover check like we did. I don't know if he did or if they just didn't listen, but five minutes later, we heard an emergency radio call that the other D-model was in the river. The pilot was a 20-year Veteran, and apparently, he thought he could get it up to transitional lift speed before they reached the water, but he was wrong. The grunts were wearing heavy packs and the crew was wearing armored vests, all of which were pretty heavy. The rescue choppers picked up the co-pilot and crew chief, but the AC, door gunner, and five grunts drowned. Their bodies were not recovered. The door gunner was a friend, and it got me mad.

The weather wasn't very good that day, so we had to split up on our return to base. As if losing seven guys wasn't enough, one of our gunships never made it back. Three weeks later an infantry company found the wreck. It appeared they flew into jungle at about 60 knots and everyone died on impact. Two of the four crewmen had kids born after they were in Vietnam that they'd never seen.

One day in the last half of November '69 I was not scheduled to fly. As the flight left that morning, I watched them leave from the top of the barracks with some other guys. They were about five miles away and maneuvering into formation, when we saw black smoke. The ships began flying around like a swarm of bees and someone asked, "What the heck is going on over there?" A half hour later, our platoon sergeant told us there had been a midair collision. One helicopter flew too close to another, and their rotors hit. The resulting impact broke the rotor mast off the other ship. It fell 350', went in nose down, and exploded on impact. The second ship had no control, but the pilot got it in a left-hand descending turn until it hit some scrub brush on the ground. Fortunately, it didn't turn over or catch fire. A sad day.

There was an ongoing argument about jumping out of a falling helicopter. Someone said that if you jumped upward at the last moment, you could nullify the fall and survive the impact. I said a free-falling helicopter was going something over 100 miles per hour. No way is anyone going to jump up at 100 mph. Still, when it's your only option, you do what you have to do. That is what the crew chief of that helicopter tried. Just before it hit, he jumped up, and my theory proved correct. He died with the rest of the crew, but at least the Army had a body to send home.

One evening I heard a gunner laughing. His girlfriend wanted him to quit flying because she didn't want him getting killed. "No way I'm quitting, and I ain't gonna get killed," he said. The next day, while they were attacking a VC position, he tossed out a grenade at an enemy bunker, but it exploded as soon as he threw it, killing him and seriously damaging the helicopter. Turns out it was a "booby trap" grenade. That meant it was supposed to be left on the ground where the enemy would find it and try to use it on us, but the case was mislabeled. His "ain't gonna get killed" didn't work very well.

I made it through most of two tours without getting shot down. Then, one night when we were sent to deliver a radio repairman to another base, we were diverted to help a ground unit. Sure, why not? It was only a couple gooks in a rice paddy, someone said.

Right? We came in from the same direction as the VC were and turned on our search light, but we flew by without seeing anything. So, we turned around and made another pass. As we came over the top of the troops again, about 100 feet up, we turned on the light again.

They said a helicopter crew's life expectancy was seven seconds under fire. As soon as we turned on the light that second time, we started taking fire from all over the place, and I noticed a guy directly ahead of us standing in front of a hooch shooting at us with an AK-47 on full auto. Lots of muzzle flash. The gunner saw him too. We both tried to shoot the guy, but we couldn't get our guns turned around far enough in the mount to get him. It didn't much matter. Suddenly, we were falling like a proverbial rock!

It was the old "time slowing down" thing. I was amazed at how much went through my mind in just one or two seconds. The impact was tremendous. Then it was absolutely silent, until I heard our passenger moaning. The co-pilot and I seemed to be fine, but the AC couldn't move his legs, and the gunner's ammo can, with 2,000 rounds of 7.62 ammo, had bounced up, landed on one of his legs and it didn't work too well either. The pilots were disoriented. I used my radio to contact the grunts, but our radio must have been broken. That's when I realized we could have ruptured fuel tanks, so we shut the systems down.

The co-pilot and I were the only ones still mobile. We decided our passenger, who seemed to be hurt the worst, would have to lay there till medics arrived. The gunner stayed behind his gun, so the co-pilot and I tried to get the AC out to where we could lay him down flat. The guy only weighed 145 pounds, but in that cramped space the two of us together couldn't even begin to pick him up and we gave up on that idea. I got back on my M-60 and waited for help. The grunts were only 200 feet away, but they were trying to avoid booby traps and bullets in the dark, and that took time. Meanwhile, I wondered what happened to that VC with the AK who had been shooting at us. The nose of the helicopter ended up about one foot from the front wall of his hooch and a rotor blade had torn up his roof. So, where was he? Smashed flat under the helicopter? If nothing else, he was probably cleaning out his pants!

When they finally got us Medevaced out and we were on our way to the hospital, I couldn't sit. My butt was burning and hurting something fierce. Maybe I pinched a nerve? Turns out I had a compression fracture of the spine and spent eight days in the hospital flat on my back or stomach. They wouldn't let me out of bed, not even to sit up. Still, I was the only one from the crew that remained in-country. Everyone else was shipped back to the States.

When they released me from the hospital, I was reissued my flight suit and noticed it reeked of JP-4 jet fuel. That was when I understood why my butt was burning on the Medevac flight. It was the fuel-soaked flight suit that burned my skin. One of the fuel tanks had ruptured and soaked me and I didn't even notice. I'm sure glad there were no sparks at the time!

The photograph is of my helicopter after they slung loaded it and flew it back underneath a Chinook helicopter; that's how they brought them all back to their home base. You might say it was unflyable. We were shot down at Rach Kein, which is in a populated, rice-growing area fifteen miles south southwest of downtown Saigon. We had come down partially on top of a hooch pad, the built-up area in the rice paddies that they build their houses on. So the front part of the helicopter came down on the pad and the rest was in the

rice paddy. That's why it looks sort of broken down at the door posts behind the pilots, because the rice paddy was about two feet lower than the house pad. The adjacent photo shows the pilot holding onto the bearing that was shot-out, pointing to the bullet that caused all the problems.

When I was finally released, I was grounded and put on light company duty. Our platoon sergeant had rotated out and since I was an E-5, they made me Acting Platoon Sergeant. I scheduled the enlisted crews to fly and on which aircraft; but as my tour in Vietnam was ending soon, I really wanted to take one last ride in a Huey. My medical profile still wouldn't let me fly, so I got to scheming on how I could make it work. I found a pilot who would let me go with him, so I just scheduled myself in. It was Easter Sunday, 1970 and I went to the flight line as per normal to see the flight off. This time, I got on the chopper and away we went. Once we were away from base, the co-pilot and I changed places and I got up front. I had had a fair amount of stick time and could do most everything required from start up to shut down. The AC even let me fly it for the next 4 ½ hours. Boy was I in hog heaven! When we got to the end of the day, I made the call to Flight Following, "This is Thunderbird 521, destination termination, rotation, separation. See ya back on the block!" The tower laughed and said, "Have a good trip, wish I were going with you."

Ten days later I was on a "Freedom Bird" heading home. I was discharged at Oakland Army Terminal and wore my uniform all the way home to get the military discount with the airlines. A lot of negative things happened to returning Vietnam Vets, but for me it was different. Even though I went through San Francisco International Airport in the daytime, no one said anything to me or treated me differently. Since then, I have never at any point in my life received disrespect in any form.

I was awarded a Bronze Star with "V" for valor, a Purple Heart, and 16 Air Medals. By the end of my tours, I had about 1,625 flight hours, which should have been enough for 65 Air Medals, but no one was counting.

After I got home, I went into industrial construction as a millwright. I have a disability from my back injury when the helicopter was shot down and have been treated for Agent Orange-induced prostate cancer. Now, I'm retired, and enjoy backpacking, woodworking, working around my church, and enjoying my ten grandkids.

Looking back on it, I hated the Army, but I loved flying the Huey and I'm proud of my service to my country. I would suffer unmercifully if one of my kids had to go through what I went through, them being away at war like my folks went through with my older brother Perry and me. Even though both of us came home with Purple Hearts for being wounded in action, the Lord was merciful to us and our parents. I can only hope there will always be "the young, the dumb, and the immortal," like me and all the others who were willing to put their lives on the line for our freedom!

HARTMUT LAU'S WAR

**U.S. Army, Platoon Leader and Troop Commander, B Troop,
3rd Squadron, 5th Cavalry, 9th Infantry Division,
Quang Tri, Khe Sanh, Dong Ha, and Route 1 in I Corps, 1968-69**

My family emigrated from Germany to the USA after WWII. My father arrived in 1949 and, after he had saved enough money for the trip, my mother and we kids followed in 1952. My youngest sister, who was born in New Mexico in 1954, is the family's first US citizen. My father was an engineer who worked for the US Air Force at Holloman Air Force Base near Alamogordo, New Mexico, which is where I grew up. As a kid, I had a lot of jobs, including paper boy, yard mower, babysitter, and gas station attendant. I was orphaned at a young age but in our family it was very important to go to college even though there was no money to do that. That made West Point very appealing, so I applied and received an appointment. After their experience in WWII, I'm certain my parents would never have approved of my going into the military, but it felt

like my best choice. When I went to Vietnam, I wrote to my grandmother in Germany that I was stationed in San Francisco so she would not worry about me. Our Vietnam postal address, APO San Francisco, made it plausible.

I began at West Point in 1963, graduated with the class of 1967, and was commissioned an armor officer. West Point is an experience you appreciate more as you grow older. I can't say it was fun, but they kept us busy with classes and athletics and you can't help but learn.

When my class graduated, we were all required to attend our respective branch basic course and Ranger School

before reporting to a unit. Those of us assigned to an airborne unit went to airborne school as well. We were also required to have some troop duty before they sent us to Vietnam. Mine was with the 1st Squadron, 17th Cav, 82nd Airborne Division at Fort Bragg. My first deployment was to Washington, DC, for riot control duty after the Martin Luther King assassination. Shortly thereafter, in July 1968, I reported for duty in Vietnam with the 3rd Squadron, 5th Cavalry, 9th Infantry Division. This was the summer after the Tet Offensive and the big battles at Hue and Khe Sanh. The VC had been badly mauled all across Vietnam and the NVA had retreated west into the hills and mountains to rebuild. The bulk of the 9th Infantry Division was down in the Mekong River Delta, but, since our vehicles needed firmer ground, the 3rd of the 5th Cav was up north in the Quang Tri area; our mobility ensured that we moved around a lot throughout I Corps.

For the first few weeks, I was one of several lieutenants assigned as S-3 duty officers manning the squadron's Tactical Operations Center 24/7. The unit's missions included "reconnaissance in force" or "search and destroy" where we traveled through the bush hoping to make contact with the enemy, looking for a fight. We also provided security for other units, such as engineers building and repairing roads. And we rolled whenever infantry units got into trouble, especially if the weather hindered flight operations.

Working in the TOC gave me a good understanding of our area of operations and tactics. Initially, the squadron was attached to the 1st Cavalry Division, then to the 101st Airborne Infantry Division and finally to the 1st Brigade, 5th Mechanized Division. We were the mobile fire department, and from a platoon leader perspective, who the squadron commander reported to was irrelevant.

As soon as a lieutenant slot came open in one of the three troops, the new lieutenants were assigned to those jobs. I thus became platoon leader of 3rd Platoon, B Troop. My platoon consisted of six ACAVs and three M-48 tanks and their crews. ACAV stands for Armored Cavalry Assault Vehicle, the Army's hyperbolic name for an M-113 Armored Personnel Carrier with a couple of extra machine guns on top. We called both the ACAVs and the tanks our "tracks." Most of the time, we went out as a platoon, occasionally as a whole troop. We also had an M-113 that carried a 4.2-inch mortar, which remained in base camp with the artillery.

I stayed in that job for about six months until I was appointed the Troop Executive Officer. That only lasted about a week. My replacement at 3rd Platoon, B Troop panicked during his first firefight and was evacuated. I was sent back to my platoon until I became the troop commander about a month before my tour was over.

Living conditions weren't too bad. Our base, when we were there, was Camp Evans. We had wooden hooches with a roof, screens, and cots. In the field, we slept on the ground next to our vehicles, but we always had one man on guard on each vehicle. We ate a lot of C-rations. We would open the boxes and the men would choose and trade. By tradition, officers chose last and got whatever was left over. My sister always sent me dehydrated onions and hot sauce, which made even the worst Cs palatable.

When I first got there, we worked along the coast in I Corps. Vietnam has some of the most beautiful beaches in the world. Many of us felt if they would just stop shooting at each other, they could set up some gorgeous resorts and prosper. Inland was mostly scrub land until we reached the hills. We provided protection for the engineers building a road into the A Shau Valley and to Khe Sanh, adding culverts and stones to firm up the roadbed. When we got a movement order, we had to pack up and roll. Sometimes we had a few days' notice, sometimes an hour. Supplies and fuel were airlifted to us – a CH-47 carrying a huge rubber bladder full of diesel fuel is a sight to behold.

On our "recon in force" we would pass through villages occupied by old men, women, and children. The kids would run out asking for goodies, and we would toss them items from the supplemental packs that came with the C rations. Hershey Tropical chocolate bars were so bad the village kids threw them back at us. One day a kid ran in front of a moving ACAV and was killed; that ended the candy tossing. There were no villages further west. Out in the hills and mountains it was all hostiles.

We set up defensive positions every evening, circling the tracks like the wagons in an old Western movie. Once my CO realized I had Ranger training, I got to lead night patrols, putting out Claymore mines, setting up ambushes and listening posts. Most of the time, nothing happened; but one night we heard noise and movement in the brush and called in artillery fire on that area. In the morning, we sent out a patrol and found a few dead wild boars. Turns out boar meat is pretty tasty.

While we couldn't sneak up on anyone in the tracks, if we found a camp or bunker, our .50-caliber machine guns or the shape charges we set off would make short work of them. However, the enemy rarely stood and fought. They used hit-and-run tactics and every now and then one of them would pop up and fire one of their RPGs or B-40s at us. Those could punch through the thin aluminum of an APC and out the other side with no problem and even disable a tank.

As usual, we went out looking for a fight and we found a big one in February 1969. We ran into an underground NVA regimental headquarters with about 400 troops. I think the only reasons we made it through was that we caught them off guard and we had a lot of firepower — the tank's main gun fired canister rounds, each ACAV had a .50-caliber and two M-60 machine guns on top, and quick got air support. The Air Force forward air controller in his spotter plane not only called in tactical air but also helped me direct our fire and movement on the ground. I learned that when things get really tense, folks on the ground are simply too busy to worry about much else. I also learned that Medevac pilots and crew are crazy. They can see what's happening on the ground and yet they keep coming in to get the wounded. Many Veterans are still with us today thanks to those crazy heroes.

I have some intense memories of that particular day: the smell of cordite and sap from all the trees and other vegetation that the bullets chopped down and using an M-60 from my own track to "fire up" NVA soldiers who were climbing all over one of our tanks. We fired our machine guns and cannon for what seemed like all day long and then dismounted with our M-16s to police the battlefield when things had settled down. One problem I had that day was that my troops would pop up out of their cover to cheer whenever an F-4 came in for a bombing run immediately to our front, exposing themselves both to the enemy and to bomb shrapnel. My yelling at them was totally futile. We lost 2 KIA and I don't remember how many WIA, but the other side lost a lot more. Three of us B/3-5 troops were awarded Silver Stars for that day's work.

One day my platoon's task was to run some tracks up Highway 1 near Camp Evans looking for mines. When we got to the gate to leave it was locked and the MP in charge wouldn't open it and let us out until 6:00 a.m. I radioed my troop CO and explained the situation. I had the radio on speaker as my CO shouted, "Tell him to open that goddamned gate, or just run it down!" The MP guards couldn't open it fast enough.

One day, when the squadron was attached to the 101st Airborne, my platoon was providing security at a bridge after being on patrols for nearly a month. Early in the morning, a Huey came in and landed next to the bridge and the 101st Airborne commander and his sergeant major jumped out. They were both wearing tailored, pressed fatigues, and spit-shined black leather "jump boots." You can imagine what my men looked like: ragged and dirty. When the general stood on the back deck of one of our tanks, his sergeant major looked at our cavalry guys in their badly-worn canvas jungle boots and announced, "Sir, there's two kinds of soldiers: airborne and those that want to be airborne." That really pissed our guys off. Soon thereafter, the commander of the 1st Brigade, 101st Airborne, just as spiffy as his general, flew in to have a look at us. On the way back out, he griped at one of my platoon leaders about his men's ragged appearance (after three weeks in the field) and how he should get them squared away.

At that point, the platoon leader had had enough and said, "Sir, we killed more damned NVA in the past month than you and your damned brigade did the past year!"

I fully expected trouble but the brigade commander just blinked, turned on his heel and returned to his helicopter. We never saw him again.

Sometimes we had infantry support with us, typically a company of Army or Marines attached to the squadron. The Marines were usually from the 3rd Marines and the Army infantry came from whatever division our squadron was attached to at the time. One day, when a new Marine company came to relieve the Marines who had been with us, I saw what I thought was a Marine major showing the Marine company commander where to set up. I figured the major was their battalion XO or S-3. I met the major that evening and discovered he was a Navy chaplain who had previously been a Marine infantryman. I guess it's like they always say, "Once a Marine, always a Marine."

One of the best examples of leadership I saw during my tour was when our 3-star corps commanding general pinned a silver star on our troop commander, Jimmy Pitts. Pitts promptly turned, took it off, pinned it to the troop guide-on, then turned to his men and said, "This is yours, you earned it."

After Vietnam, I was assigned to a tank battalion in Germany, where I got well acquainted with the Hohenfels and Wildflecken training areas and also, because I heard it numerous times a day, with the Grafenwöhr tank gunnery range control radio procedures: "Graf range control, this is unit 31A, request permission to commence firing. OIC initials are Hotel Lima; safety officer initials are Whiskey Mike." Anyone who has served in an infantry, artillery, or armored unit in Germany knows exactly what I'm talking about.

I had the privilege of serving with American soldiers in the US, Korea, Vietnam, Belgium, and Germany in various command and staff positions. My last five years on active duty were with the US Mission to NATO Headquarters in Brussels, where I got a unique perspective on the changes in the Soviet Union, the fall of the Berlin Wall and the dissolution of the USSR and the Warsaw Pact.

After 24 years, I retired as a colonel and then spent seven more years in Germany, at the *George C. Marshall European Center for Security Studies*, a joint US/German program teaching officers and civilians from the former Soviet Union and Warsaw Pact countries the basics of democracy and civilian control of the military. I finished my career as a civilian working on the Army Staff at Headquarters, Department of the Army.

DOUG THORNBLOM'S WAR

U.S. Army Captain and Advisor, 2nd ARVN Airborne Battalion, Tay Ninh, Nui Ba Din, and Rung Sat Special Zone, 1968-69

The "Blue Max" saved my life and my unit during a fierce battle with the NVA in May of 1969. I was a very junior captain and the "acting" Senior Advisor to the 2nd Vietnamese Airborne Battalion. We had been operating between the Cambodian border and Tay Ninh City for about twelve days, with only one or two light contacts, and I was supposed to be a six-week temporary replacement for a major who had broken his leg in a parachute jump. Late that afternoon, we arrived in a wooded area and set up our defensive perimeter. We were all tired, filthy, and hungry. That night I dug only a shallow foxhole, less than a foot deep, next to my jungle hammock.

I always ate with the battalion commander, Lieutenant Colonel Thac, and all we had to eat that night was a bowl of rice and a cup of green tea. Sometimes we had preserved water buffalo or chicken, and nuoc mam, a fermented fish sauce, to eat, but not that evening. After the brief meal, I walked our perimeter and recommended to Thac that he put

out a listening post, an LP as it was called, between our perimeter and a nearby wood line, which was between us and the nearby Cambodian border.

Shortly after midnight we were hit by an NVA attack, but we were warned by that LP via radio that they had sighted NVA soldiers "low crawling" toward their position. Then an enemy mortar barrage began, followed by a ground attack that overran our

LP and penetrated part of our perimeter for a short time. Later, intelligence reports said it

was two NVA regiments that hit us that night, a lot of "bad guys" for one battalion to hold off.

I heard "Phao Kich!" (Incoming!) cries from the ARVN soldiers, and was out of my hammock and on the radio before the first mortar rounds landed. I immediately called for gunships and then ran over and told the Vietnamese battalion commander, Lieutenant Colonel Thac, and his executive officer what I was doing. By the time I got back to my foxhole, my U.S. artillery forward observer had come over, laid down beside it, got on his radio, and got our artillery support working. They were big, 8" howitzers out of Tay Ninh, but they were having a hard time putting steel on the wood line we were targeting about 300 meters from our position where the NVA mortars and machineguns firing at us were located. And by then, the NVA infantry was right on top of us.

"Blue Max" responded to my request, flying Cobras out of Tay Ninh base camp. They were the 2nd Battalion, the "aerial rocket artillery" of the 20th Artillery Regiment attached to the 1st Cav Division. They were a new piece in the evolution to armored cavalry tactics. In addition to the "pink," "red," and "blue" hunter-killer teams with various mixes of infantry, observation helicopters, and gunships that the Cav had developed to find and kill the enemy, the new "aerial artillery" helicopters added an overwhelming mobile firepower to the mix and helped the Air Cav reach its full potential. By 1969 they flew Cobra gunships armed with seventy-six 2.75 rockets, two M-60 machine guns, a minigun, and a 40-millimeter grenade launcher in the nose. It was said the 2nd Battalion of the 20th Artillery Regiment had as much firepower as three conventional artillery batteries, and they operated like airborne artillery, not a conventional air assault or cav helicopter company. They even called their companies "batteries," not squadrons, and each battery consisted of 12 helicopters. That was a lot of firepower to throw at enemy infantry.

Regarding the attack that May on the Cambodian border, as an article in the *Army Times* later reported:

> "Huey Cobra attack helicopters recently dived through a wall of anti-aircraft
> fire to smash enemy hopes of overwhelming an ARVN battalion near here. The
> 1st Cavalry Division (Airmobile) gunships were returning to their base camp at

Tay Ninh after having completed a fire support mission, when the whine of their engines was momentarily broken by the crackle of their radios. The message came in loud and clear: Assist the 2nd ARVN Airborne Battalion. Quickly changing course, one section of choppers flew to the contact area, led by First Lieutenant Donald McKinney and Warrant Officer Gary B. Vander Veen. "When we got over the area," McKinney said, "it looked like the Fourth of July. There were tracers flying everywhere."

Just as they arrived, another section of Aerial Rocket Artillery (ARA) choppers reached the scene. "I don't know how many anti-aircraft positions the NVA had," said Vander Veen, "but we were drawing a lot of fire." The pilots soon realized they couldn't stem the enemy ground attack and deal with his anti-aircraft fire at the same time. Quickly they radioed base camp for a "heavy section," a Cobra equipped with 2.75-inch rockets. Within 10 minutes of their call, Captain Melvin Finch and First Lieutenant Steve Roemer were on station. "When we first got there," said Warrant Officer Thomas G. Porter, "we'd dive at one .51-caliber position, but we'd get laced with fire from another position. We confused them with the rocket ship. They never expected to run into a three-ship section." The enemy pressure soon began to ease on the ARVN outpost. As daylight approached, the enemy fled toward his jungle sanctuary, leaving 24 comrades dead on the battlefield."

The *Army Times* account differs slightly from my remembrance, and although we counted only eight bodies in the dry rice paddy between our positions and theirs, we found about twenty more in the woods, along with dozens of bloody bandages and blood trails. I still have *The Army Times* article in my Vietnam scrapbook, along with some great photos of the helicopter pilots that I took later. They looked like they were about 19 or 20 years old – and a couple were.

We lifted the artillery fire when the first two Cobras arrived on station, followed by an unexpected third ship. They saw my strobe light, and I directed them in via azimuth and distance from the light toward the target. They began their first pass along our perimeter and drove the NVA soldiers back. Then they attacked the tree line where the mortar and machinegun fire were coming from.

On the lead Cobra's first pass, three separate .51-caliber anti-aircraft guns opened up on him. They were Russian World War II DShK or "Dushka" heavy machine guns, or the Chinese copies of them. Those were powerful weapons and very deadly to American aircraft, or anything else for that matter. The next pilot respectfully requested permission to address the machineguns first which I, of course, granted. His response was, "Roger, I'm rollin' in." He and his wing men salvoed their rockets on their next passes and silenced all three machine guns. It was quite a sight, with tracers firing up at the ships while they were in-bound on their run – streams of tracers going up and streams of tracers going back down from the Cobras – until they got closer and fired their rockets. It was some of the bravest flying I've ever seen. One of the Cobras was hit, but the pilot was able to make it back to base, switched aircraft, and returned to the fight. They were quickly replaced by two more Cobras, as the first three had to return to base and rearm. And so the rotations continued – even after a fourth antiaircraft gun opened up on them – until near daybreak, when the enemy broke contact and disengaged.

I called to my Forward Observer who was lying beside me but got no response. Alarmed, I shook him and called his name, "Gene! Gene!" (First Lieutenant Gene Foo Fong) thinking he had been wounded or killed. He looked up at me and said, "Wha…" I couldn't believe it. He was so tired he had fallen asleep during the hours of the battle after he had nothing to do once the gunships arrived. He woke up and got on his radio and got artillery working following the enemy all the way back to the Cambodian border. Since we couldn't see beyond the other side of the wood line, he was shooting blindly, but I'm sure the NVA took still more casualties as they retreated.

Funny, when it was over, I realized I had fought the entire battle in only my skivvies, flip flops, and steel helmet. I had no time to get dressed when the first mortar rounds were coming in. Afterward, I took a minute to put on my uniform and boots, and after coordinating with the Vietnamese battalion commander, I called for some airstrikes to make sure the NVA hadn't left any rear guard in the wood line before we advanced. Two U.S. F-4s cleared out the wood line with bombs and cannon fire. Once that was done, we advanced into the enemy positions and found a lot of bodies, blood, and bandages, but no live soldiers.

We had lost 9 men killed and 24 wounded, as I recall, one of which was self-inflicted. He had shot himself in the foot to get out of future combat. Still, the enemy got the worst of it by far.

A few days later we set up camp in a relatively secure area on the edge of Tay Ninh city for rest and resupply. I made it a point to drive into Tay Ninh Base and find out where the Blue Max headquarters was. I talked to the commanding officer of that "Aerial Rocket Artillery Battery," and thanked him for his unit's support. I wrote up an after-action report for him, and recommended all the pilots for awards, including the Silver Star for all the pilots who returned and repeatedly hit those woods, even changing aircraft after theirs had been damaged by enemy fire. Having coordinated with my Vietnamese battalion commander, who was also extremely grateful for the Blue Max fire support, I invited the American pilots who flew that day out to the woods, where our Battalion was resting, for a party. I swung by the "Class VI Store" (booze and cigarettes) and bought lots of booze and wine, and my battalion commander sent his executive officer to arrange food from a local restaurant.

The next day we set up tables and plastic tablecloths under some palm trees, spread out the food, wine and booze, and I drove in and escorted four pilots out for the party. Much drinking, speechmaking, eating, and war stories followed. We then gave the pilots some battlefield souvenirs, which we knew those guys never got to see, and amid many thanks and back slaps, sent them home with two "designated drivers."

I grew up as an Army brat and went to school all over the world. In 1958-59, my dad was one of the first advisors to work with and train the ARVN. I entered West Point when I was only 17 years old as part of the class of 1966. After Ranger School, I was assigned as a platoon leader in the 509th Airborne Infantry Regiment, which had been an old, storied, WW II parachute unit. By the 1960s, it was an airborne/mechanized infantry unit stationed in Mainz, Germany. I later served as the Battalion S-2 (Intelligence Officer) and as a company commander as many  units were short-handed due to the buildup for Vietnam. When I came down on orders for a MACV advisor slot in Vietnam, I was sent to a six-week Vietnamese crash course in El Paso. One thing I learned was that Vietnamese was very hard to learn, especially in six weeks.

Our advisor teams usually consisted of an American major, who was the senior advisor; a captain, who was the junior advisor; two senior NCOs, and an ARVN radio man for each American who spoke some English, to communicate with his people, and an American forward observer and his radioman, to communicate with supporting US air and artillery. I was six feet, one-half inch tall and weighed 181 pounds. The average ARVN soldier around me was five feet, four inches tall and 127 pounds. To say I stood out was an understatement. We ate with the Vietnamese officers and ate what they ate – a lot of rice and green tea. We never ate US food or even C-rations. I took gamma globulin shots and was never sick; I used Halazone tablets for the water. They worked. When we were on patrol through the jungle, I noticed the Vietnamese soldiers would often pick plants and shove them in their packs for dinner. Years later, I was an advisor in El Salvador and got sick from the food within days of my arrival.

The South Vietnamese 2nd Airborne Battalion, to which I was an advisor, was part of the ARVN Airborne Division, an elite, well-trained and well-led combat unit. They wore camouflaged jump uniforms and distinctive red berets, and had grown to a force of 13,000 men, all volunteers.

In February 1968, I became the part time, then full time, battalion Senior Advisor to Lieutenant Colonel Thac, Commander of the 2nd ARVN Airborne Battalion. I had already completed my six-month "field time." and was sent down from headquarters for six weeks until the real senior advisor was back on both legs after breaking one. Apparently, the major was always butting heads with Thac. He thought he should run the battalion, and Thac didn't like that. I had only been in the army all of two and a half years at the time and knew not to butt heads with anyone of Thac's experience in combat. Thac had fought against the Japanese as a teenager when they invaded Vietnam, then fought against the French, then

with the French against the Viet Minh, and now with us against the Viet Cong and NVA. He was a professional who had come up through the ranks of the ARVN, a scrawny dude who had been wounded eight times and had scars all over his body to prove it. When I got there, I told him I would act as a second pair of eyes and ears for him, make some suggestions, and coordinate artillery, helicopter, and "fast mover" fire support. I would be his assistant. He liked that.

I had no pretensions of him learning anything from me. However, in that first big battle when I suggested he put out a night listening post in front of our position, it probably kept us from being overrun; and he knew it. Then, I coordinated the artillery and Cobra gunship fire that beat back what turned out to be two NVA regiments that were attacking his battalion. After the battle was over, he flew back to brigade headquarters and told them he wanted me to stay as his permanent dude.

The ARVN brigade US advisor I reported to was Lieutenant Colonel Jack Nicholson. I later served as his S-3 when I was still a captain and he took over the 1st Brigade of the 1st Infantry Division, the Big Red One at Fort Riley, Kansas, in 1976. Anyway, he sent a bird to pick me up and fly me to the brigade headquarters to ask me if I wanted the job. I was supposed to go back to the staff position I held before they sent me in as a temp; but I immediately said yes. It was unheard of for a very junior captain to be made a senior advisor to an ARVN airborne battalion. There were senior majors who wanted the job, including the guy who had been temporarily sidelined with the broken leg. There was lots of hostility toward me up the chain of command, which I learned about after we got back to Saigon a month or so later for replacements and resupply. However, I was kept in the job and did almost six more months in the field with 2nd Battalion.

During one firefight, we had some seriously wounded. We called in a Medevac helicopter and an old ARVN Sikorsky H-34, a relic from the early 1950s, came in and landed. They would load the most seriously wounded ARVN soldiers aboard, the pilot would fly

them to the field hospital, and come right back for more, three times, under heavy fire. The last time he came, two mortar rounds struck the wounded who were lying on the LZ, but he came in anyway, loaded more wounded, and took off. He was as brave as any pilot I saw.

Lieutenant Colonel Thac's tactics and movements to contact were superb, along with his reactions and the quick deployment of his companies on contact with the enemy; and we had many contacts. I never once advised him to do anything different than what he did; and frankly, I learned a lot from him.

Only once did I disagree with his actions, but I reminded myself to stay out of the military business of a different culture. The morning after the big night battle referred to above, Lieutenant Colonel Thac called out his soldier who had shot himself in the foot with his M-16 in front of the entire battalion and yelled at him, calling him a coward and other things that I didn't understand, and then beat him with a tree branch. I went back to my team and told them not to interfere.

After Saigon fell to the North Vietnamese, many of the ARVN officers were sent to "re-education" camps – a nice term for a prison camp. I am told that Lieutenant Thac refused to be "re-educated" and lived for another one and one half years after being put in an underground "tiger cage" before he died. He was a very stubborn man. Many officers and government officials, seeing the inevitable, converted and went along. I'm confident Thac would rather die than submit.

During my tour in Vietnam, I wasn't wounded and have had no Vietnam-related disabilities except for a little PTSD. I remained in the Army and retired as a Colonel with 30 years in 1996. I commanded two battalions; served in Korea, Panama, and Spain; taught Spanish at West Point; and was the Military Attaché to Spain. I went on to work on Wall Street for Lehman Brothers and taught Spanish at Flagler College. Now, I enjoy investment management, working out in the gym, reading and writing. I have authored three books.

ROBERT HAYS'S WAR

U.S. Navy, Senior Corpsman, Delta Company, 1st Battalion, 4th Marines, 3rd Marine Division, I Corps, 1968 – 69

When I graduated from high school in 1962, I wanted to enlist, but my mother put the quietus on that one and made me go to college: Belhaven University in Jackson, Mississippi. I went, but with an attitude. I had no intention of studying, and figured I'd get kicked out by my second year, so I joined the Navy Reserves, so I'd be ready. What I didn't figure was that they were so desperate for male students that they wouldn't let me flunk out. So, I graduated.

The unit I joined had two specialties – radioman and Corpsman. I went for radioman; but after two weeks of electronic theory and Morse code, I decided Corpsman might be a better choice. After all, I was a biology major and the medical field might work with what little I learned in school. This was 1964 and Vietnam was just getting cranked up. I knew corpsmen could be attached to the Marines, but my attitude was, "Let's get it on!"

I graduated and went on active duty with the Navy in June 1967. I attended Hospital Corps School in San Diego followed by Field Med School at Camp Pendleton. After that, I was stationed at the Naval Hospital in Memphis until I came down on orders for Vietnam in October 1968, to the 3rd Marine Division. When I arrived in-country, I was sent to Delta Company, 1st Battalion, 4th Marines. Our area of operations (AO) was as far northwest in the country as you could get, bordered on the west by Laos and on the north by the DMZ. The Tet Offensive and the siege of Khe Sanh were over. I was in-country a month before being mortared the first time. Our ordinary missions were "search and destroy" or fire base security. We

were ambushed a few times walking through the jungle, but there wasn't much happening at that time.

Then came the assault on Fire Base Argonne. My letters home say it was March 19, 1969, but the official report says it was on the 20th. Whichever, it was the northwestern-most fire base in Vietnam. It had belonged to us back in December, and we had no real reason to believe otherwise. Our battalion commander, Lieutenant Colonel Sargent, sent a Huey up there with a pre-assault recon team to look things over and the Huey got shot down. Even though the colonel knew there were NVA up there, the decision was made to assault the hill anyway.

We had six CH-46s to launch the operation. Each could only hold 12 or 13 men, and we sent two in at a time, so we didn't exactly overwhelm the NVA holding that hill. I was on the third pair of choppers in. By then, we had landed about 50 men and had been engaged

for maybe ten to fifteen minutes, at the most. As my chopper began its descent, I heard gunfire everywhere. Our machine guns were firing, and stuff was happening all over. Looking out the window, I saw a pitched battle in progress. The ground was exploding everywhere on the hill as rounds of small arms, mortars, RPGs, and other munitions landed all over it.

As we hurtled toward the LZ, they told us to roll off in a hurry when the bird got six feet off the ground. We could either get off while it was going down or ther get off while it was going up, but it wasn't waiting. By the time it touched down, the helicopter was empty, sort of bounced, and got out of there fast.

On the ground, enemy resistance was heavy, with small-arms fire everywhere, mortar rounds going off, and utter chaos as we fanned out across the fire support base. When we neared Hill 1308, we were hit by deadly blasts of enemy automatic-weapons fire from well-constructed bunkers. They halted our progress but one thing that ran through my mind was to get to the top and kill all the people on the other side before they could kill us. I discovered that there is a drive which takes hold of a person and makes him do something he would not usually do – go through bullets to stop the bullets and hope there's not a bullet there that is destined for him. But to stop and try to hide would be suicide. In the end, it's the fastest guy who survives in action like that, or at least, the one who has the best chance.

So we shot our way to the top and destroyed the last enemy fortification. The hill was now ours, but it was getting dark and we had a tiger by the tail. There was smoke everywhere from burning trees, and we were still taking small-arms fire and mortar rounds from neighboring hills. During the assault we lost six men killed and eleven wounded, and found a few dead NVA in the ruined bunkers.

Dr. Sheppler, our battalion physician, had come in with us – he wanted to see what war was like, he said – and a couple of other Corpsmen, Rick McGaffick and Bob Biebel, came with him. We found a depression in the hillside and began to construct a hooch over it before the NVA got mad and decided to take it back. After the battle was over, there were several dead Marines laid out on the LZ to be flown out. One of them was a fellow who, just a few days earlier, had asked me to cut off all his hair because of the heat – I also served as a company barber – but I had refused. I told him that if he got killed, I didn't want his mother mad at me when he got home with no hair. Instead, he went home with a good haircut.

The next morning, Dr. Sheppler, McGaffick, Biebel, and I were trying to dig a hole in which to jump in case of mortar attack. The going was slow, because the mountain seemed like it was solid rock. We were digging between where two officers were standing and where our big guns were located. The two officers and the guns were about 25 feet on either side of us. All of a sudden, an NVA 82-millimeter mortar round landed right at the feet of the two officers. The more senior one was decapitated, and the other was killed with no apparent mark on him that I can remember.

The four of us digging the hole decided it was time to try it out, so we jumped inside. That's when the reality of how shallow it was set in. It could not have been more than eight or so inches deep, but we flattened out and waited for whatever was ahead. Then another mortar round landed and went off. This one hit between where the two men had been standing and our "hole." The NVA were trying to zero in their mortars on our gun pits, and the next round landed inches from the lip of our hole, on the right side. I was the right-side man, and it couldn't have struck more than a foot away from me. Dirt and shrapnel flew somewhere. God had kept me safe thus far, but I wondered where the next round would land. It hit on the left side of the hole, flying right over us! They then dropped a few among the guns before they stopped. We decided to quit trying to dig a hole in rock and went back to reinforcing the hooch we had found with ammo boxes and anything else we could find. That's me and Biebel sitting in front of it.

One of the officers that got Medevaced out had left his pack. Later, some guys found a bottle of Christian Brothers brandy in it, and we invented a new drink. The recipe was the officer's brandy and anything else: canned peach juice, Kool-Aid, whatever. It was all fine, as long as there was brandy in it. It wasn't very good, but we had a good time joking about it.

FB Argonne was high stress. We were mortared several times a day from an adjacent hill. Some guy sitting on his hooch would hear the Whoosh, Whoosh, Whoosh of the rounds leaving their tubes and yell, "Incoming!" and everyone would jump in a hole for a few minutes. We had lots of rounds land on top of our hooch, but none ever got through. A lot of dirt rained down on us, but who could tell or even care after a while?

Airstrikes were called in day after day against the adjoining hill where the NVA were tunneled in. The jets would roar past and drop their bombs, but as they flew away you could hear NVA machine guns firing after them. Their tunnels were something else in that hill. Not even a five-hundred-pound bomb fazed them. We tried to spot them, but we couldn't. The NVA were better at that stuff than we were.

Our patrols got ambushed every day. We would send them out, the NVA would leave them alone until dusk, and then ambush them. Around 10 p.m., the patrol would get back to our perimeter with their wounded and dead. My job and that of the other Corpsmen would be to start IVs on the LZ using red-lensed flashlights, as if the NVA didn't already have the LZ zeroed in. We'd call in Medevac choppers and arrange stretcher teams to carry the wounded on board as quickly as they could, because the mortars would start landing with the chopper.

We were mortared all day and harassed all night. I had at least five mortar rounds land within five feet of me, and no telling how many landed on top of our hooch. This went on night after night until April 4th, seventeen days of non-stop stress. By then it had been some 25 days without a bath. Sleeping, eating, living in dirt. We had dirt in our beards and in our hair, in the skin, and everywhere. It would take days after we got to the rear before we could get all the dirt washed out of us.

When we left FB Argonne, I wrote home that I left the hill with no regrets except that there were still NVA up there. The doctor put Rick McGaffick, Bob Biebel and me in for Bronze Stars for our part in the action on Argonne, but there had been no heroism on our parts. We had simply done our jobs. They were downgraded to Navy Commendation Medals with Combat V devices for valor under fire.

As I look back on it now, I realize being on FB Argonne was the most satisfying and fulfilling time in my life. It was the place in the military where I have many fond memories, because there is no greater honor I could have than to say I was a Navy Corpsman attached to the finest fighting force in the world – the United States Marine Corps.

On April 9, 1968, after six months in the field, they rotated me back to the battalion aid station at LZ Stud, officially known as Vandergrift Combat Base. One evening, I was sitting on my cot writing an old college friend when I heard an explosion. I looked up and saw a

ball of fire rising from the ammo dump, about 200 yards from our battalion area. The dump was big, about 300 yards long and 200 yards wide, covered with pallets of ammo of every size and description. A CH-53 helicopter had been lifting a load which was not centered right in the sling. He dropped down to allow the ground crew to adjust the load and his tail rotor hit a pallet of artillery shells. The chopper went around a time or two and crashed in the middle of all those explosives. The fireball I saw was the helicopter going up in flames as it exploded.

Rick McGaffick, Con Costillow, and I jumped in our jeep ambulance and raced to the crash site. As we drove in, what seemed to be scores of men were running out, as fast as they could. We got to within seventy-five feet of the burning chopper and saw a man walking around naked, except for his boots. Everything else had been burned off. We ran to the burning chopper and looked inside to see if anyone else might be in there. We wound up taking the naked guy and the door gunner, who had a big gash on the back of his head, to Charlie Med, the aid station, roughly a mile across Stud, for emergency treatment. As we were leaving, a second huge explosion went off. We were about 500 yards away, and it felt like it was right next to us.

When we dropped our patients off, we returned for a second trip. By that time, artillery rounds were beginning to explode. We drove onto the ammo dump LZ again and it was a raging inferno. Explosions were everywhere. We found another man with a big shrapnel wound and took him to Charlie Med. On the return trip – this would have been our third time in there – someone stopped us and said there was no one else left. We three corpsmen were the only men on the entire base of several thousand to respond to the crisis and go into the burning ammo dump, and had gotten all the wounded out. No one died in the fire and explosions.

As we were racing back to our battalion area, a piece of shrapnel about a foot long from an exploding artillery shell tore through the canvas cover of the ambulance, about a foot from my head. I heard "Whoosh, Whoosh, Whoosh" and each side of the canvas had a slit in it which hadn't been there before. When we got back, we could not believe we had done what we did. We just sat and shook for a while.

We watched the fireworks until about midnight. Nothing else in my life will ever match it for pure adrenalin-pumping excitement and sheer spectacle, I'm sure. Later that evening, some colonel came to the battalion aid station and commended us. As a result, we were awarded the Navy and Marine Corps Medal. I'll have to admit I was proud of what I did in Vietnam, and I am still proud of it. I received a Navy Commendation Medal with Combat "V" device and the Navy and Marine Corps Medal, the highest military medal awarded by our nation to Navy and Marine Corps personnel for heroism not occasioned by enemy action.

Later, I was assigned to Operation Sparrow Hawk. That meant that we spent 24 hours a day at LZ Stud, in case somebody needed help in the bush. Then they would immediately send us out. It was pretty easy duty except I got a slight case of dysentery. One night, I woke with my belly hurting something awful. I made it the fifty yards or so to the nearest four-holer, which was when things got dicey. You never wanted to stick your hand out in the dark in Vietnam to grab anything. Toilet paper was no exception. No telling what you might find – a rat, a scorpion, maybe a snake. The latrine was pitch dark, so I lit a match.

As background, the standard Vietnam "waste disposal system" consisted of sawn-off 55-gallon oil drums placed under each hole in a latrine. Once a day or so, the drum halves were pulled out and set on fire to burn the waste. No one who spent time in the Nam will ever forget that smell. After they cooled down, more diesel fuel was poured in to cover the mess, and they were shoved back inside under the holes, or at least that was the way the Marines in our area did it. But the day I had dysentery, apparently, they had run out of diesel fuel and used gasoline. It works just as well as diesel, but it is far more volatile. And, of course, I had no idea the switch had been made.

So, after I lit that match and found the toilet paper, I was standing there with my pants down, flicked out the match, and tossed it into the hole. The match must not have completely gone out. A big ball of flame shot up through the hole and began to burn the latrine down with me in it!

The only thing I could think of to put a fire out with was water, so I ran back to the tent hitching up my britches, grabbed my canteens, ran back to the four-holer, and began to pour the pitiful little streams into the barrel. It hadn't even occurred to me that water won't put out a gasoline fire. Finally, I ran around to the back of the four-holer, ripped the swinging door off its hinges, and placed it over the burning barrel. That worked. It put the fire out, so I went back to my tent, and went to sleep.

The next morning, there was a stir like you wouldn't believe. Everybody was looking for the guy who had turned the whole inside of the four-holer black. It was sooty from top to bottom and virtually unusable. You better believe that I joined in the search and beat the bushes with just as much zeal as the rest of them.

The Seabees were some of the sorriest folks around, to our way of thinking. They were the ones who built latrines but wouldn't do anything unless you paid them with something in trade. We had nothing to trade at the moment, and they had little sympathy for Marines who didn't have any better sense than to burn their own latrine down, so they wouldn't build us another one.

Because my reserve active duty commitment was only for two years, I rotated out in June 1969 and was discharged. I went into sales for a few years, and then to seminary. I earned a Master's and then a Doctorate – something I never thought I could do before I went over to Vietnam – and became a pastor in the Presbyterian Church of America. I have been ordained now for forty-two years, the last couple of them retired.

I live in central Mississippi, am still married to my first wife of 51 years. After 22 years of living on our own nine acres, we moved to a no-maintenance golf course condo community and enjoy life. God has been good. Because of what we went through in Vietnam, I came home knowing in my heart that there was nothing required of any mortal of which I was not capable. The words "I can't" were no longer part of my vocabulary. I went to Vietnam a grown boy and returned a man who lived up to the challenges of running into the face of enemy fire to do his job, praying to God that He would get me through.

I wouldn't take a million dollars for my service. It earned me the respect of men I have the highest respect for, the greatest fighting force in the world, the United Sates Marine Corps.

Because of the way it changed my life, I always encouraged my son and then his sons to enter the service. My son retired from the Army after twenty-eight years as a helicopter pilot, and both of my grandsons are in service, one in the Army and one in the Air Force. I am very proud of all three of them, by the way.

RAYMOND "FRED" REES'S WAR

U.S. Army Captain, Troop Commander, and S-3 Air, Headquarters and D Troops, 2nd Squadron, 17th Cavalry, 101st Airborne Division, Camp Eagle, I Corps, 1968-69

I grew up in Helix, Oregon, a high-plains dryland farming area – wheat and canola – near the Washington and Idaho borders. My five uncles all served in WW II and as kids we grew up hearing stories about that war and Korea. I also remember an early TV show on West Point that I watched every week. For me, deciding to pursue a military career was easy, and I wanted to attend West Point and become a Regular Army officer.

When I enrolled in the United States Military Academy in 1962 as a member of the class of 1966, our military was focused on Korea, the last war fought, and on conventional war, the Cold War, in Europe against Russian tanks. We were aware of Vietnam and other pressures in Asia, but we were a peacetime army and West Point was a peacetime school, at least until my last year or two. As a cadet, I wasn't an NCAA level athlete. I played on some club teams, like water polo, but I concentrated on academics and on the cadet brigade, serving as a Cadet Lieutenant and then on a company and battalion staff. One sign that Vietnam was becoming more important was that Ranger School became mandatory for my class and future classes after graduation. Prior to that, it had been voluntary.

After graduation, commissioning as a second lieutenant in the armor branch, and attending Ranger School, I was assigned to the 2nd Squadron, 2nd Armored Cavalry Regiment in Bamberg, Germany. I was immediately assigned as a platoon leader, patrolling the East German border near Coburg. Armored Cavalry was to be the "new big thing" in the Army at that time. World War II and Korea may have been fought by straight-legged infantry, armor, and airborne divisions, but the world scene in the late 1960s with counterinsurgency and Third World asymmetrical conflicts demanded more flexibility. American division after American division was being converted to more mobile mechanized infantry equipment and tactics; and, with the rapid introduction of helicopters and airmobile equipment and doctrine, to air cavalry and air assault units. It was the biggest change to the Army since the horses were put back in the barn. Being part of that evolution in the Regular Army and the Army National Guard became the focus of my career.

My assignment to an ACR unit in Germany was doubly fortuitous, in that the German-based units were being heavily levied to supply troops for the expansion in Vietnam. All the experienced officers and NCOs were gone. My 2nd Squadron (a battalion) had a Lieutenant Colonel, a Major, a Captain, and a lot of Second Lieutenants. I was immediately

given command of a platoon for my first four months, followed by a tank company for five months, all as a second lieutenant. That was a most remarkable way of gaining experience. After those assignments, I became the S-4, in charge of supply, and then S-3 in charge of air operations. What tremendous responsibility and a learning opportunity for a second and then a first lieutenant. Unfortunately, the Army soon began to pay the price for that lack of experienced officer and NCO leadership in Germany with steadily increasing drug and race problems, particularly in the combat arms units in northern and eastern Germany closest to the East German and Czech borders. When I left Germany in November 1968, I attended Jungle School in Panama on my way to Vietnam.

When I knew I would soon be headed there, I asked for assignment to the 101st Airborne Division, because I knew they were beginning the transition to an air assault/air cavalry division. With its expanded air mobility, the 1st Air Cavalry Division had proven successful in Vietnam, and the Army wanted more of that. The 101st was the next division to go through that transition. By the end of spring 1969, the 101st had been completely converted over and was a mirror-image of the 1st Cav. The 101st may have had a proud tradition of making parachute jumps into Normandy and Holland during WW II, but by 1969 they rode into battle on helicopters. They didn't jump out of airplanes any more than the 1st Cav rode in on horses. However, the addition of all those helicopters, the supply and maintenance facilities that went with them, and the flight and maintenance personnel was a massive undertaking. With my cav experience in Germany, my assignment to 2nd Squadron of the 17th Cav of the 101st in Vietnam was an easy decision, and exactly where I wanted to go. The 101st was a top notch, proud organization, with experienced, career NCOs and officers. By then, the enlisted men were a mix of draftees and volunteers, but for the most part they were well-motivated and lacking the "unhappy" baggage that so many other units had to put up with.

I served as the Assistant S-3 for Air Operations for my first ninety days in-country, and then as commander of D Troop (a company) for the remainder. We were based at Bien Hoa, near Saigon, and then moved to Camp Eagle, south of Hue in I Corps. D Company had a unique mission, to perform active small unit reconnaissance. The division had gone north after Tet. The local VC forces all across Vietnam had been wiped out or driven underground and were now being replaced by regular NVA regiments coming into I Corps and the Central Highlands, bypassing Hue and Phu Bai. We would receive rocket attacks, but only rarely an infantry attack. By early 1969, we were working out west in the hills and mountains beyond the coastal plain, working the A Shau Valley and other infiltration routes from the Ho Chi Minh Trail, trying to cut off the supply of men and arms.

We were an Air Cavalry Squadron. We would send out scout helicopters: small, bubble-nose Loaches to find the bad guys, often by drawing their fire. When we did, we would send in gunships and our own infantry from the squadron's aero-rifle platoon and engage them. It was integrated use of the air, infantry, and aerial firepower. If the battle escalated, we would send in even more troops and call on even more firepower, as needed. Because we had our own infantry, they were also required to provide the security patrols around the base. D Troop had three identical platoons and was equipped with jeeps and light trucks with machine guns, recoilless rifles, and mortars, which were used as a mobile force to patrol roads. Whether it was by helicopter or vehicle, the tactics were the same: find them, fix them, and attack them.

One platoon was typically out on the road, one on security patrols around Camp Eagle, and one back at camp on standby and to provide the "Blue" Team infantry when the scout helicopters found anything to pursue. As the troop commander, if two or more of my platoons were deployed, or if we were on a troop-level sweep, then I would also go to provide command-and-control. Those type of larger operations happened maybe once per month, if we were working the A Shau or one of the other hot spots.

When my tour was over in December 1969, I was assigned to the Army Training Center at Fort Lewis, Washington for six months as the Chief of the AIT Training Section. At that point, I applied for flight school, figuring that would be a good skill to add as the Army continued to transition. But by the time I finished training at Fort Walters and Fort Rucker in April 1971, the drawdown from Vietnam was continuing to escalate. I was scheduled for a Vietnam assignment, but there were too few slots and I was sent to the Armor Officer Advanced Course at Fort Knox instead, followed by the 1st Squadron of the 17th Cavalry Regiment of the 82nd Airborne at Fort Bragg. It too was converting from Airborne to an Air Assault Division. I served as a platoon leader in an aviation troop, and then as the troop executive officer until August 1973, when I made a major career change and resigned my regular Army commission. When I left active duty, I had been awarded a Bronze Star, an Air Medal, and an Army Commendation medal.

In 1973, I returned home to Oregon and earned a law degree from the University of Oregon. Rather than settle in as a civilian, I joined the Oregon Army National Guard, with whom I would continue to serve in various reserve and active duty capacities for the next 30 years, until I retired from the National Guard in 2013 with the rank of Major General. For the succeeding five years, from 2014 to 2019 I have served as a Deputy Assistant Secretary of the Army in the Pentagon.

My initial assignments with the National Guard were as an operations and training specialist at the headquarters in Salem. I held increasingly responsible positions with the 41st infantry brigade, the 141st support battalion in Portland, and the 162nd Infantry in Corvallis, followed by a series of armored cavalry leadership positions in both the Oregon and Idaho National Guards, commanding the 116th armored CAV Regiment in Twin Falls, Idaho. I also held positions in Washington, DC, as Director of the Army National Guard Bureau, the vice chief and acting chief of the National Guard Bureau, the Chief of Staff US Northern command and North American Aerospace Defense command at Peterson Air Force Base Colorado and for eight years as the Adjutant General of the Oregon National Guard.

The Oregon guard was an active member of the Pacific command, PACOM, and participated in various international search and rescue partnerships and natural disaster planning with other countries to help spread training and "best practices" throughout the Pacific region. We were a partner with Bangladesh; and, while I was Adjutant General, a partner with Vietnam, as a people-to-people bridge-building exercise. It was when we sat down at the table and began talking that I learned that the Vietnamese representative across from me, General Que, had been an enlisted sapper up in I Corps when I was there, one of those guys who were trying to crawl through the wire and blow us up. We both learned that as you get older, shared experiences can be beneficial, and you gain a new perspective on the enemy.

In my early years with the National Guard, what became known as the Laird Doctrine, named for Secretary of Defense Mel Laird, who served under President Nixon, was implemented. President Johnson chose to fight the Vietnam War with the draft as opposed to calling up Reserve and National Guard units, to the detriment both of the active Army and of the Reserves and the Guard, whose readiness, training, and equipment steadily declined. The Laird Doctrine was a commitment to the Reserves and the Guard units that this would not happen again. The Guard and Reserves would be trained and equipped and serve as an adjunct to the active duty forces, to be called up to active duty and expected to participate fully in any future conflicts, which is exactly what happened in both Iraq wars and in Afghanistan.

During my time with the National Guard, I have received numerous awards and decorations, including the Defense Distinguished Service Medal, Army Distinguished Service Medal, Legion of Merit with Oak Leaf Cluster, Meritorious Service Medal with two Oak Leaf Clusters, and others.

Now, I am fully retired and have returned to our family farm near the small town of Helix in northeastern Oregon.

MIKE PLUEGER'S WAR

**U.S. Army, Sergeant E-5, Managed Battalion Helicopter Pad and
M-60 Machine Gunner, 1st Battalion, 14th Infantry, 4th Infantry Division,
Central Highlands, Pleiku, Kontum, Ban Me Thuot, An Khe, and Qui Nhon,
1969–70**

After growing up on a farm in Scotch Grove, Iowa, in the eastern part of the state, I attended Iowa State University, majored in Animal Science, and graduated in 1967. I had a college deferment from the draft during my four years of college, but that ended with the diploma. I was called in for a physical shortly before graduation. I flunked it. I was 6 feet 6 ½ inches tall barefoot, and the draft had a height limit of 6 feet 6 inches. A year later, when they needed more bodies to fight in Vietnam, that height limit was miraculously raised two inches, to 6 feet 8 inches; and I was promptly called for another physical. Surprise! I passed. And I was inducted into the Army on September 19, 1968.

There were still a lot of tricks and games you could play, as some guys did; but rather than try to get into the Reserves or enlist to get some particular job, I thought I might as well just get drafted and get it over with. I felt a sense of duty and was ready for a little adventure. But my story is different than most of the guys I served with – I was four years older than most draftees; I had a college degree; and I was very tall. For some reason I thought my college degree would keep me out of the infantry. I was wrong. My family dropped me off at the Greyhound bus stop on Main Street in Anamosa, Iowa, and I was off to

Fort Polk, Louisiana. My mother is now 95 years old and still says the year I was in Vietnam was the longest and worst year of her life.

Fort Polk… They said the Army could drop you off in the Mekong Delta and you'd think it was an improvement… and that the natives were more friendly. After Basic Training, they loaded us on trucks and hauled us up to North Polk, "Tiger Land" as they called the AIT, or Advanced Infantry Training site. I will always remember the sign hanging over the entrance. It read, "Through These Portals Pass the Best Trained Killers in the World." That got my attention.

On March 8, 1969, I arrived at Cam Ranh Bay, on the central coast of Vietnam. Getting off the plane, I'll never forget the horrible heat, humidity, and smell. To this day, I don't travel much off our acreage in eastern Iowa. I got on a plane to visit my sister in California in 2018. That was my first time on an airplane since I came home from Vietnam nearly 50 years ago. I tell my family that I traveled enough during the war for a lifetime.

Firebase Short: March – April 1969

After a few days at the reception station, we were flown to Camp Enari in Pleiku in the Central Highlands of Vietnam, the home of the 4th Infantry Division. From there, some of us were sent to Firebase Mary Lou near Kontum where the 1st Battalion of the 14th Infantry Regiment was located then. As I soon learned, the Central Highlands were full of firebases. Two weeks later, on March 23, four of us were flown by Huey helicopter to Firebase Short where we joined Alpha Company as replacements. Firebase Short was at the top of a very big hill in the middle of the jungle. There was a battery of artillery there with us and everything had to be flown in by chopper – including water which was hauled in on water trailers by Chinook choppers.

I was promptly handed an M-60 machine gun – the largest weapon you can carry – because I was the biggest guy in the squad at nearly 6 feet 7 inches tall. We were on that hill for five weeks except for a few patrols. Four of us went on a short-range recon patrol (SRRP) and we found a trail of elephant tracks. You don't see that in Iowa!

While at FB Short, we saw no enemy and saw no combat, but it was a miserable place. At times we were short of water. One time we were so thirsty that we took a patrol down to the bottom of the hill to a small stream. We took a bunch of canteens to fill and we took our weapons too. After filling the canteens and resting, we headed back up that massive hill, but it was so hot and humid that we drank most of the water by the time we got back to the top.

A few years ago, I found a 1969 abbreviated battalion journal on the internet. I was shocked to learn that on March 10, 1969, just 13 days before I joined the company, Alpha Company had been in a big battle. Five men were killed, and many were wounded. Nobody said anything about that to us new guys. The battalion memorial page verified the five men killed. Looking back, I should have suspected something like that happened, since no one ever talked about past experiences. Evidently, I replaced someone who had been killed or wounded, since they just handed me the M-60 machine gun without saying who carried it before me.

Firebase St. George: April – November 1969

At the end of April 1969, we were flown out of LZ Short and then trucked to Firebase Mary Lou for a stand down. I had my first shower in five weeks. After a few days, the entire battalion took a convoy to Firebase St. George, which was located about ten miles southeast of Pleiku. It became the battalion headquarters until the big attack on November 6, 1969.

St. George was a pretty good place as far as firebases go. It was easily accessed by truck and there was a mess hall and showers. The headquarters company ran the battalion from there. One company provided security for St. George while the rest of the companies were in the bush or at smaller firebases. The companies rotated in and out of St. George. My Alpha Company was on patrol for 22 days in May 1969 including one 14-day stretch.

We did not see much action during the summer of '69 except for an occasional sniper, nor did we have any men hurt during that period, but I would still hit the dirt whenever I heard the distinct crack of an AK-47.

One time while we were on patrol in the bush, a couple of Viet Cong took some shots at us. One of our guys saw one duck behind a tree. Since it was quite a distance away, they told me to use the M-60 machine gun. I couldn't see the guy, but I fired 10-15 rounds at the tree. I hit it but nothing else. I remember chugging a warm beer that I had in my pack after it was over. That was the only time I ever shot at anyone.

Toward the end of June, we got some replacements for guys who were rotating home. One guy was big and well-built, about 6 feet 4 inches tall, named John Barker. My squad leader, Sergeant Steve LeChina, promptly gave him my M-60 since I had carried it long enough. He said that my eyes lit up when I saw Barker join the squad because I knew my replacement for the M-60 had arrived! I spent the next couple of months as an assistant gunner.

On another patrol near the Cambodian border we came across a lot of "punji stakes." They were razor-sharp bamboo sticks the VC stuck upright in the ground, usually in the tall grass where we would not see them and might run into them. A couple of times I had some stick in my boots and boot laces. I saved a couple and tried to figure out a way to send them home, but I finally gave up and destroyed them.

One time while on patrol we accidentally crossed the border into Cambodia. At that time, we weren't supposed to be there. Nothing happened but at least I can say that I've been to Cambodia.

Another memory from the summer of '69 was a "bushmaster," that's what we called an ambush, which my squad set up along a trail. We had our Claymore mines and trip flares out and we were settled in for the night. Sometime after dark we smelled the very strong and distinct smell of marijuana, but none of our guys were smoking! Evidently, the Viet Cong were very close for the smell to be that strong. We didn't get any sleep that night, but nothing happened. In the morning, we packed up and went back to the rest of the company.

At the end of August, I got lucky. The company first sergeant needed someone to work at the helicopter pad at St. George. For some reason, he picked me. I think the fact that I was older than a lot of the guys may have influenced his decision, because the job required being responsible for organizing the pad and sending out supplies on choppers to the guys in the field. The guy I was replacing trained me for a couple of weeks before rotating home and I usually had another guy helping me. We had a radio so we could talk to the pilots. The chopper pad was outside the firebase perimeter and we would sit out there most of the day, not knowing when we would get a resupply chopper coming in. I got a really good tan and it was an easy job most of the time.

St. George was a firebase with about 225 men, counting headquarters company, a company that provided perimeter security, an artillery battery, and others who were always coming and going from various companies. There were bunkers around the perimeter where the company providing security stayed. Beyond the bunkers were three rolls of barbed wire with trip flares and Claymore mines. The interior of the firebase had a big bunker for the battalion headquarters, tents with a couple of feet of sandbags around them as blast protection, a mess hall, sleeping quarters, and a road down the middle. I slept on an Army cot in a tent with about 20 other guys. We had it pretty good compared to the guys in the field or those living in bunkers on the perimeter.

One thing I will always remember about St. George was the rat infestation. We could hear them running around at night and several times I felt a rat run over my legs while I was lying in my cot. Our chaplain got bit by a rat and had to go back to the rear for rabies shots.

The Day All Hell Broke Loose: November 6, 1969

Everything went pretty well up at St. George until the early morning hours of November 6, 1969. All hell broke loose shortly after midnight. We were hit by a ground attack as well as rockets. Some Viet Cong had gotten through the wire with satchel charges and were inside the compound throwing them around.

I woke up to all the racket, ran outside the tent, and met a sergeant looking for me. He said we had wounded men and a Medevac helicopter had been called. We were going to use part of the motor pool to land choppers inside the wire and I was given a strobe light to direct them in. A lieutenant was nearby with a radio and he coordinated the choppers and talked to battalion headquarters.

When a Medevac chopper came in, I was supposed to stand out there in the open with a strobe light so the pilot could see where to land. I had never even seen a strobe light before and now I was standing in the open waving one in the dark during an attack for all the Viet Cong to see. As a chopper came in, it was accompanied by Cobra gunships blasting the perimeter. Additionally, all the men on the perimeter opened fire to keep the enemy back. We loaded the choppers with wounded guys as fast as we could and then they took off. It wasn't continuous, but the attack went on for about six hours until daylight. Artillery from other firebases was called in and illumination rounds were used to light up the place.

At one point, even Spooky was called in. This was an AC-47 cargo plane with three 7.62 mm mini-guns pointed out one side. Spooky would bank to one side, circle the target, and shoot around the firebase perimeter. Each mini-gun could fire 2,000 rounds per minute. Every fifth round was a red tracer so they could direct the fire, and it looked like a red neon light show that night. Spooky also dropped flares to light the place up.

In total, 31 guys were wounded and nine killed that night. One of those killed was Tom Putman who had joined Alpha Company with me and two others at Firebase Short back in March. He was only 20 years old and left behind a young wife. You can Google Firebase St. George and read more about that battle.

In the morning, a truck driver was checking out his truck that had the tires shot out. He found a live NVA wearing black pajamas up in the truck's wheel well. He was taken prisoner, but fortunately was not armed when captured. I had been standing near that truck during the entire attack. Replacements arrived that morning. They were put on a detail to pick up the bodies of the enemy killed during the attack. What a way to start your tour! They loaded 29 bodies in a truck. After a couple of days, the battalion brass decided to bury the bodies in a mass grave. A bulldozer was brought in and a trench was dug. The truck driver backed the truck up to the trench and tossed in the bodies. As this was happening, about fifteen to twenty Vietnamese women and children showed up and watched. They were all crying and screaming. It got extra loud at times when they recognized one of the bodies. That memory still bothers me deeply to this day.

On November 11, 1969, the whole battalion was moved to LZ Lois near Ban Me Thuot. Firebase St. George was abandoned and bulldozed. I wrote home to my family to let them know they will see news of a bad attack. I told them we lost a lot of guys, but I was okay. I was awarded a Bronze Star with "V" Device for valor, when I waved the strobe light to land the Medevac helicopters during the attack.

LZ Lois: November – December 1969

The battalion headquarters stayed at LZ Lois until the end of December. I worked out of the airfield at Ban Me Thuot sending out supplies like I did at St. George. Part time, I worked as a radio operator at LZ Lois.

December was a good month because I was promoted to Sergeant and had a seven-day R&R to Australia. Those seven days plus travel to and from Australia took up about half of December. At the end of the month, the entire battalion moved to Camp Enari near Pleiku for another "stand down" or rest for a few days.

Camp Radcliff: January 1970

We rang in the New Year by moving the entire battalion to Camp Radcliff near An Khe on January 1, 1970. This was a big base that was being downsized. It was 16 miles around but there was a lot of wasted space. Also, it wasn't very secure. They even ran security patrols inside the perimeter.

Headquarters Company stayed at Camp Radcliff while the rest of the companies were out in the boonies. I oversaw the battalion chopper pad again. The hills around Radcliff were rough and there were no roads to the place, so all resupply came in from the depots and was sent out to our companies by chopper. Some large loads had to be sent in nets hooked under Chinook helicopters. One time I hooked on 5,000 pounds of mortar shells. At one point in the trip the net broke or something went wrong. We lost the whole load. I don't know what happened, but nobody ever said anything.

Sometimes I rode along on the Hueys when resupply was sent out. This was partly to ensure stuff got to the right people and partly for a joy ride. The scenery was great. One time when coming out of a tight LZ the chopper blades hit tree branches on both sides because we were overloaded. I quit going on joy rides after that!

Firebase English: February 1970

In the first part of February, our battalion moved to Firebase English near Qui Nhon. I worked out of English as well as a couple of smaller firebases. February was pretty uneventful, which was a good thing, because I was getting "short." Short was a sacred word in Vietnam. We all counted the days until we left, every one of them; and short meant I didn't have much time left. At that point, when you had a few weeks left, they finally cut you some slack. My one-year tour was up on March 7 and I was sent back to the rear around March 1 to begin processing out.

Boarding the Freedom Bird: March 1970

After 364 days in Nam, I boarded the "Freedom Bird" to go back to the "World" as we called the United States. That was another sacred act, terrifying, because you were convinced the war wasn't really going to let you go, that it would get you at the very last moment. But as the plane lifted off the ground in Cam Ranh Bay, I'll never forget the overwhelming feeling of relief that came over me. I remember thinking "I will never have to sleep with a gun again."

For my service, I was awarded a Bronze Star, a Combat Infantry Badge, an Army Commendation Medal, and an Air Medal.

When I got home, I still had five months left on my Army service. I was a Sergeant E-5 by then and was assigned to Fort Riley, Kansas. When I was finally discharged, I went back home, farmed and sold real estate. My interests now include horses, spending time with my wife, two daughters and five grandkids, following Iowa State sports, and attending the Great Jones County Fair. The only time I missed the fair in 74 years was the summer of '69 when I was in Vietnam.

Looking back after fifty years, I realize that I was very lucky. I got out without a scratch and do not suffer from any Vietnam-related health problems.

WALLACE "EARL" WALKER'S WAR

**U.S. Army Captain and Armored Cavalry Troop Commander,
3rd Squadron, 5th Armored Cav, 9th Infantry Division, Dong Ha,
Northern I Corps, 1969-1970**

I grew up in Decatur, Illinois, a city in central Illinois. It had a population of around 78,000 when I graduated from MacArthur High School in 1962, and has about the same population today. We weren't from a military family, but my father talked up the academies quite a bit and was relentless on grades. I took the competitive test for West Point offered by our US Senator, Paul Douglas, but I came in second and attended the University of Illinois for one year. My mother had gone there, and I enrolled in their ROTC program. When the West Point test rolled around the next year, I took it again. This time I received the appointment and on July 1, 1963, I was sworn in at the US Military Academy at West Point as part of the class of 1967.

My class was full of tall, blue-eyed, good-looking athletes... and then there was me. I was 6' 2" tall and weighed 180 pounds. I lifted a lot of weights and did what I could, but I would never be a standout athlete. I decided that my niche was academics. If you finished in the upper 5% of your class, you were designated a Distinguished Graduate and that came with a lot of perks. You tended to get your career choices, so that was my goal. After the first year I never finished lower than the top 5% and graduated #26 out of 583. It was the top 5%, but barely. West Point was an engineering school. I was never terribly strong in math and was bored by engineering, but the top students

were very good in these fields. My preference ran to English and history and I graduated as the top-ranked graduating cadet in social sciences. One other thing that finishing in the top 5% got you was the chance to later attend graduate school for two years for free. Vietnam came first, of course, but I tucked that chit away.

At West Point I was allowed to take a summer program as an exchange cadet with the Argentine Military Academy in Buenos Aires. We stopped in Panama, where I met an "American Army brat." Later in my senior year, I started dating her. On our third date I proposed. On our fourth date she accepted. We were married in June 1968 at Fort Myer, near Arlington and the Pentagon, and across the Potomac from the Lincoln Memorial. When your future father-in-law is a 4-star General Officer, scheduling the ballroom at Fort Meyer wasn't a problem.

On commissioning, I chose Armor as my branch because I liked the officers I met from that branch and its modern approach to warfare. For my duty station, I picked Bamberg, Germany, and the 2nd Squadron of the 2nd Armored Cavalry Regiment. I was assigned an armored cavalry platoon patrolling along the East German border facing the Russian armored divisions. Before I went to Germany, I attended Ranger School and the Armor Officer Basic Course at Fort Knox, and later the armored cavalry platoon leader course at Vilseck, Germany, and the Army Airborne School at Fort Benning, Georgia. I arrived in Bamberg, Germany, in January 1968. I was hoping to get a troop commander position after my time as a platoon leader, but my squadron commander needed an adjutant, so we cut a deal. I would take the adjutant job and get the troop at the end of the year. Of course my orders for Vietnam came down first.

After some counter-insurgency training at Fort Lewis, Washington, I arrived in Vietnam in March 1969. I was a first lieutenant and was assigned first to a corps headquarters. I worked in the Tactical Operations Center, the TOC, at the 24th Corps Headquarters as a watch officer. My time was spent with phone and radio calls and pinning things on maps. I figured if I wanted to get out of there, I'd have to do it myself. I heard there was an armored cav unit further north that might have an opening, so I went up to see the CO. Turns out he was one of my professors at West Point, and he hired me for the 3rd squadron of the 5th Armored Cav Regiment assigned to the 9th Infantry Division in northern I Corps. When you mentioned the 9th Infantry Division, most people remember photos of the infantrymen slogging through the mud in the Mekong Delta chasing Viet Cong. That was true for the leg-infantry battalions, but the division's tanks and tracks were of no use down in the Delta. They were sent to more solid ground up north to chase the very formidable NVA regiments in I Corps.

Again, I did not get a troop. For my first three months from June 6th to September

11th, I worked as the Squadron Maintenance Officer. I commanded a maintenance platoon, but it seemed I spent most of my time trying to find replacement engines for our ACAVs. An ACAV, an Armored CAV Assault Vehicle, was a fancy name for an M-113 APC with two more machine guns on top and even more weapons.

Finally, on September 12, 1969, I was given command of C Troop of the 3rd squadron of the 5th Cav, which I held for six months until March 15th of the next year. In Germany,

with the units so badly stripped down, there were almost no experienced or qualified NCOs. That was not the case in Vietnam; we had all ranks filled with the proper officer and enlisted grades. Just before I arrived, C Troop had been badly mauled. They were in a troop-sized "laager" around a small hill – a laager is an old military term from the Boer War for an encampment which the cav had borrowed. Unfortunately, C Troop didn't realize that the hill they were surrounding was a former NVA base, full of spider holes and tunnels. The NVA came in one night and a lot of men were killed and wounded, including the troop commander. So, the troop had been pulled back to be rebuilt and put on convoy-escort duty on the road up to the A Shau Valley. The truth was they had not been doing much of anything other than running the roads and sitting around base camp when I took over, so we had to do a lot of retraining and re-motivating.

A cav troop had three platoons plus the headquarters group, and generally 150 to 200 men. Each platoon had seven ACAV vehicles and three tanks, which were M-48s and later the Sheridan. It's a heavy unit with a lot of firepower. At night, we would go into platoon-size laagers, with the platoons close enough to each other to provide mutual support with their mortars. We set up our machine guns, put out barbed wire fencing around the perimeter, put up stakes and mesh fencing in front of the vehicles to catch RPGs, and planted trip flares and Claymore mines in the bush in front of our positions. Our guys seemed to have a terrible time with the trip flares. They kept going off and our men would get injured and burned. So we had to stand down for a day for retraining.

An ACAV or an APC was made of lightweight aluminum. It would stop a bullet, but an RPG would go right through it. An RPG could also disable a tank, but they offered more protection inside. At night, one man always slept inside each vehicle to get it quickly moving if necessary, but the rest of the crew slept outside on the ground because the vehicles were always the enemy's main target and if you got caught in one it could be dangerous.

Our armored cav units were at their best operating in the lowlands where we could bring our armor and firepower to bear. They were less effective in the jungle or the mountains. After two or three weeks, we moved further north, around Dong Ha, where the squadron and troop had set up headquarters, and around Cam Lo, which was a Vietnamese resettlement district. The cavalry's main mission, as it had been for centuries, was to go out and look for bad guys. Because of our firepower, they left us alone during the day, except for mines and booby traps, and came after us at night with rockets, mortars, and occasional infantry probing and attacks.

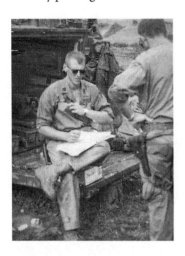

I would be out in the field with one of my platoons two days out of three, rotating between them, and never going anywhere without my own ACAV and the radios it carried, plus a second ACAV as backup in support. When we were moving, it was always in column formation with a tank in the lead. If you hit a mine, and mines were always our biggest threat, it would destroy an ACAV and kill people, but probably only knock a track off a tank.

One night, we had a Marine platoon attached to us. Those guys had been out in the field and hadn't even been fed for a couple of days. We rounded up a bunch of C rations for them and got them all settled in.

We always had a lot of C-4 explosive with us. We used small pieces to heat our Cs, and larger pieces to blow holes in the ground to make foxholes. Everyone had to have one for a night fighting position, and using the C-4 to blow holes in the ground made digging them lot easier. Anyway, after the Marines got settled in for a few days, we sent them out to patrol. Unfortunately, they got caught in an ambush, and we had to go out and bail them out. Things were pretty hot, and I even had to call in Spooky to work over the countryside.

There was a Marine Corps company about 5 km down the road from us and we would stay in touch. One night, I got a phone call from their CO saying they were being hit hard and asking if we could provide any assistance. I cranked up two of my platoons and started rolling down the road toward them. We got halfway there when I got another call from the guy saying they didn't need our help and we could go back. I asked what the heck was going on. We had a lot of firepower and could really wreak havoc on enemy infantry. Finally, the guy admitted that when his boss heard he had called me for help, he told him that they were Marines. If they needed help it would be from Marines, not from the Army. The next day I went down there and saw that they had lost at least six men killed. How stupid can you be?

The biggest fight we were in occurred just prior to my turning over command of the troop in the spring. They had moved us west to block a valley where intelligence thought the NVA would be coming down to hit us. I put two of my platoons on hills on each side of the mouth of the valley and placed myself with the third platoon in the center. They had sent us a special AN/PPS 5 Doppler ground radar unit with an operator, and I put them right in the middle of my laager with me and near my forward artillery observer. Earlier, I told the FO if he got more than ten feet away from me, I'd shoot him.

I was a little skeptical about the whole thing; but sure enough, around 9 p.m., the ground radar operator called me over all in a sweat and said his radar unit was picking up a very large enemy force coming toward us. From the number of shapes he counted and the direction they were headed, he figured it was probably a battalion-sized force; so I told my FO to dial up the artillery and to put 100 rounds on that area.

The artillery guy at the other end wasn't too happy about that and started giving him some static. Maybe he could give us 64 rounds. I got on the radio and told him I'd go right up my chain of command and say he was unable to sup-port us if he didn't deliver exactly what I was asking for. The artillery hated that, and I'm pretty sure I got my 100 rounds although I really wasn't counting. There were explosions in that valley, and we also fired our own 4.2-inch mortars. Each of our platoons had a track-mounted "Four-Deuce," as they were called, a 4.2" diameter mortar, and they were big, powerful weapons. By 10:30 p.m or so, all movement had ceased on the radar; so at midnight, I went to bed. I always believed the worst thing a commander could do was let himself get groggy and tired, and I knew I needed some sleep.

I got up before dawn the next morning, but we still had no idea what was going on in that valley. I didn't want to send troops out to look, so I radioed squadron and asked for a helicopter. I was supposed to be turning over command of the troop later that day, and they didn't want to give me one, so I never got the chance to look myself. Later, some troopers did go out and found a whole lot of bodies scattered around in the bush. By all appearances, we had caught an NVA battalion in the open with artillery and destroyed them.

Later the next day, on March 15th, I did in fact turn over command of the troop. There was a USO show coming through with an African-American woman singer and her husband. They needed an escort officer to take them around, so that's what I did for the next 10 to 12 days. Then I got on the plane and went home.

What was Vietnam like? How did it affect me? The biggest single memory I have was the intensity of that six-month period when I was the Troop Commander and was responsible for all those people. The responsibility and intensity could be overwhelming. I was on the radio all the time talking to squadron and to my platoon leaders, always fussing with them and the enlisted men about something. Usually it was about them not wearing flak jackets. The weather was hot. We had the old-fashioned heavy jackets, and everyone hated to wear them.

It was very serious work. If you are in daily contact with the enemy, like many soldiers were, the pressure could be very bad. Lots of us came home with great memories, and lots came home with a lot of PTSD. To me, the most important thing was to kill bad guys, but equally important was to take care of my men and keep them safe. I lost none of my troopers in combat, although I did lose one man in an accident and I lost a Vietnamese Tiger Scout to a mine.

As expected, it took me quite a while to come down after I got home. Branch sent me to the Armor Officer Advanced Course at Fort Knox. I arrived a few weeks early, so they put me to work as a Tactical Officer for newly arrived second lieutenants going through their Basic Course. One of the guys who came in as a new lieutenant had just earned a PhD in psychology. I felt it would've been a complete waste to have him continue on the armor officer track, so I picked up the phone and called the Psychology Department at West Point. They immediately grabbed him and put him on the faculty teaching for his three-year tour.

My dream had always been to teach at West Point myself, so in 1971 after the advanced course, I pulled out that graduate school chit that I mentioned previously and called the Department of Social Science at West Point. With my grades and record I probably could've got into most universities, but they had developed a relationship with MIT, which I did not realize had a really top-ranked political science department; so that's where I went for two years, earning an MS in political science, concentrating in American politics, national security affairs, and international relations. The armor branch must've thought I was having too much fun in Boston, so when grad school was over, I was assigned to Fort Hood, Texas, for two years to command a tank company. I then went back to West Point and became an Assistant Professor in Political Science and spent the rest of my career on the military-academic track; I became a full tenured professor with the title of Professor of Public Policy and a division chair. I taught there for 18 years.

Also, I was a Distinguished Graduate of the Command and General Staff College and had the honor to be selected by President Jimmy Carter as a policy advisor and White House Fellow in Washington, taught at the National War College, and earned my PhD in Organizational Behavior and Political Science at MIT in 1980. I was a DoD and NATO research fellow and did research at the Department of Defense Headquarters in Brussels.

After 26 years on active duty I retired with the rank of full Colonel, having earned two bronze stars and numerous other awards and medals.

My personal and professional area of specialization has been organizational behavior, creative leadership development, organizational culture, training, and management – exactly the same things that they attempted to teach us as new cadets at West Point so many years ago. After I left the Army, I thought I would try the private sector and became involved in creating company-wide management training programs for a major Walmart subsidiary. Then I found work as a Dean of a Business School at a private university in Texas, was Dean and Professor of another university business school MBA program in Kansas City, and then became the Founding Dean and Professor of management and leadership in the School Of Business Administration at the Citadel in Charleston, South Carolina.

I have been married to Susan Porter Walker for over 51 years. She has a master's degree in library science and has served as a librarian and docent at a number of fine museums as we moved around. We have two adult children, Kathryn and Allen. Allen is a regular Army Colonel, airborne and Ranger qualified, with a degree in computer science and service in Iraq, Afghanistan, and many other places. Kathryn is a practicing attorney in Michigan and graduated from the University of Michigan Law School. Both children are married; Allen has two children, and Kathryn has one. So we are grandparents of three strapping, energetic boys.

I now enjoy spending my time as the director of the Citadel's distinguished scholars' program, reading, traveling, and sustaining a family farm in Virginia. Of course, I've only very recently retired, and I'm certain I will find many other activities to keep me busy.

JIM CALI'S WAR

U.S. Army Captain, 6th Battalion, 20th Artillery,
1st Infantry Division, 1969–70

I grew up in Garfield, New Jersey, graduated high school in 1963, received an appointment to the US Military Academy at West Point, and graduated in June 1967. In our senior year, we got to choose a career branch, but as Regular Army Officers that would be one of the "combat arms" for our active duty commitment. When the day came to choose, all 583 of us sat in the auditorium. There was a big world map on the stage, and we got to stand up in the order of our class rank, top to bottom, and announce our choice. You'd say "I pick (name the branch) and want to go to (name the Army post I'd like to be assigned to). The cadets who picked early usually got what they wanted, the earlier the better. The cadets who picked later got what was left. Most of the brains picked the Corps of Engineers and Germany. That would delay a Vietnam assignment, but the brains who were really "Gung Ho," and wanted to rack up career points, picked the Infantry.

When it was my turn, about half-way through the class, only US posts were left. As for branch, back then I think we could pick Infantry, the Corps of Engineers, Armor, the Signal Corps, Air Defense Artillery, and Field Artillery. I lost interest in Armor when I cracked my head getting out of a tank during training, so I picked the Field Artillery and Fort Carson Colorado, one of the better US assignments.

After graduation we attended our branch schools, and many of us got married. After that, we all went to Ranger School, which was three months of agony at

178

Fort Benning Georgia and other places during the winter. We also did rock climbing there. We scaled a vertical cliff covered in ice with a buddy pulling us up. I'm not the tallest guy and the crevasses in the rocks were too far apart for me to reach. Thankfully the guy on my rope was strong enough to literally pull me up the wall.

That was where I learned that when I am really cold, my back sweats. But I also learned I'd go back to Vietnam for another year rather than repeat Ranger School.

Each morning at 5:00 a.m., we ran the obstacle course. The first group to go was the one that finished first the day before. Their reward was they didn't have to go through the cold water that was sprayed on the course after the first group went through, but everyone had to finish. I was one of the stronger runners and used the butt of my rifle to move the slower guys along. In some cases we had to carry the guys that were in trouble. I don't think my group ever finished first.

Another training exercise was to climb a pole that was perhaps thirty feet tall. We also had to shinny on a rope out over a pond and drop into the water. We were in the bleachers watching an Instructor demonstrate. When he hit the water, we heard a SPLAT. The

other Rangers Trainers pulled him out, but he had hit bottom and broken both legs. Fortunately, they canceled the event that day because the water level was too low.

When I finally got to go and I yelled the required "Ranger!" on the way down, but my mouth was open when I hit the water and I lost a tooth. The Instructors pulled me out because I was bleeding. I didn't know it and I didn't feel a thing. I was too cold. That cost me "one million" pushups for making the Instructors go into the water. I won't even talk about the chickens, sleeping standing up, or the guys who finished the course with broken bones, so that they wouldn't be recycled and have to repeat the training they missed.

One objective of the course is to find your weakness – food, sleep, or exhaustion. Mine was food. To this day, when I get hungry, I dream of a scrambled egg sandwich on white bread. That's my go-to food. When Ranger School was over, my family had a second Thanksgiving dinner for me. And after that big meal, I went out for hamburgers. My wife Geri was in awe!

My first duty assignment was with the 4th Infantry Division at Fort Carson, Colorado, where I was assigned as the Executive Officer of an artillery battery, the equivalent of a company. After a while, they asked me if I would be the Battalion S-1, who is in charge of personnel. I accepted and discovered my true love in the Army – administration. I put in for a branch transfer to the Adjutant General Corps, which can be a lengthy process. As expected, I received my orders for an artillery assignment in Vietnam. Before I left, we learned that two of our friends at Fort Carson had been killed in Vietnam, soon after they were deployed. Worse still, one week before I deployed, I learned that my best friend from West Point had been killed too. That was the worst time in my Army career.

I arrived in Vietnam in June 1969, two years after I was commissioned, and had been promoted to captain. The photo above is of four of my classmates, with me in the middle, in-country. My initial assignment was in the Mekong Delta. I'm not sure what division that was, maybe the 9th Infantry, but I was quartered on the second floor of a two-story barracks. I returned from the shower one day and saw several Vietnamese with war wounds at the other end of the barracks. One was missing a leg, one an arm, etc. I later found out they were "Hoi Chanh," VC or NVA defectors who had come over to the ARVN side. Some of them became "Kit Carson Scouts" and some served with US units as guides.

I heard someone yell, "Incoming!" and had no idea what that meant. I took my time getting dressed and noticed that the Vietnamese were gone. As I walked to the door there was an explosion that knocked me to the ground. I got up, heart racing, and ran down the stairs. Everyone was headed for a bunker, so I followed. As I entered, there was a lot of yelling and screaming. Some US soldiers were holding others back, stopping them from going after the ex-VC. They were yelling, "Those Vietnamese set us up!" and other things, until another rocket hit the barracks door, presumably the one the ex-VC and I came running out of, killing one US soldier and wounding a few others. Fortunately, the next day I was reassigned as the S-1 of one of the artillery battalions in the 1st Infantry Division! Welcome to Vietnam!

When I arrived in Lai Khe, I was assigned to the S1, the Personnel Office of the 6th Battalion, 20th Artillery Regiment. The 1st Infantry was one of the first divisions sent to Vietnam in 1965. It consisted of seven battalions of light infantry, two battalions of mechanized

infantry, an armored reconnaissance unit, and four artillery battalions, one of which was mine. Throughout the war, the 1st Infantry Division guarded the approaches to Saigon from Cambodia. To help the local population, my unit also took a local orphanage under our wing and helped them out, as many other units did. My son was born while I was in Vietnam. Perhaps that was why I was drawn to help the orphans.

Lai Khe got rocketed almost every night and hit with several ground attacks each month. I was on duty at the Artillery Battalion command post when a volley of rockets came in. Standard procedure was to send surveyors out to take back azimuth readings at the crater and determine where the rockets came from. But before I could fire, I had to get permission from the local village chief, who we knew was playing both sides in the war.

The first incoming volley had hit our hospital, but I was still waiting for the village chief's permission. That was when our CO walked in. After telling him what happened he asked me why the hell I hadn't returned fire! When I said I didn't have the village chief's permission yet, he said "F*** that! Fire!" So I did. After an inquiry, the CO was relieved. I should have had some action taken against me as well, but the CO took the hit. More importantly, we got the bastards. The infantry confirmed the bodies the next day.

We lived in bunkers and I commanded a dozen or so "artillery" soldiers that served as an "Attack Repel Team." One night we were all anxious because we had just been attacked a few nights before. We were hunkered down in our bunker expecting another attack when we heard a loud "click" as one of our mousetraps caught a mouse in our bunker. Everybody jumped up, put the lights on, and I heard rounds of ammo being locked and loaded. There was a mouse in the trap, and it was still alive, so I told my sergeant to get rid of it. He said he wouldn't touch the trap, but he'd shoot the mouse. Some of the others also volunteered to shoot the mouse, including one soldier with a grenade launcher. I finally picked up the trap and discovered the mouse was dead; but by then I was more concerned that we were all so uptight about a mouse "click" that I collected all the ammo. Thankfully we had no attack that night. The next day, I got reamed out by a lieutenant colonel because I had collected the ammo, but I told him I'd do the same thing under the same circumstances.

The Division was involved in major battles along Highway 13, known as "Thunder Road," and with major reconnaissance-in-force and ambush operations, as part of *Dong Tien,* or "Progress Together" with the ARVN to get them to take a more active role in combat.

Six months after I arrived in Vietnam, my transfer to the Adjutant General Corps was approved and I was reassigned to the Division staff. Soon afterward, it was announced that the 1st Infantry, the Big Red One, was returning to Kansas and I became the Chief Administration Officer to handle all of those plans and paperwork. Soldiers who had been in-country less than six months were transferred to other units. Soldiers who had been there more than six months went home with the Division. This prompted many complaints and Congressional inquiries. One of my responsibilities was to write to each of those Congressmen to explain why his particular soldier was not coming home even though he was with the 1st Infantry Division.

After my tour was over, I worked on the staff at West Point, and got out of the Army when my commitment was over. I received an MBA from St. Mary's in 1977 and went into the private sector as an executive with a large corporation, owned my own manufacturing business, wrote three books on business, lectured, and consulted in New Jersey, Pennsylvania, and Massachusetts.

I am a cancer survivor, having contracted prostate, kidney, and pancreatic cancer as a result of exposure to Agent Orange. I now spend my time playing senior softball, senior stickball, golf, and serving as the president of a local Veterans' group.

Looking back on my brief Army career, the worst job I had was serving as a "Survivor Assistance Officer" during that last year when I was stationed back at West Point after Vietnam. That involved knocking on doors and informing a family that their husband or child had been killed. I had to do that three times and each time was heartbreaking.

The first visit was to a very poor family that lost their "good" son in Vietnam. Their "long-haired hippie son" was still at home. I was escorted to the house by the local sheriff, who said the area would not be safe for me to go into alone. Our standard orders were to not allow the family to open the casket. I had several soldiers with guns with me, not loaded of course, as part of the escort. At the funeral, the family went nuts wanting to open the casket and began coming after us. Thankfully, the Sheriff and his deputies were there to control the chaos, which included the mother trying to jump on the casket. After we got beyond that, the family's only concern was who would get the $10,000 GI Death Benefit, and when.

The second time I had Survivor Assistance duty was as tough on me as it was on the family, who "adopted" me as their lost son. They took it very hard, as could be expected, and wouldn't let me or the priest who accompanied me leave after we gave the notification.

The last time was unusual. The deceased was a young West Point lieutenant who was killed in a fishing accident. His pregnant wife had already been notified and I handled the funeral at West Point. Unfortunately, no body had been recovered, but the young wife insisted on having a Mass and a cemetery burial, except there was no casket. It seemed very strange to go through the whole process for a small headstone. I don't think I will ever forget that.

Most Memorial Days, I give a speech at various commemorative events in the central New Jersey area. Here is a brief excerpt of that speech:

MEMORIAL DAY Remarks by Jim Cali

Today you will hear eloquent tributes to the millions of military Veterans that lost their lives for our freedom. For many of us, Memorial Day is even more personal as we have lost a loved one or a friend.

I would like to share the story of one young soldier and his wife during the Vietnam era, in the 1960s. Several of his friends were killed in Vietnam just prior to him leaving for combat:

1. He played high school baseball with his hometown's first Vietnam casualty.

2. His West Point mentor was killed in Vietnam a few months after the young soldier entered West Point.

3. Two friends who preceded him to Vietnam were killed shortly after they arrived.

4. His best friend from West Point, who was an usher at his wedding, was killed in Vietnam one week before he was to return home.

The young soldier left for Vietnam with his wife six months pregnant. She returned home to live with her parents in northern New Jersey and gave birth to their first child, a boy.

There is good news to part of this story as the young soldier did return home safely. The young soldier's wife is here with us today. Please meet my high school sweetheart and wife of 53 years.

As a side note, many of you are old enough to remember the protests by tens of thousands of Americans against the Vietnam War; but I don't think too many of you are aware that when many of our soldiers, sailors and airmen returned home from Vietnam, they were advised to remove their military uniforms before they reached a US airport or traveled in the US. There was concern that American protesters would attack American soldiers. This may be hard to believe but it did happen. Our soldiers were sweared at, spit at, and had blood thrown at them. Hopefully, our nation learned a grave lesson from the Vietnam War – don't blame the young soldiers and sailors for the war. They proudly served our country and should be honored and not victimized. Today, many Vietnam Vets greet the young men and women coming home from Iraq and Afghanistan. They do not want these young service Veterans to experience the rejection that the Vietnam Vets received when they returned home.

The Vietnam War will always be a major event in our history. More than nine million

Americans served in the war. They represented 10% of their generation. Six million of them volunteered and would serve again if called. More than 300,000 were wounded, to include 75,000 who were severely disabled. It is hard to believe that the first known casualty of the war was over 60 years ago on June 8, 1956.

America paid for its involvement in the Vietnam War with many lives. There are 58,286 names engraved on the Vietnam Memorial in Washington, DC, known as "THE WALL." Their names are inscribed on this polished black surface in the order they were taken from us. And let us not forget the more than 1600 who are still missing and unaccounted for.

Most Americans only see or hear those numbers. To those of us who served and survived the war, and to the families of those who did not: we see the faces and we feel the pain that these numbers created. And we are, until we too pass away, haunted by these numbers; because they are our family members or friends.

There are no noble wars, just noble warriors.

In conclusion, I carry in my wallet a list of 30 of my West Point classmates who were killed in Vietnam and the location of their names on the "WALL" in Washington, D.C. They truly gave ALL for our freedom, and my wife Geri and I will never forget.

BLAIR CRAIG'S WAR

U.S. Army, Captain, Platoon Leader and CO of D Troop, 2nd Squadron, 17th Cavalry, 101st Airborne Division, I Corps, Republic of Vietnam, 1969–70

I graduated in 1962 from Summit High School in New Jersey, twenty-five miles west of New York City, and enrolled at Rutgers, "The State University of New Jersey" intending to become a veterinarian. I joined their Army ROTC program and enjoyed it. But in the beginning of my third year, in 1964, I took a semester off. There was an Army Reserve Special Forces unit at Camp Kilmer, New Jersey, which I had the opportunity to join. The draft was in full swing. Everyone without some deferment was trying to get into an Army National Guard or a Reserve unit. However, no one, except me, wanted to go into a Reserve Special Forces Unit! After Basic, AIT and BCT at Fort Dix, New Jersey, I went to and completed Airborne Training at Fort Benning, Georgia. I became a 111.07 Light Weapons Specialist. Then, I re-enrolled in Rutgers in May 1965 and rejoined the ROTC unit, who were very glad to have me with my additional training.

I graduated in May 1968 from Rutgers and was selected as a Distinguished Military Graduate (DMG) from their ROTC program. That carried some important perks with it. First, DMGs were commissioned on the same day the West Point graduates, giving us the same date-of-rank that they had. Second, it helped in getting your branch choice and duty assignments. I requested Armor, deciding I would like that rather than Infantry due to the ease of inter-unit communications. Armor Officer Basic School was at Fort Knox, Kentucky, following which I had an interim troop assignment to

185

the 1st Squadron, 6th Cavalry Regiment at Fort Meade, Maryland, plus some of my first Armored Cavalry training. That was followed by Ranger School at Fort Benning, Georgia. I completed the jungle phase of Ranger School at Eglin Air Force Base in Florida on May 19 and was in Vietnam ten days later, on May 29, 1969.

By the luck of the draw, there happened to be a vacancy for a lieutenant in the Cavalry troop assigned to the 101st Airborne Division. One month before, it had converted from an all-track unit to an airmobile unit that rode into battle in helicopters. I was made the platoon leader of 3rd Platoon, D Troop, 2nd Squadron 17th Cavalry Regiment, 101st Airborne Division. Normally, a lieutenant would only serve six months with a troop unit, followed by six months in a staff job. But D Troop, 2nd of the 17th was so unique and rewarding of an experience that I stayed with it for nineteen months. For the first year, I was a lieutenant and platoon leader. For the last seven months, I was a captain and troop commander.

We were the aviation recon unit for the 101st based in northern I Corps, its eyes and ears in enemy country, like the cavalry has done for thousands of years. Our area of operations was from the DMZ in the north, to Danang and Marble Mountain in the south, and from Laos in the west to the South China Sea in the east. The unit was highly specialized

 and along with L Company of the 75th Rangers and a handful of other special ops units were the only ones allowed to operate on the western side of President Nixon's "Presidential Blue Line" in I Corps. In June 1969, he drew that line on the eastern side of the A Shau Valley, beyond which regular US units were not permitted to go. The line went through a series of firebases along the eastern edge of the A Shau Valley, leaving the A Shau and the Ho Chi Minh Trail in enemy hands. Other special op and recon units that operated in I Corps included the US Special Forces, their Mike Force militias, Marine 3rd Force Recon, and L Company 75th Rangers. But as the drawdown and departure of units accelerated, the remainder of the decreasing number of conventional US forces could only operate on the coastal plain east of the mountains in South Vietnam.

We operated mostly at the squad and platoon level and were inserted into enemy country on "specially directed missions" to go after known enemy units or positions that had been located by aircraft or radio intercepts. We performed a variety of other missions as well: bomb damage assessments, rescue of downed airmen, snatching enemy for interrogation, reinforcing and extracting Ranger Teams and Marine Recon Teams in contact, escorting convoys, special G-2 directed missions, ambushes, determining the actual enemy strength by engaging them, bringing back prisoners, their equipment and documents, and occasionally serving as a reaction force.

Delta Troop usually worked in small elements, inserted by combat assault, often rappelling from helicopters 100 feet down through the triple canopy jungle. As 1970 and 1971 passed and US troop drawdowns continued, the NVA became bolder and bolder, moving more and more main force units further down into Laos, Cambodia, and western and northern Vietnam. That made our reconnaissance and special operations even more important.

In August 1969, two months after I arrived, Operation Richland Square began, when the 3rd Brigade, 101st Airborne Division and ARVN 3rd Regiment went into the A Shau

Valley on a clear-and-search-operation. The remainder of that year was spent on small unit level operation throughout Thua Thien Province, the Laotian border, and northern I Corps. The monsoons of November '69 through February '70 were particularly strong and kept the number of missions down, but Operation Randolph Glen began on February 15 and lasted two weeks, with the 101st Airborne Division and the ARVN 1st Division conducting a clear and search operation on the edge of populated lowlands in eastern Thua Thien Province. This was in response to elements of the 9th NVA Regiment being identified in that area.

In early March 1970, Lieutenant Colonel Robert F. Molinelli assumed command of 2nd of the 17th Cavalry. He proved to be the finest soldier and unit commander I have ever served with, and just what 2nd of the 17th needed in this time of daily enemy contact and large NVA movement into South Vietnam. He was a real soldier and died from cancer as a Major General. The 101st began another large operation, Texas Star, which ran from April 1 until September 5.

As my twelve-month tour in-country came to an end, I extended to become Commander of Delta Troop on 8 May 1970, about a year after I joined the Troop as 3rd Platoon Leader. Delta Troop was now often being employed beyond the range of any supporting artillery and could not be reinforced by the decreasing number of US ground units, only by a special unit of the 1st ARVN Division known as the Hoc Bao, or Black Panthers.

On May 11, 1970, Team Kansas from L Company of the 75th Rangers was three days into a five-day reconnaissance mission when they missed a 0430 hours commo check. At 0600 hours, when they failed again to check in, Squadron launched an OH-6 Light Observation Helicopter, a Loach, to investigate and found the six-man team dead. A reaction force was inserted to recover their bodies and found that all six had apparently fallen asleep, been caught by the enemy, and shot in the head. In response to that tragedy, Delta Troop took over all the Ranger reconnaissance, ambush and sniper missions in I Corps for four-weeks while the Ranger Company went into retraining.

In June the Squadron moved its Tactical Operations Center to the city of Quang Tri. The Cav had found evidence of a regimental base camp belonging to the NVA's 66th Regiment. Delta Troop was inserted on June 24th and found a large hospital complex with supporting bunkers. Most of the enemy had fled, leaving a small security element for Delta Troop to eliminate. Left behind were weapons, medical supplies, surgical instruments, food, and over 100 pounds of documents.

In July, having destroyed a large part of the 66th NVA Regiment the previous month, the 2/17th was targeted against the 9th NVA Regiment believed to have arrived in South Vietnam from its sanctuary in Laos. At approximately 1130 hours on July 8, a "Pink" team of Loaches and Cobra gunships conducting a visual recon in the Fire Support Base Snapper area, observed 150 to 200 NVA in the open, moving along a fresh, well-beaten trail. The Cav pink team struck with Cobra gunships and supporting Aerial Rocket Artillery gunships. In the initial engagement 50 NVA were killed. Two hours later, Delta Troop, supported by A and C Troop Aero-rifle platoons, was inserted into two locations directly on top of what turned out to be a 600-man North Vietnamese Regiment. In the ensuing firefight, 139 enemy soldiers were killed and 4 captured, along with many documents, individual and crew-served weapons, and the elimination of the NVA Regiment's Command Group. The number of NVA wounded or dead who were dragged away will never be known.

That day, Delta Troop did what no other unit in I Corps could have done. By destroying that NVA regiment we saved the lives of many Americans and Vietnamese. As important, Delta Troop captured all the 9th NVA Regiment's maps and battle plans to attack American bases in I Corps. Unfortunately, Delta Troop lost six great men KIA: Platoon Sergeant Walter L. Walker, Sergeant Allen R. Stroud, Sergeant Stanley J. Cruse, Sergeant Harold L. Frank, Specialist Joseph F. McDermott, and Private First-Class Harry McEwing. As we say, "They wait for us to join them, in our time, halfway down the trail to hell… at a place called Fiddler's Green," from a poem about the legendary Cavalrymen's afterlife.

Later, Brigadier General Sydney Berry, the 101st Airborne Assistant Division Commander who ordered the attack, said that while it had to be made, he was expecting a 90% US casualty rate, not an overwhelming US victory.

In August 1970, Delta provided extensive ground reconnaissance, downed aircraft crew security and airframe recovery, a ready-reaction force for ground units in contact. We spent thirty-one days on convoy escorts, ambushes, and performed security sweeps around Camp Eagle. Finally, we provided the security reaction force for Camp Eagle with jeeps mounted with M-60s and 106-millimeter recoilless rifles. There weren't very many ground units left to retrieve pilots in helicopters that went down in enemy country, so that often fell to us. In addition to retrieving the pilot and crewmen in triple canopy jungle, we had to secure the site and retrieve the aircraft, if possible, by sling loading it under a larger helicopter to be lifted out. Other times, we went into places responding to seismic sensors dropped by air or fired by artillery in and around trails to detect enemy activity.

On August 16, Delta was inserted with the ARVN Hoc Bao unit to secure and recover two downed aircraft. Additionally that month Delta reinforced and extracted two Ranger Teams that were in contact.

In September, increased enemy activity in "Elephant Valley," a thick jungle northwest of Danang, called for the Cavalry. On September 8th, 2nd of the 17th elements to include Delta Troop established a command post at Marble Mountain. The Elephant Valley now belonged to the Cav.

On September 29, two platoons and the headquarters element of Delta Company rappelled down through the triple canopy jungle twelve kilometers south of Fire Support Base Fist in a recon-in-force. While enroute, the Division G-2 reported to me that a 120-man NVA unit was seen on the river, downslope from our insert point. He cautioned me to avoid contact, because the weather was closing in and a major engagement could not be reinforced. We located several hundred pounds of rice and stores, but the early monsoon arrived, and the Hueys could not return to extract us. The 101st Division had declared "No Fly" for all aircraft.

We remained on that hillside for five days in continuous driving rain with only one day's ration per man to eat, being sporadically probed by the enemy. On the evening of the 4th day, our Squadron Commander, Lieutenant Colonel Molinelli, called for pilot volunteers to attempt to get us out early the next morning. Everyone stepped forward. At first light, without informing the Division, the Cav lifted off for the Rung Rung Valley. A single Loach maneuvered up the river through the rain and fog and established radio communication with me. At this point, our Squadron CO declared a "Tactical Emergency" and told the Division the Cav had lifted off to rescue Delta Troop. The Loach had only about thirty feet of visibility and had to fly sideways up the mountain so he could see the ground and trees to be avoided. I could hear his rotor blades and talked him upslope into a clearing. What followed was a string of LOHs and UH-1 Hueys one at a time, each risking the very hazardous flight in almost zero visibility to come in and recover the Delta teams two to four men at a time until all 52 Troopers were lifted out.

Those glorious pilots and "Men in the Doorway!" Cavalry all the way!

In October and November, the monsoon and two typhoons severely restricted operations for both aviation and ground Cav elements. However, Delta continued to provide daily patrols and nightly ambushes into the foothills east of the A Shau Valley, protecting the area around Camp Eagle to the South China Sea. It was miserable weather for both the friendly and enemy forces.

In late-November, my second tour was over, and I relinquished command of Delta Troop.

Vietnam was a "come as you are" war. After the first year or two, there were few new arriving units, only individual replacements on the "trickle down" system. You came in by yourself, you left by yourself, and you went home to family and friends who couldn't understand where you'd been, what you'd done, or why. And they didn't want to talk about it.

From Vietnam I was assigned to Fort Knox where I taught Armored Cavalry tactics and then went to the Armor Officer Advanced Course. I was subsequently assigned to the 25th Infantry Division in Hawaii, as Commanding Office of Alpha Troop, 3rd Squadron, 4th Cavalry for over two years.

I earned a Master's Degree in Asian Studies and Political Science from the University of Hawaii in 1976. Graduated from the Army Command and General Staff College in 1980 and the Defense Language Institute's Korean language program in 1981. Subsequently I was assigned as a student at the Korean Army Command and Staff College. I made Korea my secondary military specialty and spent over three years in Korea as a Foreign Area Officer, Aide de Camp to Lieutenant General James Vaught, Commander of the U.S. and Korean Combined Field Army, and in G-2 Psychological Operations for the Combined Forces Command, Korea.

Departing from the Republic of Korea in 1984, I attended and graduated from the Defense Institute of Security Assistance Management program and was assigned for the next four years to HQ Pacific Command as the Northeast Asia and Korea Desk Officer.

In 1988, having been diagnosed with bilateral necrosis of the hips, I was medically retired in the rank of Lieutenant Colonel at the 25th Infantry Division parade field at Schofield Barracks, Hawaii. During my time of service I am honored to have been awarded the Silver Star, two Bronze Stars, three Air Medals, two Defense Meritorious Service Medals, the Meritorious Service Medal, two Army Commendation Medals, the Vietnamese Cross of Gallantry with Palm, the Combat Infantryman's Badge, Parachutist's Badge and Ranger tab, plus others.

Since being medically retired from the Army I switched focus to homeland security, civil defense, and natural disaster planning in Hawaii and in the Pacific Basin. Working for the National Aeronautics and Space Administration, the State of Hawaii, and a variety of other agencies, we helped people through better emergency and disaster risk assessment and operations planning.

Moving to Florida in 2006, I have become involved in many Veterans-related activities in the Saint Augustine area, including the Veterans Treatment Court in St. John's County. In coordination with the attorneys and the judge, we arrange for Mentors, or "battle buddies," for Veterans who have found themselves in trouble with the law, often due to anger management issues, substance abuse, or PTSD. For the past three years, I have been a Mentor myself working for a year with each of my total of eight Veterans. I do this to acknowledge their service to our country, provide an alternative to a year in jail, and hope to help them re-integrate back as great contributors to their family and community.

On April 1, 1972, the 2nd of the 17th Cavalry re-deployed from Vietnam to its home station with the 101st Airborne Division at Fort Campbell, Kentucky. Thirty-six Delta Troopers died in combat during the 2.5 years from April 13, 1969 through September 11, 1971 in the Republic of Vietnam. Exactly the same number, thirty-six Delta Troopers, have died during the 43 years between 19 September 1972 and 25 September 2015, at home. My narrative stands as a tribute to all of the men of Delta Troop. It was their personal valor, teamwork, and looking after each other that enabled them to conduct some of the most diverse and dangerous missions during the Vietnam conflict.

FRITZ WALTER'S WAR

**U.S. Army Specialist-5 and Small Engine Mechanic,
523rd Engineer Company, 20th Engineer Brigade,
Vung Tau and Binh Thuy, 18 months, 1969–70**

I graduated from high school in Delavan, Wisconsin, in 1965, attended college for three years, half at University of Wisconsin-Oshkosh and half at Milton College, and worked road construction during the summers. I became disillusioned with college, but the war was heating up and I decided to enlist to avoid getting drafted into the infantry. Later I found out that the infantry wouldn't have taken me because I was colorblind, so the joke was on me.

I went on active duty in January 1969. After Basic at Fort Campbell, I was sent to Fort Leonard Wood, trained as a 62B20, a Small Engine Mechanic, and arrived in Vietnam on June 29, 1969. The neat thing about that was I got a full month of combat pay for only being there fifteen hours on the last day of June. I was assigned to the 523rd Engineer Company, part of the 20th Engineer Brigade. We were headquartered at Vung Tau, a big base and port complex southeast of Saigon. The 20th Engineers handled all of the non-divisional and specialized engineer units, like us, in the III and IV Corps areas. The 523rd was one of those. We had four platoons, which did port construction and built permanent bridges, sea walls, piers, and bulkheads, and even had an ancient steam-driven pile driver.

There were other companies in the brigade that handled Bailey bridges and other temporary structures; but by and large, what we built was meant to be permanent. We used heavy timbers, steel girders, and steel plate, so that old pile driver came in handy. We fixed welding machines, water pumps, motors, engines, and about everything else. There was a rock quarry nearby with a rock crusher which was used to make gravel for road construction, and a truck company that hauled the rock from the quarry to the river, where it was put on boats to go up to Saigon and other places. While I was with the maintenance platoon at Vung Tau, I worked in the shop and only rarely went out to the field.

Vung Tau was a big base and port complex at the mouth of the Saigon River. It was part US Navy and Coast Guard, and part Australian and New Zealand, all of whom had units there, and it had all the conveniences. Next to the base was an ammo dump that had guard towers around it. One night there was a new guy up in one of the towers. About midnight, he began shooting his M-16, and the place went on full alert. They didn't find any VC, but they did find a nine-foot-long python up in the guard tower. After that, no one slept on guard duty.

Every two weeks, the company would send a 2 ½ ton truck into Saigon to get some equipment resupply. In addition to the bench seat in the cab, this truck had a seat up be-

hind the cab for a guard to sit in with his M-16. I made that trip several times. It gave you a good view of the road and the surrounding Vietnamese countryside, but I always thought it made you a pretty good target, too.

After I was there six months, around Christmas 1969, the whole company was moved from Vung Tau to Binh Thuy, southwest of Saigon in the middle of the Delta near Can Tho on the Song Hau River, one of the tributaries of the Mekong. We loaded up everything we had, and then had to erect our own prefab barracks and other facilities after we arrived. The maintenance platoon stayed at our base at Binh Thuy, but parts of the engineer company were always working out at scattered sites throughout the area. Equipment always needed repairs, so mechanics like me were always being sent out to remote locations and we were rarely there.

I was a Spec-4 then and was frequently working seven days a week as I bounced around to all of the platoon bases fixing small engines that broke down. Our company equipment included a variety of barges and boats. The barges tended to have quarters for their own crew on board. One of them had four steel Connex containers with beds inside. We slept in them while we were building a seawall at a base up near the Cambodian border on the river. We built that during the dry season and when the water went up in the spring, they discovered that somebody's calculations were wrong, and the thing went underwater. The lieutenant in charge was reassigned.

Binh Thuy was a big base, like Vung Tau. The US Navy and a US Air Force base were there, as well as a hospital that served the middle part of the Delta. There wasn't much combat going on, but we did get rocket and mortar at-tacks at night. One of the boats assigned to the com-pany was an LCI and we had two smaller bridge boats we used for construction projects. The rivers could be dangerous, so our boats and barges had machine guns and guards. One of the things we were always looking for were floating mines. The enemy would put them in the river and let the current take them down into the shipping channels. After I left, one barge did get blown up by a mine.

We didn't have a mess hall when we were out at construction sites, but we did have a cook who would prepare our food. On other sites, we would have hot meals sent out to us in mermite cans, insulated metal boxes that kept food hot. The meals were nothing elab-orate. Sometimes we ate C-rations, but not very often. But when we were at Vung Tau or Binh Thuy, we had big, regular mess halls.

The area around Binh Thuy was part of the Mekong Delta. In the wet season, all the low-lying areas and fields were flooded and there would be water as far as the eye could see. For the NVA and the VC, the Mekong Delta was their "rice bowl." They had a lot of troops there and it was heavily fought over throughout the whole war. One thing that I will always remember is the weather. In monsoon season it rained heavily eighteen hours a day,

nonstop. But when the dry season came around in the summer, it became very dry and dusty and any breeze, a vehicle, or even a footstep would send up clouds of dust. Binh Thuy is on the Song Hau River, one of the tributaries of the Mekong River, and the tides were ex-treme. When the water came up, everything flooded, like you see in the US upper Midwest in the spring. The bulkheads we built weren't needed in the dry season, but they had to be very tall in the wet season.

As my tour was coming to an end, I found out that guys who had more than one year left were being sent to Germany. I didn't want to go there, so I extended my tour for six months. When you extended, you got a 30-day leave to go home. When I went to Vietnam the first time, they flew me out of Oakland, California. The second time, I flew back from Fort Dix and McGuire Air Force Base in New Jersey, which made for a long trip.

One day after I was back, I was working on a welding machine at our main base at Binh Thuy, trying to fix the governor on the motor. I was careless for a moment and got my hand too close to the radiator fan. When it started up, it split my fingers open. There was a big gash and the knuckles were shattered. Fortunately, we were only a quarter mile from the Army's Binh Thuy hospital, so I was treated right away. Initially, they thought they would Medevac me out to one of the larger hospitals or back to the States, but there were worse casualties than me. I spent a couple of weeks there, until I finally was returned to my unit and put on light duty. I spent the next eight weeks driving a jeep. Even today, those fingers are stiff and don't work very well.

After my Vietnam tour was over, for the rest of my enlistment I was assigned to the Engineer Company at Fort Rucker, Alabama. I was a Spec 5. We were responsible for the normal road repairs, electrical work, and facilities maintenance on post. When I was discharged, I had received the usual service medals, plus an Army Commendation Medal, and a Vietnamese Civic Action Medal. In addition to the bad hand, I have had a number of health issues but none that can specifically be attributed to Agent Orange.

When my enlistment was over, I got out. I went back to Wisconsin, enrolled in college and got my degree in History. I bummed around after that, until I got a job in a manufacturing plant. That lasted 14 years until it closed. So, I got a job with another company and six years later they moved to Mexico. Finally, I got a job with Kikkoman, and stayed there for 12 years until I retired. For twenty-one years, I also served on the Delavan Volunteer Fire Department.

In 2015, my wife and I went on an 18-day tour of mostly the III Corps and IV Corps area of Vietnam where I served. We went to Saigon, up as far as Ban Me Thuot and Qui Nhon, and down into the Delta. We even had a chance to eat some of the local food. The new development, hotels, businesses, industries, and highways were strikingly different from the way the country used to be. One thing I discovered was that when it came to the former US bases and facilities, they fell into three categories: sites that were now totally overgrown with weeds or jungle, sites that had been totally rebuilt for some other use and you could find no sign of any American presence, or sites that were now Vietnamese Army bases, which the government wouldn't let you anywhere near.

Now, I spend my time doing some volunteer work, play golf, and attending estate auctions looking for collectables.

FREED LOWREY'S WAR

**U.S. Army, Rifle Platoon Leader and Recon Platoon Leader, 3rd Bn,
503rd Inf, 173rd Airborne Brigade, II Corps 1968–69 and
Company Commander, 1st Bn, 52nd Inf, 198th Inf Brigade,
23rd Infantry Division – Americal, Southern I Corps 1970–71**

I am an American soldier. To be more specific, I'm an infantryman from a long line of soldiers and infantrymen, an Army brat who grew up all over the world, graduating from high school in Fayetteville, North Carolina, where Fort Bragg is located. Lowreys fought in every American war from the Revolution through Vietnam. My sixth great-grandfather Adam Lowrey served as an officer in Washington's Continental Army, fighting throughout the Carolinas and Virginia. My great-great-grandfather fought in the Mexican War and was a brigadier general in the Confederate Army during the Civil War, commanding a brigade at Shiloh, Chickamauga, Murfreesboro, Chattanooga, Missionary Ridge, Atlanta, Kennesaw Mountain, and many others. Major General Patrick Cleburne, the "Stonewall of the West," called him "the bravest man in the Confederate Army."

My father began his career in the National Guard and was commissioned an Infantry Officer in 1940 with the 153rd Infantry. He remained on active duty until 1960 and fought with great distinction in World War II in the Aleutian Islands and then Central Europe. In Korea he commanded the 3rd Battalion, 31st Infantry Regiment during some of the bitterest fighting there. His military service had a huge impact on my brother and me.

Like my older brother, I attended the US Military Academy at West Point. He was in the class of 1960 and I was in the class of 1967. When I started, in the summer of 1963, the nation was at peace. By the time I graduated, we had been embroiled in the charnel house of the Vietnam War for over two years and the worst was yet to come.

Following the family tradition, I chose the Infantry and reported to Ft. Benning in

August 1967 for Infantry Officer Basic Course, followed by Ranger and Airborne schools. My first troop assignment, in December, was as a rifle platoon leader in B Company, 2nd Battalion 508th Airborne Infantry, 82ndAirborne Division at Ft. Bragg. It's not very well known, but Vietnam took its toll on the stateside Army and the Army in Europe. Most rifle companies were down to 120 men versus an authorized strength of 166 enlisted and six officers. Most infantry companies and artillery batteries were commanded by new first lieutenants as opposed to experienced captains. That weakness became glaringly apparent in late January 1968, when the Tet Offensive struck, and the 82nd was ordered to deploy a full-strength brigade to Vietnam immediately. To do that, the rest of the division was stripped of soldiers to fill the three battalions of the 3rd Brigade. My platoon was left with eighteen soldiers, all recently returned from Vietnam and non-deployable. It took six months to replenish those units.

Soon, I received my orders for Vietnam in July 1968, to the 1st Infantry Division. I was thrilled to finally have a chance to prove I was up for the task, especially since my brother had already served a Vietnam tour with the 1st Division.

I arrived in Vietnam on 4 September 1968 and learned my assignment had been changed. Instead of going to the 1st Infantry Division, I was sent to the 173rd Airborne Brigade in the Central Highlands. Two weeks prior to my arrival, two of their four infantry battalions had lost a lot of lieutenants and needed airborne-qualified replacements. Again, I was thrilled. The 173rd had carved out an incredible history and I would remain on jump status. That extra $110 per month was huge!

I arrived at my battalion's base at Bao Loc in southern II Corps, assigned as a rifle platoon leader in B Company, 3rd Battalion, 503rdAirborne Infantry. I was issued an M16 and my combat gear, and at 1630 got on a Huey helicopter with the mail and hot chow and was flown to a small hilltop firebase to join my company. My battalion had undergone a great deal of tough combat over the previous six months and suffered accordingly. In that part of Vietnam, the enemy was Viet Cong main force and local force units. There were some NVA around Dalat and Ban Me Thuot, but my battalion had mostly been fighting VC, and had destroyed them. As a result, Hanoi sent regular NVA troops into the area to replace them. It changed everything. Platoon and company firefights now quickly escalated to multi-company and even battalion-size battles.

We were an elite airborne unit and every soldier in the brigade was a volunteer on at least one level: they all had airborne training. Most of the men in my platoon had enlisted; they weren't draftees. Best of all, my NCOs were all professional career soldiers. I was blessed to have E6 Staff Sergeants as squad leaders and a grizzled old E-7 sergeant first class as my Platoon Sergeant, and it was his second tour. Morale was high, and in those days the attitude was positive. We all believed we had been sent there to win the war, and we were going to do that. In short, no new platoon leader in combat could have hoped for a better situation and a more positive leadership climate than I had. I was very lucky.

It was a great opportunity for me to learn the ropes. On my first full day with the company I took my platoon out on a lengthy patrol and had my first enemy "contact." We had crossed a small stream near a village and were climbing a hill through waist-high elephant grass. My two-man point element was about 25 meters ahead of me and had disappeared over the top of the hill. Almost immediately, the calm was shattered by automatic weapons fire from the hilltop. I did my best John Wayne impersonation, threw off my rucksack, turned to my men and yelled "Follow me!" I sprinted to the sound of the guns, and just as I reached the crest, I was met by my point team running for their lives right at me. I looked behind them and saw a 1,500-pound water buffalo, head down, charging right for me. Discretion being the better part of valor, I joined my point men in full flight. Fortunately, one of my M-60 machine gunners solved the problem, but this was not the glorious introduction to combat I had envisioned. My men, on the other hand, thought it was great and gave me the nickname "LT Buffalo Slayer."

On my second night in the field I led an ambush patrol along a heavily traveled trail into a nearby village. It gave me a perfect opportunity to show my men that I was in charge, part of the team, and knew what the hell I was doing. It was a textbook operation right out of the Ranger School handbook, and I was proud of what I accomplished.

My real introduction to combat came on my fourth full day with B Company. There were numerous reports of enemy activity near the village of Di Linh, the site of two previous large battles with VC main force units. At about noon, my company was airlifted into an LZ near the village. It had been heavily prepped by artillery and Cobra gunships, and the first five Huey slicks carrying about thirty men touched down with no problems. I was in the second lift, about two or three minutes behind them, and as we were on final approach, the tree lines on both sides of the LZ erupted in gunfire. I was sitting in the door of the lead helicopter, with my radio operator on my right and my medic on my left. Both were hit by machinegun fire, killing the medic and seriously wounding my radio operator. Welcome to the real war.

That fight lasted about an hour and resulted in ten casualties from B Company. Due to the surprising strength of the enemy force – at least one VC main force company – a second rifle company was flown in, and what was expected to be a one or two day search and destroy mission turned into a major ten day running fight, during which we uncovered a major underground hospital complex, an elaborate training facility complete with a ringing field telephone, several tons of rice and quite a few fresh graves, all occupied by enemy soldiers.

By the end of that operation I was a well-established Veteran and had earned my first decoration and the coveted Combat Infantry Badge. My men and I had established a rapport and a relationship based on mutual trust and respect, and I was a happy soldier.

The next month was more routine grunt work – patrols, ambushes, brief firefights, an occasional incoming mortar round or two. We seldom went more than two days without some kind of enemy contact, but it was all low level. That all changed on October 22, 1968. Late in the afternoon, both B and C Companies were airlifted into an LZ at the base of an 1100-meter-high mountain with strong evidence of a major enemy presence at the top. We spent the next day climbing until we reached a false crest just before dusk. We dug in, in a two-company perimeter, and surveyed our route for the following day across a narrow saddle, followed by a steep climb up a narrow ridge to the crest.

On the morning of October 24, B Company took the lead. The ridge was very narrow and covered in triple canopy jungle. About 45 minutes into our climb all hell broke loose. The lead platoon was completely enveloped in a U-shaped ambush. One of the left flank security men triggered it when he realized he was too close to the main body and tried to move farther off the trail. Two large Chinese Claymore-type mines were detonated at the top of the U, and two 12.7-millimeter heavy machine guns began firing, as did at least a company of AK-47s and RPD light machine guns. The flank man was badly wounded and his platoon leader, First Lieutenant Tim Porter, was killed in the initial burst. Almost immediately, I received a call from my company commander, who was behind my platoon in the column. He told me Porter was dead and instructed me to take my RTO forward, take command of Porter's platoon and stabilize the situation. I turned the platoon over to my platoon sergeant and started forward with my RTO. We moved in short sprints from tree base to tree base but when we reached the point, he and I were both shot by the same bullet, him in the shoulder, me in the leg. His wound was far more serious than mine, his ticket home, and he made a full recovery. But once again, I became my own radio operator.

Long story short: it took most of the rest of the day, both rifle companies and a great deal of artillery, napalm and 500-pound bombs to secure the top of the mountain; but secure it we did. On top we found an NVA regimental headquarters and training area. It was a costly fight. B Company lost close to 20 men killed and wounded. I don't know the number of NVA we killed, but it was enough to get them off the hill. I was finally Medevaced out at 1400.

After a week at 8th Field Hospital in Nha Trang, I was transferred to the 6th Convalescent Center, located on the beach at Cam Ranh Bay, one of the prettiest beaches on the planet. It was for patients who could return to duty in 30 – 60 days. The downside was that we knew we would be sent back to the meat grinder when we were pronounced fit for duty.

Officers had our own ward – "Ward P." There was a chain of command, but the real pecking order was why you were there. There was one lieutenant from Military Intelligence who had broken a collarbone playing flag football at Long Binh. His injury didn't count for much. The guy with highest honors was a Special Forces lieutenant who had to answer an urgent call of nature and got bit on the ass by a snake when he squatted down in elephant grass to do his business.

Sometimes in the mornings we would go outside and watch the Korean troops do their hour of PT. Their entire contingent would fall in at 0600, face toward Korea, sing their national anthem, and then punish their already wounded bodies, after which they would run laps around the hospital compound. Everyone participated, even those on crutches or hooked up to IV bottles. Very impressive.

On 15 December 1968, we were all diagnosed with an unspecified but highly dangerous upper respiratory infection. No medications were prescribed, no limitations were placed on our activities, no one died, and no one was declared fit for duty. On Christmas day, we were sitting front and center at the *Bob Hope Show*, live and in person. I guess that was the Army's way to guarantee a suitable front-row audience of the noble wounded. Bob was at his best, Ann Margret was in her prime, and all the nubile lasses in his entourage were visions of loveliness. Halfway through the show it rained like hell, but nobody cared, and nobody left. It was a far better Christmas than any of us had expected. The next day, twenty of us were miraculously declared cured, fit for duty, and discharged back to our units. All good things come to an end.

Two weeks later, I learned one of my fellow patients, an infantry lieutenant from the 199th Infantry Brigade, was killed on his first day back with his platoon. About a week after that, the Special Forces snake bite hero was also dead. And the following August, the VC launched a rocket attack on the hospital while sappers came through the wire and ran through the hospital throwing satchel charges in all the wards. Thirteen soldiers died, 103 were wounded and Ward P was destroyed.

I returned to my battalion on 2 January 1969 and was given command of the Battalion Recon Platoon. While disappointed at not rejoining my combat brothers in B Company, this new assignment was quite an honor and treated as a promotion. Unlike a rifle platoon, the recon platoon operated independently, usually far away from the rest of the battalion in six-man teams performing clandestine scouting and ambushes. It was hugely challenging and rewarding. I did that for the next six months until I was promoted to captain. They included everything that anyone who served as a small unit infantryman in Vietnam experienced – periods of excruciating boredom punctuated by intense, terrifying combat; humor, pathos, melancholy, horror, depression and intense pride. During this assignment I was wounded twice more.

After being promoted to captain, I was reassigned to the 173rd Brigade headquarters located at LZ English, just outside Bong Son and at the mouth of the An Lau Valley. It was the scene of many tough battles involving the 1st Cavalry and 101st Airborne Divisions in 1965 and '66. I spent my last three months in-country as an assistant Brigade S-3, the operations officer. I was very happy with my new assignment. I wore clean clothes every day, could shower daily, ate my meals off trays in the Commanding General's Mess, and no longer had to hump over hill and dale carrying an 80-pound rucksack.

My first tour in Vietnam ended on September 9, 1969, one year after I arrived. My new job was commander of C Company, 2nd Battalion, 509th Airborne Infantry, 1st Airborne Brigade of the 8th Infantry Division in Mainz, Germany. At that time, duty in Germany was not fun. There was a shortage of soldiers, and the severe drug and race problems, and deteriorating German American relations, made it an agonizing grind. After ten months, I requested a transfer back to Vietnam; after all, that's where the war was, and I had been trained to go to war.

I arrived in Vietnam for my second tour in late October 1970 and was assigned to headquarters troops at Long Binh, but I managed to talk my way into an infantry unit and command of D Company, 1st Battalion, 52nd Infantry, 198th Infantry Brigade, in the 23rd Infantry Division, the "Americal." We were located in southern I Corps near the coastal town of Chu Lai. This area was the birthplace of the Viet Cong and the location of the infamous My Lai Massacre in 1968, carried out by soldiers in the 11th Infantry Brigade of the Americal Division. Suffice it to say, there weren't many friendlies in the area.

My battalion was headquartered at LZ Stinson, surrounded by rice paddies and farmland about 10 kilometers east of the mountains. Affectionately called "Happy Valley," those mountains were also home of the 2nd NVA Division. The tactics we used in the lowlands were quite different from what we used in the mountains. In the lowlands we'd go on "Eagle Flights," wherein a company or platoon would air assault near a village, conduct a quick sweep, jump back on the helicopters and repeat that elsewhere until contact was made. This was wide-open country with an incredible network of tunnels and spider holes dating back to the French Indochina War when it was called the "Street Without Joy." A remarkably fast and accurate enemy communications network made our work challenging and very dangerous. Contact was frequent and sniper fire was constant, but we had as many casualties in the low country from mines and booby traps as by gunfire.

Operating in the mountains was decidedly different. It consisted of a lot of intense close-in fighting. A rifle company or two would be airlifted into an LZ the size of a postage stamp perched perilously on the side of a ridge. That meant it took a long time to get our unit in place. Once there, we'd spend two to three weeks patrolling, ambushing, and climbing up and down triple-canopied jungle-covered mountains looking for trouble, which we frequently found. This was a major NVA enclave, a very target-rich environment, and a free-fire zone as late as 1971.

In the seven months I was in command, I only had two face-to-face contacts with the other company commanders in the battalion, and not one of us escaped this tour unscathed. On May 28,1971, I was wounded during a particularly vicious firefight inside an NVA basecamp near Happy Valley. It proved to be my ticket home: ten days in the 91st Evac Hospital in Chu Lai, three weeks in the US Army hospital in Camp Zama, Japan, and over two months at Brooke Army Medical Center at Fort Sam Houston, Texas.

In hindsight, this tour was very different from my first one. By late 1970, everything had changed. Public support for the war had eroded significantly and there was increasing political pressure to find "the light at the end of the tunnel" and disengage. We were turning the fighting over to the ARVN and sending American combat units home. The first to go was the 9th Infantry Division in August 1969, followed by the 1st Infantry Division and the 3rd Brigade of the 82ndAirborne Division. More units were sent home in 1970, but with one caveat: a soldier had to have been in-country with the unit for at least nine months to be sent home early. Those soldiers who didn't meet that criterion were reassigned to other units in-country – typically units up north like my 23rd (Americal) Division.

This created a major leadership challenge. As soon as a unit was told it was going home, that unit effectively ceased aggressive combat operations, going from "search and destroy" to "search and avoid." Everyone knew the war was effectively over. It was the ARVN's war, any US casualty was a waste of good manpower, and "search and avoid combat" was the norm. The problem was, when those soldiers arrived in their new units up north, like mine, they were in for a rude awakening. We weren't avoiding anything. We were fighting our asses off, being as aggressive as possible, and we expected new soldiers to do the same. It was a huge leadership challenge. The reality was, we were eventually going home, and we weren't trying to win the war either.

And there was a third factor. Most of my men were draftees, not enlistees, and many were the products of Secretary of Defense McNamara's "Project 100,000," where the IQ and entrance standards for recruits were reduced to make up for plummeting enlistment rates. Also, the luxury of having old-line, professional, career NCOs was a thing of the past. Many squad leaders were "instant NCOs" or "shake-and-bakes," recruits who had performed well in Basic and AIT and were sent to instant NCO schools. Nine months after entering the Army they were E-6 Staff Sergeants on their way to squad leader positions in combat in Vietnam, with zero experience. As a result, platoon leaders had to perform many of the duties traditionally performed by NCOs, because they couldn't trust these "shake and bakes" to get it right. This problem became so pervasive in the Army that it took many years – two generations of junior officers and NCOs – before the roles of each were properly realigned and relearned.

Despite all that, my troops performed magnificently. If they believed their leaders were competent and that they would be taken care of, there was nothing they wouldn't do or sacrifice. They did not hesitate, they did not refuse, they did not question; they performed, and I loved them for it and I always will. Of course, they did it for each other, not out of some false patriotism about country, freedom, and Mom's apple pie. But then, soldiers were always at their best when serving each other.

One last word, this about my West Point class. We graduated 583 young men in 1967. Three were foreign cadets, and five were not commissioned for medical reasons. Of the remaining 575 graduates, 538 served at least one tour in Vietnam. Thirty were killed in action. The first was Jim Adams, on March 20,1968, during the battle for Hue. The last was Ellis Greene, on May 23,1970, during the incursion into Cambodia. No West Point class suffered more. I have accounted for 362 decorations for valor, including 3 Distinguished Service Crosses, 79 Silver Stars, 25 Distinguished Flying Crosses, and 156 Purple Hearts. It is a legacy of service and sacrifice we are fiercely proud of.

This class went on to give 8,239 years of uniformed service in the Army, Air Force, Navy and Marines. Nineteen of my classmates became General/Flag officers with a total of 38 stars, including three 4-star generals in the Army and one 2-star Admiral in the Navy, the only West Point graduate to achieve that distinction. One classmate, Tom White, became Secretary of the Army; another, Ty McCoy became Assistant Secretary of the Air Force. We have two former NASA Space Shuttle astronauts with a total of three flights, and two members of the Ranger Hall of Fame. Unsurpassed!

I dedicate this story to my 30 fallen classmates.

JIM MYERS'S WAR

U.S. Army E-5 Platoon Sergeant, B Company, 1st Battalion, 52nd Infantry Regiment, 198th Light Infantry Brigade, Cu Chi, 1969–70

I grew up in Sunset Beach, California. As a boy, I would go quail and dove hunting with my dad on the Irvine Ranch or "surf fish" in the Pacific Ocean right in front of our house. The most traumatic thing I did back then was to kill a dove or gut a fish. After I graduated from high school in 1969, I didn't know what I wanted to do, so I enrolled in a two-year college to stay out of the draft and Vietnam, even though I knew college wasn't for me. One day my math teacher came up to me and asked, "Myers, why are you here?" When I replied, "To stay out of the draft," I guess he didn't think I had much academic motivation, not that it mattered. Two or three weeks later I received my "Greetings from Uncle Sam" letter.

Like most guys, I thought I knew everything and if anything happened, I'd be ready and was smart enough to handle it. Boy, was I naive! Some guys were going to Canada or Sweden, but I couldn't do that. When I received that "Greetings" letter, I was going, and that was that. Today, even fifty years after serving in the infantry in Vietnam, that drive has never left me. The Army refined me. It taught me discipline, respect for my buddies wherever they came from, and it made me into the person I am today.

In March 1969, after I was inducted in LA, they handed me a bus ticket to Fort Ord to begin Basic and AIT, Advanced Infantry Training. When I graduated, I was an 11 Bravo Infantryman. This was late 1969. They weren't wasting time, and my orders assigned me to the 198th Light Infantry Brigade in Chu Lai. After I landed at Long Binh near Saigon on September 1st, I was flown to a forward firebase, LZ Stinson, one of many forward firebases in the Chu Lai area, with about twenty-five other "FNGs," or new guys. After we arrived at Bravo Company, we had a short orientation, were issued our combat gear, and met our CO and what was left of the company. There should have been 150 guys or more, but all that was left were 75 or 80. The CO explained about the hill we were on and the huge valley that lay in front of us. I didn't understand much of it, but I looked out and saw a lot of smoke and shit happening down there.

The old guys were only looking us over. You could tell they thought we were going to get them killed, so we had to learn and adapt as fast as we could. We were told to load up with as much ammo as we could carry and get ready for a CA, a combat assault. We were going to help Alpha Company get out of the heavy combat they were in. After wrapping belts of M-60 ammunition on me, plus two M-16 bandoleers and at least six hand grenades, I thought if I fell down, I'd explode. We were standing there waiting for the helicopters that would land to pick us up. But after an hour or so, we were told to stand down. It seems Alpha Company got their shit together and fought their way out by themselves, so we didn't have to go. That was my introduction to Vietnam. And that was my first day! This was real!

I spent the next year with Bravo Company. I saw a great deal of combat at the age of 19, and I was scared shitless most of the time, as were all the other draftees. All that any of us could think of was to save each other and help each other come home alive. But why would anyone want to make a career of the most horrific tragedies of life? I wanted out! No such luck, after two or three days up on LZ Stinson getting ready, it was our turn to go on patrol.

As an 11-Bravo Grunt Infantryman, I knew I would be in the bush for the rest of that year, or as long as I stayed alive. And as a FNG, I also realized I had to learn from the old guys about how to do that. Worse still, I was only 5' 7" tall and weighed 145 pounds, just the right size for a tunnel rat. And if I didn't get stuck with that, my other career position would be walking point. There was no way I wanted to do either one of those jobs, so I asked to carry the radio. Everybody told me I was nuts because the radio guy was always the first one to get killed, but I had made up my mind and they realized I was set with my decision. From that point on I felt I was accepted by the old guys.

People ask me what I remember of those days. Well, I am 69 years old now, and I remember EVERYTHING! I can't forget any of it. There was a guy from Chicago in the unit. His name was Francis E Dymbroski, one of the new medics, and we became good friends.

When the company got into shit walking on top of those rice dikes or trails, and if it was our platoon, Frank was always there doing his medic thing and I would be right up front with him as the Company RTO. He stayed in the field for that entire year.

Another name I've never forgotten is Sergeant David B Magruder. He came into our company just after they let me come in out of the field and made me the mail clerk. I would take the mail out to the platoons, distribute it to the sergeants, and they would give it to their men. Dave became someone I respected because of his unselfishness, his leadership, and the respect his men had for him. He was killed and I was the one who had to go to Graves Registration and ID his body; because, as mail clerk, I pretty much knew everybody in the unit and what they looked like, especially guys who had lost their dog tags. I've never forgotten his name in all these 50 years. When I go to any memorials, and they ask, "Is there anybody you want to recognize? Please stand," I always say, "Sergeant David B Magruder."

After the war, I had a job that took me to Chicago every year. Somehow, I found Francis (Frank) Dymbroski's mother's phone number. Every year I would call her, and I'd be told that Frank wasn't home. I'd always leave a message with my phone number and ask him to call me, so we could get back together. After maybe eight years, we did meet and went to a bar to catch up. Well, that wasn't where we should have met. He told me that he had re-enlisted for two more years as a field medic after that tour with me, and I couldn't understand why. So I asked him what he was doing now. He said he really didn't have a job. At night, he'd get on the "El" train with his knives to scare and rob people. That was the last time I tried to get together with Frank.

Combat medics were always called "Doc." Ours was called "Doc" Frank. The company had just returned to our base camp at LZ Stinson from five or six days in the field and we were getting back in the routine of being on the Hill. Maybe it was the second day when the other guys started complaining that both the Medic and the RTO were exempt from "burning the shit." Everyone who was in Nam knows what that means. Fifty-five gallon oil drums were cut down and placed under the latrines to collect the waste. Someone had to pull them out with a shovel or something, pour fuel oil or gasoline in, and set them burning each morning. Bad duty. Lots of smoke, lots of smell. Our lieutenant came over to Doc and me and told us that it would be a morale booster for the unit if the two of us volunteered to do it.

I turned to Doc and said, "Let's show 'em how to really do it!" Now, what you were supposed to do was pour in about an inch of diesel fuel and a quarter of an inch of gasoline on top of the diesel to get the diesel to ignite. Well, we poured in four or five inches of diesel and three or four inches of gas over the diesel, then stood back, and threw in a match. Wow! It looked like our whole firebase was on fire! Unfortunately, it just so happened that the wind blew the stinky smoke right into our command headquarters while our officers and NCO's were having a big meeting with the higher-ups. The next day our lieutenant came over and told us that he was ordered never to let the Medic and the RTO burn shit again. What a laugh we had!

Another time, we were on patrol walking through a rice field with several wooded tree lines around us when we realized that there was an NVA or VC platoon or maybe a small company following us. I think it was around 8:30 or 9:00 p.m. that night when we got hit the first time. We were in our NDP, our night defensive position, and they were hitting us from the side. The attack diminished after a while, but we had two wounded. I was the platoon RTO, the radio operator. The LT called in a Dust-Off, and that's when the shit hit really hit the fan. The enemy fired AK-47s, grenades, and larger-caliber machineguns at us. I had dug my foxhole so deep that I had to get up on the back side to get higher to see what was happening.

Well, that wasn't good. I had my M-16 on full auto and was firing into this tree line as bullets were hitting all around me. You could hear them whizz past my head. That was when a grenade exploded right in front of me, and I was hit. I remember ducking back against the foxhole thinking one of those little shits was in my hole with me, but I soon realized there was no one there except me. I got up, changed magazines, and was firing back at them on auto with my M-16 in my right hand and the radio in the left. Suddenly, I felt this warm fluid running down my left side and realized it was blood. I said to myself, "This isn't good."

I was trying to give my LT updates on what was happening and let him know that I was hit. We ended up with five wounded, but we had to wait until morning to get a dust-off helicopter in to pick us up. I spent the next three weeks in the rear recovering before I had to go back to the field. That was when something happened that I will always carry with me. I reported back to the platoon and squad, who were still doing the same old patrols, sweeps, and night ambushes, day in and day out. But on this particular day, about seven of us went out. Our squad leader told us we were going to go on a night patrol to locate an enemy unit. It was supposed to be either an NVA or VC platoon or a small company. Whichever, there would be a lot more of them than us, so silent movements were essential, no talking, and we could only communicate through hand movements or whispers.

To this day I am still trying to make some sense of it. It was night and this was the jungle. Usually, we never found anything, but this time we stumbled right into them. We were undetected and lay low, hoping to slip away, when this VC soldier walked right into us where we were lying. We were all pretty scared, so somebody grabbed him, tied him up, and gagged him. He was lying there right in front of me, when my platoon leader told me that I had to kill him, without making any noise or else we'd all be killed. He said he was the enemy and it had to be done.

The VC's hands were tied behind him, so I grabbed my bayonet, got over him, and was ready to stab him in the heart. That was when I made the mistake of looking at his eyes and realized he was crying; I also realized that he was a kid, only fourteen or fifteen years old. I stopped and said to myself, I can't kill a boy; I just can't. So, I turned to the only other guy there and whispered, "I can't do this!" He told me, "Okay, I will," and grabbed my bayonet. "Hold him down!" Without thinking, I did what he said. I grabbed the kid's ankles and my friend killed him with the bayonet. I held on to his ankles until he stopped moving. Even still, I couldn't take my eyes away. Slowly and silently, we were able to back out of the shit situation we were in and make it back to our company without being seen.

I realize it was a nasty war, that they would have killed us if they found us that night, but killing a kid, up close like that, even if he was an enemy soldier, not with a gun or hand grenade or anything, was the worst thing I was involved in over there. Later, I remember asking my friend about it, the one who had stabbed the kid with the bayonet, and the only thing he said was how hard it was to get that bayonet through his chest. But that was the end of it. No one said anything more about it.

After that, I really worked hard to find a job back there at base camp. After six or eight more weeks in the field, I finally managed to get assigned to the mail clerk slot. Things definitely changed for the better after that. I would get on a chopper to take the mail out to the troops every day. But after the initial rush of adrenaline from being out of the field, I was bored. A few of our men had re-enlisted to become door gunners, so one day I asked if I could ride along. It was up to the pilot, and most of the time it was okay with them. That got my rush back. It was great!

When my tour was over and I flew back to the States, we were told to take off our uniforms and wear civilian clothes before we got off the airplane. I didn't understand why. We had been through hell. I was so proud to have made sergeant, so proud to have been the best soldier I could have been, and so proud of my country. It felt like we were in hiding and we felt bad for the 58 thousand plus that came home in body bags. They seemed to have died for no cause.

That's why I locked up all of those memories in the back of my mind for 45 years and never talked about Vietnam. Even when I was cornered and asked about what I did, I'd lie about what I went through and say anything except what I really did and had to do to stay alive. I was always trying to change the subject. Fortunately, I only had to be out in the field for around six months.

I received an early out from the Army to go back to school and enrolled at Orange Coast College. I began in the architectural program and transitioned into their general contracting program, where I earned my AA degree. While going to this two-year college, I found a job on a yacht in Newport Beach as a deckhand. We would sail to Cabo San Lucas and La Paz down in Mexico, up to San Francisco, and back to Newport Beach. The owners became interested in offshore powerboat racing. As a result, my summer job lasted eighteen years and involved winning three National and two World Titles. I was the systems mechanic, the test driver for the team, and was responsible for getting the boat to each race destination. Unfortu-nately, the owner got cancer and eventually closed the company. By then, I had my general contractor's license and worked in that field for thirty more years. I had to stop when I developed Parkinson's disease from the Agent Orange I was exposed to in Vietnam. I have also been diagnosed with PTSD. I received a Purple Heart, the Army Commendation Medal with two oak leaf clusters, and my Combat Infantryman's Badge, plus the usual array of Vietnam service medals.

That is where my life is today.

I was a boy when I was drafted into the Army but that year in Vietnam made me grow up fast and made me the man I am today. I was scared to death when I was in the bush when we were under fire and prayed to God that I would come home alive. Well, 50 years later, what my experience in the Army did for me was the best start to a life that I could have imagined. It gave me the confidence that I could be the best I could be.

PAUL O'CONNELL'S WAR

U.S. Army Platoon Leader and S-3, 1st Battalion, 22nd Infantry, 4th Infantry Division, An Khe and Tuy Hoa, 1970–71

I grew up in New Haven, Connecticut, and graduated from The Hopkins School, one of the oldest private college prep schools in the country in 1965, not the best preparation for crawling through the jungle in Southeast Asia, but it was excellent preparation for the US Military Academy at West Point, where I graduated in the class of 1969 as an Infantry officer. It was West Point, followed by Airborne and Ranger Schools that did the rest, plus a lot of OJT, on-the-job training.

The war was still very active when I arrived as a first lieutenant in-country in July 1970, assigned as a platoon leader in the 1st Battalion of the 22nd Infantry, part of the 4th Infantry Division at Ah Khe in the Central Highlands. The big drawdown of US troops had already begun; and six months later, the 4th Infantry Division returned to Fort Carson Colorado. My Battalion, the 1st of the 22nd, however, remained in-country as the II Corps

Strike Force, working with the 17th Aviation Group unit, at Tuy Hoa, further south on the coast between Cam Ranh Bay and Quin Nhon. While the 4th Infantry had been a regular "leg" infantry unit, when we were partnered up with the 17th Aviation Group as the Corps "fire brigade," we became far more airmobile, but that was the second half of my tour.

In the first half, we were "boots on the ground," and spent most of our time patrolling through the hills and jungle looking for bad guys. The most anticipated part of any re-supply in the field in RVN was not ammunition or four days of C-rations (in cans in 1970), it was those large bags of

mail that were often unceremoniously kicked out of a helicopter hovering over the clearing. Whether it contained good news or bad news from home, each piece of mail was loving- ly opened, read, and in some cases smelled by the recipient. The C-rations were picked through for the meals that were basically edible, and the remaining cans committed to a garbage dump that had been dug and booby trapped to discourage the enemy from rum- maging through it after we departed. With the typical "gallows humor" of a combat soldier, the snickers of "Sorry about that" could be heard after hearing an explosion while moving away from our previous encampment.

On this particular re-supply day, I was pleasantly surprised with two letters from my wife, and a large package. Having received packages of cookies before that barely survived the trip from the east coast of the US, I was expecting to open yet another box of very tasty chocolate chip cookie fragments when, to my surprise, I found two large mason jars full of homemade tomato sauce and meatballs that had miraculously survived intact. I proceeded to toss out the cans of tasteless c-rations and committed myself to humping these heavy glass containers of Italian treasure made by the loving hands of my Sicilian mother-in-law into the Central Highlands. Word of my good fortune quickly spread, and I was soon sur- rounded by a bunch of GIs with hungry, depressed, hang-dog expressions. Realizing that I could only defend my treasure for so long, I doled out spoonsful of the precious sauce to allow as many men as I could to at least flavor their barely palatable C-ration meal. After a few days, every drop of sauce and fragment of meatball had been scraped from the jars, and I gave them a warrior's burial before the next scheduled re-supply.

Although I did not receive another delivery of this delicacy for the rest of my tour, the moral of the story is to always marry an Italian.

Life and death decisions were daily occurrences for platoon leaders in Vietnam. Some- times those decisions had to be made using emotion and logic rather than the neat "solu- tions" to tactical problems so often outlined in Infantry training manuals and the "course solutions." Sometimes what you had to do flat-assed flew in the face of what the "book" recommended.

One night, at about 0300, my platoon was at 50% alert in our night defensive position in the Central Highlands. We had spent a back-breaking day clearing elephant grass to create a small LZ in anticipation of a re-supply next day. After checking the perimeter and plotting some protective artillery fires with our assigned Forward Observer, I faded off into a troubled sleep. I was soon awakened by the platoon medic who told me that one of our newly arrived replacements had a serious "fever of unknown origin," a FOUO as it was called, a relatively common malady in the jungle. I was relatively unconcerned until the medic told me, with a growing panic in his voice, that the soldier's temperature was 104 degrees and climbing. That was very high; and I knew death could occur if his temperature climbed above 105 degrees. During the day, I would have requested a "Dust-Off," which was an aerial medical evacuation, without hesitation. However, sitting there in the almost total blackness of the jungle night, I began to realize the dangers that this type of rescue would pose, both to the helicopter crew and to my platoon. To make matters worse, we had come across evidence of large-scale NVA troop movements in the area. Right or wrong though, I decided that we had to try to get this man to safety and radioed the request to the battalion base camp.

In what seemed like an eternity later, we heard the comforting sound of helicopter blades rumbling in the dark. While they knew our approximate position on the ground, it would have been very dangerous to try to set down a Huey helicopter through the darkness. Our perimeter was roughly outlined by the landing zone we had cut during the day, and I ordered that flashlights be turned on to outline the landing area. By, this time we were able to talk to the Dust-Off crew by radio, and the pilot told me that he was still not sure whether it was safe to land. I grabbed the radio and a red strobe light myself and made my way to the approximate center of the perimeter. Putting the strobe on my chest, I told the helicopter crew to land where they saw the flashing red light. I stayed in that position until I could see the Red Cross on the belly of the chopper coming down on top of me, and then got my rear end out of the way. We loaded the soldier onto the bird, and they took off without incident.

The next decision I had to make was what I should do with the platoon now that our position had been clearly compromised. Some might argue we should have quickly moved to a different location. I briefly considered doing just that, and then discarded the idea because of the very real possibility of taking friendly fire casualties during a move like that in almost total darkness. Also, we were already dug in and had a defensive perimeter set up where we were. On balance, staying made the most sense, so I put the unit on 100% alert/awake, and decided to wait it out until dawn.

I have always regretted that I never had the chance to personally thank the Dust-Off crew for their courage in undertaking this mission. I do not know what happened to the soldier who was evacuated since he never returned to the platoon during my time as Platoon Leader. But whenever I review the decision-making process I used that night, I still feel comfortable with it.

I remained with the 1st of the 22nd Infantry after our attachment to the 17th Aviation Group as a Platoon Leader, and then as Battalion S-3 Air after I was promoted to Captain, in charge of planning and coordinating air operations, until July 1971, when I rotated home after my 12-month tour. I received a Bronze Star, a Combat Infantryman's Badge, an Air Medal, and the usual Vietnam service ribbons. I remained in the Army for 22 years serving in a wide range of intelligence and counterintelligence operations, planning, and training assignments, retiring as a Lieutenant Colonel in 1990.

Since then, I have served in senior management positions with Sigma Group International, US Defense Systems Inc., and others, serving as a senior US Government consultant, instructor, advisor, and Operations Officer on Human Intelligence (HUMINT), Counterintelligence (CI), /Counterterrorism (CT) Operations Officer. I've led insider threat investigations that resulted in the arrest of persons committing espionage against the US, and personally conducted international operations that deterred terrorist attacks against US facilities and personnel. Other than Type-2 diabetes, some hearing loss, and PTSD, my health has fared pretty well in my post-Army years. I now enjoy mentoring USMA cadets and continuing to stay in shape with martial arts.

The years after Vietnam have passed quickly. A full military career and an equally long career as a government contractor in the Iraq War and the War on Terror have left me with many new memories of men in the crucible of combat. Yet, in the twilight of my mind, I always return to the visions of the Central Highlands and the men with whom I served. I recall my disappointment in not being able to serve with a Special Forces unit, because a "straight leg" (non-airborne) unit needed platoon leaders because they had lost so many during the incursion into Cambodia in 1970. The ironic thing is that I came to love those "dog faces" with whom I served and continue to admire their courage and devotion to this day.

I attended my first company reunion a few years ago to re-kindle those long-ago associations and friendships. At the end of the banquet, I remember hearing my name being called out from across the floor. One of my M-60 machine gunners was calling my name. I thought it amusing that he was calling out to me as "Lieutenant O'Connell." (I haven't been called that in years.) He then said, "Thank you for bringing us home." No honor or award that the Army or the government ever bestowed on me could match that simple, yet profound thank you. It brought a lump to my throat then, and it still does to this day. God Bless them all!

BOB JANNARONE'S WAR

**U.S. Army, 1st Lieutenant and Platoon Leader,
65th Engineer Battalion, 25th Infantry Division,
Cu Chi, Dau Tieng, and Xuan Loc, 1970–71**

I more or less grew up at the US Military Academy, graduated from nearby Highland Falls High School, and from West Point in the Class of '69, following the proud tradition of my family. My father graduated #1 in the class of 1938, returned as a professor of physics and chemistry, was Dean of the Academic Board, and retired as a Brigadier General. My older brother graduated in the class of 1965 and was commissioned in the Air Force. Both my father and mother were fixtures at Academy athletic events for years, and have seats dedicated to them in the basketball arena.

I am a small, short man. Uniforms never fit right. The first day as a new cadet, I couldn't go to the Swearing-In Ceremony because my trousers were way too tight, and I was dragged off to the hospital. That may sound odd, but it was 99° with 99% humidity, we were standing in formation in our new summer-weight gray trousers, white shirt with epaulets, and white gloves. By the time my squad leader came over to check on me, I was "wobbling in place," perhaps my heart was palpitating, and I could barely breathe. At the hospital, the doctor prescribed that I should leave the trousers unzipped. A month later, those trousers fit and I was put at the weight-gain table. I was down to 107 pounds.

In Airborne school, on my first jump it took fifteen minutes for me to reach the ground, when it took everyone else one minute. After Airborne and Ranger Schools I was down to 107 pounds again. I then attended the Engineer

Officer Basic Course and was sent to an interim engineer assignment at Ft. Meade, Maryland, for three months before Vietnam. I arrived in-country on July 1, 1970, assigned to the Engineer Battalion of the 25th Infantry Division, "Tropic Lightning," based at Cu Chi. Although one of my classmates in the Division, assigned to the 3rd Squadron, 4th Cavalry, was killed in January 1971, the engineer battalion mostly built roads or improved existing ones. Occasionally, one of my men assisted infantry troops by blowing up places where the enemy had hidden supplies, but that was about it.

We took a few casualties. The day I was supposed to meet one squad at a fire support base, the squad leader from my platoon in A Company stepped on an anti-personnel mine and was evacuated to Japan. I'm not sure what he was doing at the time. Other casualties were from improvised explosive devices when we built new roads. We found most of them, but two found us. One bled from his ears after a bomb went off under his road grader. I don't know how we missed that one. Another time, the Viet Cong outsmarted us by placing the IED under the wire rope that we used to tie headwalls together in a stream bed where we had placed a large culvert. The bulldozer that went over the roadbed had its belly pan blown up. Fortunately that driver was unhurt.

One time we had to repair a bridge over the Mekong River, and I held up a squadron of Armored Cavalry that wanted to cross while we were doing the work. The major in charge was livid that he had not gotten the word that the bridge was closed, and his group had to wait until we finished. I'm not sure how communications like that worked in the Cav, but I took my orders from my CO, not from a major from some other unit.

Not long after that, I got my "war wound." My driver took me to a borrow pit where a material called laterite that we used to cover roads was pushed by bulldozers into huge mounds, and then pushed into dump trucks to be hauled to the road site. For some reason, a dump truck backed up instead of going forward, and ran into the smaller truck I was riding in. Instinctively, I held out my hand as if to stop it. When I did, my hand got caught in the tailgate of the truck. As the truck pulled forward, my hand was gouged, and flesh was pulled from my right index finger. Today, it looks like a little scratch, but it looked ugly back then.

Once, I was tasked with erecting a split rail fence at Dau Tieng. It was for a check-point, to make the Vietnamese workers coming into our compound pass by the armed Military Police, and show their credentials before being allowed in. I assigned one of the three squads in my platoon to erect the fence, at the direction of an MP captain. He told us where to build it, and that's what we did. It took a long time, because the road was covered in laterite. When that stuff has the right moisture content, is properly compacted, and then dried like this was, it's almost as hard as concrete. We had only one hand-held posthole digger to cut through it, and no electrical tools; so, it was very hard work that took several hours. My men were exhausted, and I didn't think the MP captain appreciated our effort as much as he should have. But then again, this was war and we needed to accomplish the mission. That squad had light duty the next day.

The 25th Infantry Division had led the Cambodian Incursion just before I arrived, and there was not much Engineer action in our area of operations during my tour. By then, the war was winding down and it seemed to me that the enemy in III Corps appeared to be waiting for us to leave. My first assignment was at the Cu Chi headquarters of the division and of our battalion. I was then assigned to Company A at Dau Tieng, where we provided engineer support for the First Brigade. Vietnamization was well underway, and the strategy was for them to take over more of the fighting as time passed. Two of the division's three brigades returned to Hawaii in November. Short-timers returned with them, those with not much time left before they were eligible to return from overseas, but I did not have enough time in-country to leave. Neither did many of the troops in my company. Those who didn't, wanted to be in my next platoon, wherever that was to be. That was heartwarming.

I was transferred to the 65th Engineer Company (Provisional) at Xuan Loc. The first meal there was lunch. We had liver and onions. I don't like liver and onions. For dinner we had liver and onions. For breakfast the next day we had liver and onions, and we did again for lunch. Finally we had something else.

While I was at Xuan Loc, I met Sebastian Cabot. We were the only two people in the main street; he was walking one way, I the other. He was a television star of the day, a very big and tall man. I told him I liked his television show.

When I was in "Beast Barracks," where the new cadets at West Point spend their first summer, we were not allowed to heat our C-rations – the canned goods we took to the field – or to add salt, pepper, or other spices to them. The Cadet Mess Hall food was really good, and so was the Camp Buckner Mess Hall food when we went to the field. But for some reason, I drew "Ham and Eggs, Chopped," as my C-ration meal several times that first summer. It looked like green slime and tasted just as bad.

In Vietnam I spent most of my time at a base camp, where we ate "A" rations – hot meals cooked in stoves and ovens by persons trained for that work. But when we were tasked to build a new road from a tiny village to Black Horse Base Camp, we were out in the field for three weeks. We ate C-rations, but at least we could heat them with C-4, an explosive that burned well. As was the custom, I drew my meal last, after all my troops. One day I drew "Ham and Eggs, Chopped." I could have tossed it back into the basket and drawn again, since I was last anyway; but I decided that since it could be heated and I could add salt and pepper for some flavor, I'd try it. You know what – it tasted just as bad as it always did. The last two days on that job we got something new, Long Range Reconnaissance Patrol (LRRP) rations. They were freeze-dried, a new process at the time. Just add hot water and wait a few minutes. They were really good.

After that, we did some work for an orphanage served by Vietnamese Catholic nuns. They spoke French, so here was a chance to demonstrate my foreign language skills. I took French in the seventh through tenth grades, and Spanish in eleventh grade and the first two years of college. I wasn't very good at it, but I figured we could communicate. After a while, however, the nun's eyes glazed over, like she couldn't understand anything I was saying. I finally realized I was mixing French and Spanish and tried very hard after that to speak French only.

In 1970, Bob Hope kicked off his Christmas USO Tour at West Point on December 15. Since my dad was the Dean of the Academic Board and one of three generals on the post, my mom and dad got to meet him after the show. Mom mentioned that two of her sons were in Vietnam, so Hope said he would get them together for Christmas. He asked for our names and addresses, which she gave, but my mother thought nothing of it and didn't tell us.

Lo and behold, on December 23, an Army major showed up at Danang where my brother Jack, an Air Force pilot, was stationed. He was supposed to transport my brother to Bien Hoa airbase for the show on Christmas Day. My brother, a captain, went to his Commanding Officer with the major, related the situation, and the CO said, "Well, if Bob Hope says so, I guess we better do it." There was no provision for in-country leave, but a plane with my brother on it left Danang for Bien Hoa the next day.

Also on December 23, it so happened, a civilian showed up at Xuan Loc where I was a first lieutenant and Engineer platoon leader in the 25th Infantry Division. He explained there was one seat left on a chartered aircraft from Tan Son Nhut Airport at Saigon, to JFK in New York. If someone wanted to, he could take leave, pay the airfare, and go home for Christmas. I asked my junior enlisted men first, then the squad leaders, then my platoon sergeant. I turned to the civilian and told him that no one wanted to go. Immediately, my squad leaders and platoon sergeant insisted that I go. They said that there was no need for me to be a hero. We had no missions; all we would be doing is pulling Motor Stables, which was the Army term for vehicle maintenance. Reluctantly, I agreed to go.

I left the next morning for the flight to JFK, where I was met by my sister-in-law, Jack's wife, who was living at Stewart Air Force Base with other waiting wives. She drove me to West Point, where I rang my parents' back doorbell at 2 a.m. on Christmas Day. My youngest sister came to the door, saw me, and screamed "Bobby's home." I went upstairs and when my mother saw me, she fainted. But it was a wonderful Christmas.

My leave over, on New Year's Eve I had to go back to Vietnam. We left about 10 p.m. flying west to an airbase near Anchorage, Alaska for refueling. The crew had hats, whistles and confetti for the New Year's celebration on board. We went through several time zones, moving the clock back each time, so we never got to midnight before refueling. We got off the airplane and saw the Northern Lights. Once back on board, it still wasn't midnight; but most of us passengers fell asleep instantly. I was awakened by a stewardess who handed me a breakfast tray. We were somewhere over the Pacific under a clear blue sky and had crossed the International Date Line. It was now January 2, and I had missed New Year's Day.

When I finally reached my unit, my platoon sergeant told me someone had come looking for me an hour after I left. The man didn't say who he was or why he wanted me, and I didn't think anything of it at the time. It wasn't until the next Christmas, the first time Jack and I saw each other since we returned from Vietnam, that he related what had happened at his end. I pieced together the rest. It turns out that an hour after I left on the 24th, someone from the USO tour came to get me. Xuan Loc is only a half-hour jeep ride from Bien Hoa. Learning that I had already left, he called Saigon, who called Danang, who radioed the plane to turn around. Since I wasn't there, there was no point in Jack coming. Unwittingly I had spoiled Bob Hope's plan to get the Jannarone brothers together for Christmas. It's no wonder that he never spoke to me for the rest of his life.

One of the worst parts of being in Vietnam was the feeling that much of the U.S. population was not supporting us. When I was given a letter from a woman from Missouri addressed to "Any U.S. soldier" thanking us for serving, it brought tears to my eyes, as it did to many of my men. I wrote back, thanking her profusely. At least someone back home cared.

When it was my turn to go on R & R, rest and recreation, I went to Australia for the last week of March and stayed for a few days in a hotel on Bondi Beach, Sydney. The USO had sightseeing trips planned, so I learned how to throw a boomerang and went water skiing one day. Another day was a river cruise and lunch – with a one-pound steak. Several of us went to Canberra and stayed with host families for three days. That was very nice. I bought a sheepskin rug one day. I got to the shop just before morning teatime, and was browsing through the sheepskins, deciding which ones to have put together with a zipper. The staff asked me to wait until teatime was finished, saying that they would invite me in, but they didn't have any coffee. I said I would be happy to have tea with them. Several, in amazement, said together, "Aren't you a Yank?" It took me a second to understand what they meant, but then I understood that most Americans drink coffee. So I drank a cup of tea and then they were very happy to help me with my purchase.

I got back to Vietnam on April 1. Several weeks before, I had filled out a questionnaire asking where I wanted to go for the next assignment. I wrote down Ft. Devens, Massachusetts; Ft. Meade, Maryland; and Ft. Belvoir, Virginia. Imagine my surprise when I got back to my camp and was handed orders saying I was to depart on April 4, eighty six days before my "date eligible to return from overseas, or DEROS," when I expected to go home, and be assigned to Ft. Benning, Georgia I thought it was an April Fools' Day joke.

I was awarded a Bronze Star Medal – with the wrong Social Security Number on the orders – and an Army Commendation Medal for my service in Vietnam. On April 3, in the afternoon, the adjutant got hold of me and said, "Hey, Lieutenant, you're supposed to be departing tomorrow. You better get up here and clear." It wasn't until then that I understood I was really going home early.

I checked the flight and found that it was going to Travis Air Force Base in California and that I would have to make my own arrangements to get the rest of the way to West Point, where my family lived. I was able to find another flight leaving four days later to McGuire AFB, New Jersey, where my parents could meet me, so I had my orders changed. While I was at a swimming pool two days later, my locker padlock was cut off and my $140 dollars were stolen. But the next day, when I met my platoon for the last time, I was handed a plaque inscribed:

TO: LT JANNARONE.
Best Little General in
All of the Whole U.S. Army…
    3rd PLT."

I treasure that.

On April 8, I went to the airport near Saigon and we took off with a full plane. It seemed like we took the whole runway before we were airborne. After a while someone said, "We're out of artillery range." There was a deafening cheer. We made it. But there was still one hurdle to go. The day before, we heard a plane had not been able to stop on the slick runway at the Air Force Base in Alaska, where we were supposed to refuel. Several people were killed. But we stopped just fine, with everyone sticking his foot out like he was trying to push a brake pedal down, although we all knew we had no influence on the plane. Then,

I went on to New Jersey, where my parents met me. At home, there was a big sign in the yard, saying, "Welcome Home Bob."

My mother, ever the character, used the same sign when my brother Jack came home in October. I remained on active duty for five years, transferred to the Army Reserves, served for another twenty-eight years, and retired as a Colonel. I earned an MBA, became a Registered Professional Engineer, worked for the photographic film-making division of DuPont in Rochester New York, became the Associate Director of Admissions at West Point, and worked in the Resident Office of the Corps of Engineers at West Point after that.

In all, eighteen of my classmates died in Vietnam, and a nineteenth died many years later from wounds inflicted there. In talking to my classmates over the years, I was very lucky to have been where I was and not have to suffer the way they did.

In 2015 I was diagnosed with prostate cancer. I was operated on and have been cancer free since then. I had been declared 100% disabled by the VA for three years. The Army declared that cancer "Combat Related" due to Agent Orange exposure, so I got and still get some money tax-free from VA and my Army pension. However, there sure are a lot of people who are supposed to help Veterans receive the proper benefits, who know only parts of the whole. I mention the Pennsylvania Department of Veterans Affairs, the American Legion, the VFW. The IRS gave me back too much money, and after a year of letters back and forth and speaking to an agent, they still don't understand why.

Now, I enjoy grandkids, astronomy, playing the guitar and ukulele, and traveling.

BOB CANCHOLA'S WAR

U.S. Navy, E-3 Fireman and Boiler Technician, *USS Oriskany*, CVA-34, Dixie and Yankee Stations, Two Deployments, 1971–73

I grew up on the southwest side of Chicago, in Saint Justin Martyr Parish, and graduated from St. Rita, an Augustinian high school. In Chicago, people identify themselves by the Parish and the high school district they live in, as much as their neighborhood. After high school, I graduated from Washburn Trade School in auto mechanics. Unfortunately, the draft and Vietnam were just waiting for me to finish. I was 1-A and my draft number was 74. Rather than let that happen, I enlisted in the Navy in March 1970.

After Boot Camp at Great Lakes Naval Training Center just north of Chicago, my first assignment was to a destroyer. After two years I was transferred to the USS *Oriskany*, CVA-34, as a Fireman and Boiler Room Technician, and spent two long combat deployments off the coast of Vietnam in 1971, 1972, and 1973, but at least I wasn't out crawling through the mud with the infantry.

When I got my orders in May 1971, I flew to California, to the Treasure Island Navy base across from San Francisco. They bussed me up to Travis Air Force Base where I flew to Honolulu and to Guam, to Clark Air Force Base, to Subic Bay, and finally to the Cubi point Naval Air Station. I sat there for a week, "on-call" every day, waiting for a seat on the plane to take me out to the ship. The good thing was, we didn't have any duty.

The *Oriskany* was already "on-station" off Vietnam, so I didn't go aboard by walking up the gangplank from the pier as most guys do. From Cubi Point, I went in what they called a "Carrier Onboard Delivery" flying in a C-2 Grumman Greyhound. It was a dumpy, high-winged, twin-engine cargo plane designed to carry supplies, mail, and passengers to and from aircraft carriers when they are out at sea. It has a drop-down ramp in the back, like a C-130. And when they come to land on a carrier deck, steep and hard, their tail hook grabs one of the restraining wires and yanks you backwards. The seats all face backwards, toward the tail.

The *Oriskany*, the "Big O," was an older aircraft carrier, but it was still very big. It was a WW II Essex Class carrier completed after WW II and modernized several times. I worked in the "Black Gang" in one of the ship's four firerooms or boiler rooms below deck. They called us Boiler Technicians, BTs, and sometimes referred to us as "Snipes" and "Bilge Rats," but the job wasn't that bad. My job title was Boiler Technician Third Class and my responsibilities included the Fireroom, the Boiler Rooms and the Oil Shack, where I handled feedwater, fuel oil, and freshwater testing and treatment. Mechanically, the *Oriskany* was old-fashioned. Our job required us to take a lot of readings, and they all had to be done manually. Physically, with no automation. It might not have been glamorous down there, but the boilers supplied the steam to drive the ship, power the catapults to launch the aircraft, and run all the pumps and auxiliary equipment throughout the entire ship. If you read the poem "The Snipes Lament" you will get a pretty good idea what we did and what we endured down in "The Hole," but without the steam, the ship couldn't do anything or go anywhere.

During that first combat deployment that I was on, the *Oriskany*, the ship's main mission was to strike the Ho Chi Minh Trail and other targets in Laos. While there were no combat losses per se, the ship did lose four aircraft due to accidents, two of which were fatal. One was in June when an F-8 Crusader turned upside down and splashed. The other was in November when an A-7 Corsair II pilot drowned after ejecting following a catapult launch failure.

Even though the ship was big, and the ship's crew and air wing operated separately, everyone on board felt every loss. On November 1st off Vietnam, the nose wheel broke off of one of the A-7s. The pilot ejected, but his parachute didn't fully open and he was killed. On December 13, 1972, an aircraft from VFP-63, a photo recon squadron, was lost when attempting a landing aboard the *Oriskany* after flying a reconnaissance mission. The plane was an RF-8G Vaught Crusader, its serial number was BuNo 144608, and it was flown by Lieutenant Tom Scott. He ejected safely, but the airplane was lost at sea. Fifteen years earlier, that same airplane, BuNo 144608 was flown by then Major John Glenn to set the "Project Bullet" transcontinental speed record. There is a plaque on the side of the plane that commemorated the record, but it's now resting on the bottom of the South China Sea.

The ship was actually toward the end of its deployment off Vietnam when I went aboard the first time and caught the last few weeks while it was still "on-line" before it was replaced and sailed to Singapore. There's an old Navy tradition that when you cross the equator for the first time, as I did on the return trip to the US, there's a big funny ceremony on deck when you become a "Shellback." When the *Oriskany* reached the Hunter's Point Naval Shipyard in San Francisco, she received a much-needed upgrade in its SPN-41 all-weather carrier landing system. That, and our refresher training, were finished uneventfully in March, and on 14 May we left Alameda for the carrier's sixth Vietnam deployment.

That cruise seemed to be jinxed. On June 28,1972, we collided with an ammunition ship, the USS *Nitro*, AE-23, during a night-time Underway Replenishment, an UNREP as it's called. The supply ship was much smaller than the carrier, and much shorter. Their deck was about 150 feet below ours. The way an UNREP worked was we shot lines over, followed by cables to keep the ships close, and then hauled all the ammunition, bombs, and rockets across from the supply ship to our hangar deck by a system of cables and pulleys. With two big ships bobbing up and down, accidents sometimes happen as it did that day. I was in my compartment and we could watch the whole operation on TV in our bunks. All of a sudden, I felt a big thud and alarm bells went off sending all hands to General Quarters. The *Oriskany*'s damage was limited to the number three elevator, but it put a hole in the *Nitro*. I ran up to the hangar bay to look, and the ammunition ship was right next to us, literally side by side. You could've almost walked across from ship to ship.

Despite that damage, we stayed "on-line," Later the next month we lost one of our four screws, or propellers, off Vietnam. An aircraft carrier propeller is huge, and we had to go into dry dock in Yokosuka, Japan, to have it replaced along with the repairs made to the damage we sustained during our collision with the USS *Nitro*. That's me, standing in front of the bow of the *Oriskany*. In October

of that same year we lost a second screw off Vietnam and had to go into dry dock in Yokosuka again to replace it.

My section's quarters were on the starboard side of the ship. We were about three decks below the hangar deck, and there were two more decks below us. The ship had been modernized to some extent by then, in that we did have air conditioning. On a typical 24-hour day, we worked an eight-hour shift and had two four-hour watches to stand, for a total of 16 hours on duty, which included time to eat. If we went to a port for say five days, we might pull duty one of those days as well.

In May 1972, events in Vietnam heated up again. The NVA big "Easter Offensive" was the largest offensive of the Vietnam War. By July, six attack Aircraft Carriers were on-line off Vietnam: USS *Hancock* CVA-19, USS *Oriskany* CVA-34, USS *Midway* CVA-41, USS *Saratoga* CVA-60, USS *Kitty Hawk* CVA-63, and USS *America* CVA-66. That was the greatest number of aircraft carriers on station during the entire war, and the largest gathering of aircraft carriers in a combat zone since WW II.

With the peace talks in Paris stalled, we returned to Yankee Station and continued to pound Communist targets in South Vietnam. Later, the Operation Linebacker II "Christmas bombing" campaign took place and we went back on-line from December 27 to January 30, 1973. When the Paris Peace Accords were finally signed on January 23rd our planes finished up their last strikes over South Vietnam that same day. On January 28, 1973, *Oriskany*, along with the carriers *Enterprise, Ranger, and America* were all off Vietnam conducting combat operations when the Final Vietnam Cease Fire was signed in Paris, France. This photograph shows the four carrier groups sailing together for the last time to commemorate the signing.

On March 30, 1973 *Oriskany* returned home, but not before conducting one more set of combat missions in February 1973. We observed the Cease Fire and did not hit North or South Vietnam, but we did hit targets in Laos. That gave *Oriskany* the distinc-

tion of being the last of the 24 Essex Class Carriers to engage in combat in the Vietnam War. We'd been deployed on- line for 159 days. More importantly, we did not return home until all the 591 American POWs returned home.

After a short rest period at Cubi Point in the Philippines in early February, the aircraft carrier conducted one final combat line period from February 11-22 when we bombed enemy targets in Laos, but not Vietnam, in a last effort to assist indigenous allies there against Communist infiltration. After that, we sailed for home, arriving at Alameda on 30 March after completing 169 days on the line, her longest – and what proved to be her last combat tour; all in all receiving ten battle stars for its Vietnamese service.

In June 1973, after we returned to California, I was separated from the Navy, returned home to Chicago, and used the GI Bill to go back to college. The highest rank I achieved in the Navy was E-3, Seaman; earned the usual array of Vietnam service medals, but received no injury except for some tinnitus in my ears and a loss of hearing. I received a bachelor's degree in Corrections and Criminal Justice on the "six-year plan," but with my Navy record and experience I was able to get a City of Chicago "Stationary Engineers License" and got a job with the city Department of Aviation as an Operating Engineer. Thirty years later, I retired. In Chicago, it's hard to beat a city job.

My wife and I still live in Chicago, in the city. I spend my time playing the drums, reading, and doing internet military research. For exercise, I like to juggle, use free weights, a Versa Climber, a Nordic Track Incline Trainer, and a Schwinn Airdyne. Or... I like to climb to the top of the Sears Tower, the Hancock Building, and the Aon Building downtown.

BILL ZOOK'S WAR

**U.S. Army, Captain and Huey Pilot, 240th Assault Helicopter Company
and 187th Assault Helicopter Company,
Bear Cat and Xi An, 1971–72**

I was an Army brat. My father was West Point class of 1945, he stayed in the military, serving in World War II, Korea, and Vietnam and retired as an infantry colonel with a Silver Star and Purple Heart. We moved around a lot as I grew up. I graduated from high school in Newport, Rhode Island, and attended Purdue University for one year before receiving an appointment to another engineering school, the US Military Academy at West Point, graduating in June 1969. My father died at the age of 92 a few years ago, disproving MacArthur's line that "Old soldiers just fade away."

At West Point, when it came time to pick branches, I chose Air Defense Artillery. After ADA Officer Basic at Fort Bliss, Texas, my first assignment was as a Nike Hercules Missile platoon leader. It was a surface-to-air missile used by U.S. and NATO armed forces for medium-and high-altitude long-range air defense, primarily to stop Russian bombers coming over the pole. My platoon had approximately 20 missiles, each armed with the W-31 nuclear warhead. Officially, it was mobile, but it was big and cumbersome. We didn't move often or very far. Watching a missile that didn't move and was never fired became pretty boring, so I volunteered for flight school which meant another year at Fort Walters, Texas, and Fort Rucker, Alabama.

By the time I got to Vietnam in August 1971, the war was pretty much winding down, and flying helicopters was far different than it had been six, four, or even two years earlier. Vietnamization and the withdrawal of most US troops were in full swing, and all kinds of American units were standing down across the country. When that happened, the men and equipment would be consolidated into another unit, sent home, or turned over to the Vietnamese. Without all those US ground troops out there, flying became more and more dangerous. Everywhere outside an American base was "Indian country," and if you went down, you were often on your own. We no longer had US fire support, air support, rescue services, infantry backup, or artillery to call on. And the VC and NVA were everywhere, shooting at us all the time and getting more and more bold.

I was a captain then and Huey pilot. For about four months, my first unit was the 240th Assault Helicopter Company, part of the 12th Group at Bear Cat near Bien Hoa, about 20 miles east of Saigon. When the 240th stood down, I was transferred to the 187th Assault Helicopter Company at Xi An. I was the newest and most junior captain in that company when I arrived, having only been promoted two months before. There were about twenty other captains in the unit, most of whom outranked me. In the rest of the army, captains command companies and lieutenants command platoons, but not in an aviation company with all that flying hardware. In an aviation company captains command platoons and majors command companies; so the lowly job of platoon leader was a very coveted position, because it gave you combat command time, which was necessary for promotion. I was assigned to 1st Platoon. As I got there, the platoon leader of 1st Platoon was relieved of command for striking a warrant officer. That platoon leader was a former enlisted man himself, who had been given a commission and became a captain.

Our company commander was not well-liked. He was an arrogant USMA graduate and a major. For some reason, when I arrived, he decided to appoint me platoon leader of 1st Platoon, passing over all of the other guys in line for the job. That didn't sit well with anyone. The enlisted men didn't like that I replaced a former enlisted man. And it didn't sit well with all those captains with more time-in-grade than I had, either. So, for the next two months I kept a lookout, concerned about being fragged from both sides.

Fortunately, this was December 1971 and there wasn't a lot going on. Combat assaults were at a minimum and it became a pretty boring job. Since there were very few US ground troops around, we primarily flew ARVN combat troops in different operations around the Cambodian border. I would fly a Loach light observation helicopter on recon missions. In addition to the ARVN, we flew a lot of special ops troops, inserting long-range recon or LRPs. They were some seriously mean dudes. Or we would insert CIA operators, and even haul province chiefs making various stops around the area. On occasion, we would go out and strafe boats on the canals and small rivers that were bringing in supplies and reinforcements to the VC. We'd shoot them up and see who ran.

When we returned from a mission, we did the usual: have some drinks, eat a big steak at the O-club bar, and be in bed by 11 p.m. Normally we were up again at 5:30. The day I got shot down in Cambodia even started different. They came and woke us up around midnight because they had a critical resupply mission we had to fly. An ARVN Battalion had gotten itself encircled by bad guys over near the Cambodian border. We had to go in, drop off ammo, and pick up wounded. It was about a 45-minute flight from Xi An to the staging area we used. We had a briefing there, got the ammo loaded, and flew into Cambodia in flights of two, two minutes apart.

As we got close, I saw fires everywhere. The NVA were listening to our radio frequencies, knew we were coming, and copied all of our signals. We were supposed to look for three flashlight beams in a row, to find the LZ. Unfortunately, the NVA had flashlights too, and they were everywhere. As soon as we started to go in, we got shot at. The first flight got in, offloaded their supplies, and got some wounded aboard, but there were firefights going on all around them. After they got out of there, it was our turn.

Whenever you get caught in a big firefight, everything is frantic, and things move fast. We were pointing at the ammo and screaming to the ARVNs, "Get it off! Get it off!" while they laid fifteen of their wounded guys on the floor in back. The Vietnamese are small people, but that was a lot of weight back there. Even at full power, I barely got it off the ground and over the wire, then broke right. Maybe I was up to 500' to 600' when we started getting hits from one of those big Chinese .51-caliber machine guns. They hit our gas tank, and why it didn't explode, I'll never know. Gas was all over the place and the rear compartment was on fire. My crew chief and machine gunner were getting burned, we were losing our hydraulics, and the cockpit was full of smoke. We still had power, so I began to auto rotate knowing I had to get the helicopter on the ground quickly before we crashed.

We were twenty miles inside Cambodia, it was the middle of the night, and I really wasn't too sure where we were. As I came down, I tried to flare above the trees, but we hit one. We ended up hung up in a big tree with the helicopter on its side about six feet off the ground, on fire. The whole crew had been knocked unconscious or were stunned, including me. My guys were strapped in, but the wounded ARVN in the back had not been and most of them had been thrown out as we came down. There were bodies lying everywhere. I quickly woke and dropped to the ground, but I realized I had to help my guys get out. I climbed back up on a skid, got each of them unbuckled, helped them out, and down to the ground. We managed to get about 40 feet away to the edge of a clearing, and I was about to go back for the M-60 machine gun and ammunition, when the Huey exploded. I don't know if you remember high school chemistry, but if you burn a piece of magnesium it's like a fantastically bright torch. Well, there was a lot of magnesium in those helicopters, and it lit up the jungle like a big flare as it burned.

Our standard protocol for a crash was for your wing man to come back around on your heading and see if there was anyone he could pick up. We were all cowboys back then, and I had a "six-gun" holster on my hip with a .38-caliber revolver in it. I pulled it out and fired some shots so they might see us. Unfortunately, I had picked up some tracer ammo that was the same color the NVA used. I think that was green. Anyway, my wingman saw that, thought the NVA were firing at them, and took off.

So there we were, alone in the jungle somewhere in Cambodia. We had emergency radios, but whoever checks those things? Sure enough, we turned them on, and they didn't work. We hung around there until daylight, when I returned to the crash site to see what I could salvage. The whole area had already been policed up by the NVA. Even the ARVN bodies were gone. I went back to our guys and we took inventory of what we had to work with. One guy had a survival knife. I had that .38-caliber revolver with eight rounds of ammunition. And we had a small signal mirror. That was about it. I heard helicopters coming in about two fields over, maybe 150 yards away, but they started taking fire and took off; so we knew that would not be a good place to go. We even heard jets and B-52s flying overhead and there was a lot of bombing going on all around us.

About noon, I fell asleep for a few minutes. When I woke up, it was easy to see we needed to get into an escape and evade mode. We didn't have a compass, but Vietnam was south, and it wasn't too hard to figure out which way that was. We got moving, but it was thick jungle. We worked our way down some trails until we found some booby-traps, trip wires hooked up to old artillery shells and went back into the bush. We came to places where we found NVA trail markers, stones stacked together or pieces of wood in a pattern. Those told them something, although we didn't know what it was. We didn't have any machetes, but the jungle wasn't very thick. Finally, we found ourselves in a clearing and realized it was a big NVA base camp of some kind – huge, and maybe 100 yards wide in each direction. Nobody was there, but there were smoldering fires and we found an empty POW cage in the center, homemade hooches with furniture, and things like that. It finally dawned on us that the reason the camp was empty was they were all out looking for us.

We kept pushing south until we came to another clearing. It had several huts in the middle, with nothing in them but empty bowls. We set them on fire. There were helicopters passing over us all the time, but they were up at two thousand and three thousand feet, and they never saw us. We hoped the fire and smoke might bring one of them down to look. We even saw a Loach come in low, maybe 50 yards away from us, but he didn't see us either. I even fired my pistol, but that didn't make any difference.

We managed to find some water in a five-hundred-pound bomb crater from a B-52 strike and drank some of that. Finally, around 8 p.m., we were hiding under a tree in a meadow when another helicopter came by. My crew chief had a reflective lightning bolt painted on the side of his helmet. He let that catch the light from the fading sun. Someone on the helicopter saw it and sent some helicopters in to pick us up. Seeing those Hueys coming in was one of the most beautiful things I've ever seen. Prior to that, in the middle of the night I think, two of the wounded ARVN had found us and joined up. They were the only two survivors from that group, making a total of six of us.

There was a lot of luck in that flight. We should have blown up in the air. Our C&C commander said that he saw the stream of bullets shredding our gas tank. It should have exploded, but it didn't. We were in thick triple canopy jungle, with no place to set down. And we found out later that there had been a large NVA force tracking us, trying to find us, and they were right on our tail. I don't know what would've happened if that C&C chopper

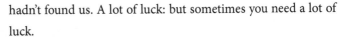

hadn't found us. A lot of luck: but sometimes you need a lot of luck.

After that, everything changed for me. I had been through my baptism of fire, I'd provided leadership, and I was accepted by the officers and enlisted men alike for what my abilities were, not for my time in rank.

A month or two later, that unit stood down and I was sent to another unit at Phu Loi before they finally sent me home after eight months in-country. I was assigned to the 101st Airborne Division at Fort Campbell, Kentucky, for two years. I served as the S-1, head of personnel, and Adjutant for the 158th Assault Helicopter Battalion stationed there. And I was put in charge of the big flyby for Westmoreland's retirement ceremony which was held there.

Then, I got out. I went to law school at the University of Texas at Austin from 1974 – 76. I became a trial lawyer and practiced law for 41 years in Austin, Paris, and Dallas, Texas.

Fortunately, I only received one minor wound in Vietnam and have experienced neither PTSD, nor any Agent Orange-induced illnesses. Now, I enjoy golf, working in the yard, fly fishing, traveling, and reading.

ROGER HAMANN'S WAR

**U.S. Air Force, Sergeant E-4, Airborne Interpreter,
Forward Air Controller, 23rd Tactical Air Support Squadron
Ubon Royal Thai Air Force Base, 1971–72**

No. 34. That was my Draft Lottery Number for the Selective Service in 1970. I was attending art school in Portland, Maine, unfortunately a non-accredited school at the time. The Vietnam War was still going on. Although it had begun to subside, the television news carried daily updates of Americans being killed, but it wasn't anything I lost sleep over. Vietnam was a long way from home, I didn't know anyone serving there, but I had a decision to make. Wait and be drafted by the Army? Join the Army or Marines? Either way, I'd end up in Vietnam. There was the Navy, but I didn't like boats or water. And the Coast Guard? Much the same. So that left the Air Force and "see the world." After all, how dangerous could the Air Force be? I was sworn in on June 24, 1970, and proceeded to San

Antonio, Texas, for Basic Military Training, BMT, at Lackland AFB. This was my first time in an airplane and my first time away from home for any length of time.

After six weeks of training in the hot Texas sun, I was assigned to Wurtsmith AFB in northeastern Michigan. I had not tested too highly on any of the aptitude tests during BMT and was one of only four airmen from my training flight to receive DDAs, or a Direct Duty Assignment, which meant we didn't go to technical school first. That was the Air Force's version of grunt or go-fer, and I was assigned to a supply squadron as a POL specialist dealing with petroleum, oil, and lubricants, in other words, a gas jock. At Wurtsmith, that meant driving a truck filled with 5,000 gallons of jet fuel, or AV-GAS for propeller driven planes, and refueling everything from B-52 bombers to KC-135 tankers, F-106 fighters, T-33 trainers, T-39s and the C-47 gooney birds. When we were refueling with a hose cart, it was mandatory that we hold the control switch in our hands, no matter how cold it was on the flight line… and believe me, it could get "wicked" cold up there in northern Michigan on the shores of Lake Huron.

Wurtsmith reminded me of my home state of Maine. The area and the weather were the same as back home. The downside was there wasn't much to do there and after a while I needed a change. So, I decided to put in a volunteer statement for Vietnam or Thailand. After all, how dangerous could refueling aircraft at an Air Force base in Vietnam or Thailand be? I was just a gas jock! Go for it!

A few weeks later, our orderly room clerk told me I had orders to go to Vietnam... oh, and they were "Special Orders." Special Orders, I wondered? What's that all about? I was to report to Phan Rang AB in South Vietnam, but not as a POL specialist. The orders had something to do with the fact that I spoke French. My family was originally French-Canadians, who settled in central Maine to work in the fabric mills and shoe shops. We all spoke French, as did most people up there. And I remembered taking an optional language test back at Lackland AFB, but I'd never given it any thought since... not until then.

What I would be doing was classified, but I'd have to go through altitude chamber testing at Wright-Patterson AFB in Ohio, survival school at Fairchild AFB in Washington, and jungle survival school at Clark AB in the Philippines. And, I would be flying! What had I gotten myself into? Flying? In Vietnam? And what about speaking French? It was on my last leg of training at Clark AB that I first heard they were sending enlisted guys to fly in the backseat of a two-man reconnaissance plane called an OV-10 Bronco as Forward Air Controllers. Wow, this was becoming more "warlike" by the minute... and I wasn't a "warlike type" of guy! But what was the French for?

I arrived at Phan Rang in October 1971 and reported in to the 19th Tactical Air Support Squadron, "The Rustics," and met Captain Murphy, the officer in charge of the enlisted back-seaters program. Turns out that with the troop drawdowns, some of us would be reassigned. I was picked to stay, but the squadron was moving from Bien Hoa near Saigon to Ubon Royal Thai Air Force Base in Thailand. An OV-10 Bronco was a twin tail, twin-engine turboprop that had been developed for forward air control and counter-insurgency operations. We worked as a team. The pilot sat in front and the GIB, or "guy in back," served as the Forward Air Controller, or FAC, and sat behind him.

But why did they need a French-speaking GIB FAC? To be an interpreter between the pilot and the ground commanders. Ground commanders? Didn't they speak English? Or Vietnamese? Some, but most only spoke Cambodian and French. Wait a minute! Cambodian and French? That meant we would be flying in Cambodia, not Vietnam, and the ground commanders were Cambodian Army officers, fighting a war against the NVA, the VC, and their own internal Communist insurgency in a war President Nixon said we were not involved in. That's why it was all secret, because we were there, and we were involved, although it all remained classified until 1996.

On November 10, 1971, I saw my first OV-10. After being strapped into the back seat with parachute, helmet, gloves, revolver and my duffel bag thrown in the cargo bay, I was off to Ubon, Thailand, a two-hour flight and the new home of the 19th, now renamed the 21st Tactical Air Support Squadron, soon to be renamed again to the 23rd Tactical Air Support Squadron, but still called "the Rustics."

After a few days of briefings on map reading, the code wheel, proper usage of radios in the OV-10, the terminology used in reconnaissance work, and of course, familiarity with the OV-10 itself, my call sign became "Rustic Yankee" and I was added to the flying schedule. On November 13, 1971, I set out on my first Cambodian adventure with Rustic 18, Lieutenant Clinch, headed for Rumlong, which had been the scene of many recent battles between the Cambodian Army and the NVA. When we arrived, we were told the enemy had finally overrun the area and we were to destroy any weapons we saw abandoned. It was ironic that my very first mission was to destroy "friendly" weapons instead of the enemy's, but it was necessary to deny the enemy an extra supply cache of weapons.

We put in four sets of airstrikes on the targets. It was a good thing my French wasn't needed, because I had all I could handle trying to keep my lunch down as we constantly pulled Gs going up and down with our dives to mark targets for the fighters. Looking down through my binoculars while making marking passes also proved worthless as I was getting nauseous just trying to keep sense of where the target was in relation to what I was seeing through the binoculars, dealing with the G forces and a pilot who was obviously delighted to have a rookie in his backseat. Still, I gutted it out and didn't use the barf bag that day or any other. We returned to Ubon almost five hours later. Upon landing, I felt like I was on top of the world, with a sense of pride I'd never experienced before. In a matter of one month, I'd gone from driving a fuel truck in Northern Michigan to flying a combat mission in the backseat of a two-man recon plane in Cambodia, from oil-stained fatigues to a sweaty, thoroughly drenched flight suit, from delivering JP-4 jet fuel to an F-106 fighter jet to directing A-37 fighter jets on an enemy target in Southeast Asia. Now THIS was what being in the Air Force was really all about; and although I never saw myself as being part of THAT Air Force, I was mighty proud to be a part of it now!

As time and the missions began to fly by, I became more accustomed to each pilot and his preferences. Some liked flying solo and having someone in their backseat cramped their style. In those cases, I just kept notes and let the pilot do the talking to the fighters as well as the ground commanders. Other pilots enjoyed having an extra set of eyes and ears along to see and hear more of what was going on. With a UHF, VHF, HF and two FM radios aboard the OV-10, having a back-seater gave the pilot the opportunity to share the workload, especially when we were involved in a TIC (Troops in Contact) situation where we could be talking simultaneously to the Cambodian ground commander, his radio operator, a set of fighters on bombing runs on the target area, another set of fighters in a holding pattern awaiting their turn to hit the target, another Rustic FAC arriving or departing over the target, and BlueChip, the 7th Air Force Headquarters. When all that was going on, we had to make sure we were all on the same page. One erroneous placement of a bomb could be devastating, and it was my job as the FAC to make sure that never occurred.

Those daily missions into Cambodia developed into a strong bond between our Cambodian allies and we Rustics. It got to the point where the ground commanders and their RO's could identify which Rustic pilot or GIB they were talking to; and we could hear the relief in their voices knowing a Rustic was covering their area, if only for an hour or so.

One of the voices we most often heard was that of Sam, a captain in the Cambodian Army. Sam was one of the most endearing characters I worked with. It was not uncommon for us Rustics to become involved in a dialogue with him about life after the war, or personal things. Sam would ask about girlfriends back home, what our favorite foods were, his seemed to be spaghetti, and whether we had any "ankle biters." Ankle biters? I'd never heard that term before. Sam laughed and said an "ankle biter was a small child, a crawling toddler... an ankle biter!" Imagine flying over a war-torn country talking to a foreign army officer about children.

Later, after I had children of my own, the children of Cambodia would come back to me in a nightmare. Was I ever responsible for dropping a bomb that resulted in the death of children? It's a question with no answer, perhaps until my own day of reckoning.

It wasn't until Christmas morning, 1971, my 32nd mission, that I actually saw enemy troops on the ground. Shortly after we "crossed the fence," the Thai-Cambodian border, I raised our Cambodian allies on the radio and heard the familiar voice of Sam in Kampong Thom. He was always cheerful, but not this day. His troops and the villagers of KP Thom had been hit with heavy mortar fire throughout the previous night, resulting in many being killed and wounded. He passed me the coded map coordinates of two hooches at a bend in the river. That was where his scouts said the NVA fired their mortars from the previous night.

We did a high visual recon of the area, high enough not to attract any attention, and I looked for any signs of activity through my binoculars. I saw nothing: no people, no enemy soldiers, no mortar pits, nothing, except for those two hooches. Sam asked us to put an immediate airstrike on them, although he knew as well as we did that approvals did NOT come that quickly. Nevertheless, my pilot pleaded Sam's request to "BlueChip," the 7th AF headquarters in Saigon. Maybe they were in a giving mood because it was Christmas, but in ten minutes we were told two A-37 Dragonfly light bombers were headed our way.

When they checked in about 15 minutes later, my pilot gave them a quick briefing, describing the target, elevation, weather, enemy and friendly locations, best possible bailout areas and so on. While this was going on, I kept in touch with Sam, advising him that we were about ready to put in an airstrike and to make sure there were no friendlies in the target area.

The A-37s were carrying old-fashioned MK-82 "dumb" 500-pound bombs. The lead plane went in and put his first bomb shy of the hooches. About 50 or so black-pajama-clad NVA came running out of the dust and debris of the hooches, heading for cover in the nearby jungle. But before any of them got that far, the second A-37 put his bomb right in the middle of them! We flew down for a quick visual reconnaissance and Bomb Damage Assessment and saw the results of the two MK-82s were total annihilation. That's the only way I can describe it. There was nothing down there but bits and pieces of black, blood, and bodies. Neither the pilot nor I said anything for a few minutes. Then, in an uncharacteristic moment, I keyed my mike and said, "Merry F***in' Christmas." My pilot responded with a double click of his mike. Anyone who knows me would say I never could have said that… but I did. And to this day, every Christmas, I think of that mission…and those words…and that scene below me.

Up until then, the targets I had been going after were usually suspected ammo dumps, VC training areas, or mortar or gun pits, always under the cover of triple canopy jungle. But this one, with these two hooches sitting in the open by the riverbank, seemingly unoccupied on a Christmas morning… It was an eye opener. This time I saw humans, obviously fighting for their own cause, much as we were doing… but for different reasons. We got the best of them that day, but other days would yield different results. Sam was ecstatic with the results of the airstrike and thanked us endlessly for our support. His people would be able to rest now, if only for a day or two before the whole process would begin again in earnest.

In truth, I barely remember most of the 169 missions I flew during my ten months as a Rustic GIB. It's surprising that those missions don't come back to me as if they happened yesterday; but they don't. Had they become "just another day on the job?" Or has my brain blocked out that chapter of my life, for reasons I may not want to know?

I flew a mission with my Squadron Commander, Lieutenant Colonel Ray Stratton. As we were finishing it up, we were told to report to Tan Son Nhut AB in Saigon to brief some generals on the current situation in Cambodia. By the time we finished, it was sunset. Once we were up in the air, Colonel Stratton asked me if I'd like to fly the plane for a bit while he organized some of his paperwork. What a thrill! A two-striper flying a plane, even if it was from the back seat!

A storm had developed ahead of us and we flew on the edge of it. The OV-10 was bouncing around and I was keeping it level... or so I thought! I glanced at my attitude indicator and saw we were in a 90-degree left bank. Colonel Stratton finally looked up and asked if everything was OK back there. I quickly straightened the Bronco out and replied, "Yes sir."

I remember flying into Laotian airspace one day, listening to music from Australia on one of our radios, when my pilot spotted something below. I looked down and saw a man sitting on a dilapidated oxcart being pulled by a water buffalo. The cart was loaded with something that was covered by a tarp. Was he a simple peasant farmer, or an NVA? My pilot asked me what I thought the guy had hidden under the tarp. In my opinion, he was some poor farmer going about his daily chores, but that wasn't what the pilot wanted to hear. He decided the cart was loaded with weapons, probably AK-47s, and was going in. That day, we were carrying a pod of flechette rockets. They were rockets filled with small darts. I almost didn't want to look as he fired one at the cart and then quickly pulled out. The pilot said whatever was in the cart, there was now one less bad guy to worry about. Fortunately, most of the pilots I flew with were more restrained before engaging a target. Maybe that's why I remember it.

We flew mostly day missions, so the tracer rounds coming up at us were rarely visible. We heard the familiar "They're shooting at you sir!" warning that we'd get over the radio and usually ignore. During my ten-month tour as a Rustic, none of our OV-10s were shot down, although three Rustics were shot down and killed before and after my tour. The names of Garrett Eddy, Michael Vrablick and Joseph Gambino are inscribed on the Vietnam Veterans Memorial in Washington, D.C.

My tour of duty was over in August 1972. I ended my tour as a Rustic GIB with 169 missions and having been involved in over 200 airstrikes. I had time left on my enlistment and was assigned to Loring AFB in northern Maine, becoming a POL jock and fuel specialist again. It was culture shock to go from driving a 5,000-gallon JP-4 fuel truck in Michigan, to "driving" in the back seat of an OV-10 Bronco in a secret war in Cambodia, and then go back to the POL truck. I took an early out and was separated in February 1974. I moved back to Lewiston and got a job as a cabinetmaker until the company closed in 2010.

In October of 2002, on the occasion of our third unit reunion, six of the Rustic GIBS were presented with Distinguished Flying Crosses, admittedly some thirty years overdue. Being the youngest and the only one not to have made the Air Force a career, I was the last to receive my three DFCs. As a gesture of thanks and to show respect for the Cambodian people and the soldiers who fought for them, I presented one of my DFCs to Colonel Sam Oum, the Cambodian Army commander the Rustics worked with from 1970–73,  and who now resides in Austin, Texas. Colonel Oum passed away on August 8, 2008, and the presentation speech I had made to him six years earlier was read again at his funeral by one of the former Rustic pilots.

Now, I spend my time as a researcher for a Facebook group USA Military Directory, which helps Vets connect with other Vets they served with.

DENIS GULAKOWSKI'S WAR

U.S. Army, Captain and MAC-V Cords Advisor to Team 89, Dat Do District, Phouc Tuy Province, 1971–72

I am a 1969 US Military Academy graduate and served one combat tour in RVN as an advisor in the Military Assistance Command Vietnam, (MACV), Civil Operations and Revolutionary Development Support, or CORDS, from November 71 to November 72. At the time, I was a 24-year-old airborne Ranger infantry captain who wound up being the District Senior Advisor for Dat Do District, Phouc Tuy Province, Team 89. That area is southeast of Saigon on the coast, north of Vung Tao. It had been a major Australian and New Zealand Army area of operations, but they were mostly gone by the time I got there.

I grew up in Ridgefield, New Jersey on the west side of the Hudson River and graduated from Xavier High School, a Jesuit school in Manhattan. I was fortunate enough to get an appointment to West Point in 1965. I was there at the height of the war and we were exposed to it 24/7. Nearly all of our instructors were Vietnam Vets and it was the focus of all of our military studies and subsequent training. But by 1970, with President Nixon's Vietnamization program being implemented and the war winding down, you had to volunteer for a Vietnam assignment. Troops were coming out, not going in, and a combat assignment was essential if you were staying in. After Branch, Airborne and Ranger Schools, I was assigned to the 5th Infantry Division at Fort Carson Colorado, which was being renamed the 4th Infantry Division, as that entire unit was coming back from Vietnam. While waiting for an assignment to Vietnam, I served as a platoon leader, and later Battalion Assistant Operations Officer and Battalion Intelli-

gence Officer. In my spare time, I played on the brigade softball team. As time progressed and I hadn't heard about my assignment, I went to my branch to see what they could do. Their quotas were filled and I was told there were no openings until 1972. Two weeks later, one of the E-5s with whom I played softball and who worked in personnel, told me my orders had come down. When I called branch to find out why the change, I was told they had received a new requirement for 150 captains. Usually they'd send an advisor to a six-month language and culture course before reporting in-country, but all of that had been cut back, and I went straight to the unit. Ironically, when I in-processed through Bien Hoa, the admin specialist who was assigning me to a unit said something to the effect of, "Holy 'ship' Sir, I don't know where to put you. I have so many captains, I don't know what to do with you guys." So much for my branch assignments officer's comment about needing 150 captains.

Team 89, in Dat Do District, consisted of two captains; the other officer, who was leaving, was military intelligence, and I was infantry. Everyone else had rotated out except for an E-7 Ranger who was on his third MACV tour and who was a great NCO to work with, and an E-4 radio telephone operator, known as an  RTO. They called me "Dai Uy," which meant Captain in Vietnamese, and called the E-7 "Ranger." The rules were that there had to be two Americans to go to the field. They didn't want us going anywhere alone.

I got there in November and we operated out of a small fortified compound that included the district head-quarters. The head of the Vietnamese unit was a lieutenant colonel who spoke three lan-guages. Unfortunately, English wasn't his best, but I had taken French at West Point, so we mostly conversed in French. We also had a Vietnamese E-5 interpreter and a translator, and both of them spoke very good English. The Australians were all gone by then, and their bases had been turned over to the ARVN; but they left a few advisors behind. The one who worked with us was a graduate of their Royal Military College, Duntroon.

The first half of my tour consisted of: "Don't get dead. Don't get wounded. And don't get captured." There were very few active American units left in-country. All our air support was either from the Vietnamese, who were very cautious, or from the US 126th aviation company, whose mission had been to shuttle VIPs and who rarely flew below 2,000 feet. Interestingly, the seats in their helicopters were leather, not the usual torn and bloodstained canvas, which pretty much indicated the difference in their mission.

The Vietnamese units in the province were "Regular Forces," similar to our reserves, and "Popular Forces," who were like a militia. All of the ARVN Regular Army units were occupied elsewhere to the north and west. The US 1st Cav division was still around, but they were packing up and leaving, and our only serious helicopter gunship support had to come out of Vung Tau and Bien Hoa, even farther away. Even regular air support was rationed, and we were told the number of "blade hours" that we could use. Fortunately, there were still a lot of Air Force and Navy fighter-bombers in the air over South Vietnam; and if their assigned targets were weathered in, they would look for alternate targets, because pilots prefer not to land with a live bomb hanging underneath the aircraft if they don't have to. So we kept a list of targets and suspect areas where there had been enemy activity or recent sightings. After all, you hated to waste a 500-pound bomb.

Time moved along, with routine patrolling and some enemy incursions into the villages, until the command decision was made in early '72 to move the district teams back to the Province Headquarters, where I became the Team Adjutant. We were there only a short time, however, when the NVA's Easter Offensive of 1972 changed that situation dramatically. With the Paris peace talks mimicking the Abbott & Costello classic comedy routine, *Who's On First?*, the enemy objective was to occupy as much territory on the Monopoly board as possible before a cease-fire was agreed upon, so they could claim it as theirs.

With confirmed intelligence reports indicating the enemy was infiltrating our AO (area of operation), our district team, comprising only myself and my RTO, (since my NCO was home on leave), was ordered back to the district. I arranged for a helicopter to take us back for an insertion. Once there, the two of us, along with a South Vietnamese Regional Force company, who were protecting the district capital, quickly became surrounded by elements of the 33rd NVA Regiment, the 274th Main Force Viet Cong Battalion and the D445 Local Force Viet Cong Battalion. Both of the Viet Cong units were pretty much street gangs – kids with guns. They weren't well trained or organized, but to some extent, neither were the Vietnamese reserve and militia units on our side. What sharply tipped the balance was the arrival of the NVA 33rd Regiment, which was tasked by Hanoi to seize the province. There were a lot of Vietnamese civilians from I Corps, whom the government had moved down and resettled in a showpiece settlement area in the province called Suoi Nghe, to demonstrate productivity and the success of Vietnamization. That made us the target of a coordinated attack, and we got jammed up quickly.

Once there, I was manning the shop by myself with my RTO. He had to stay there and communicate with our province advisors and the Vietnamese, so I had to go out alone. Even though that deviated from protocol, the urgency of the situation called for it. This was a critical area for the government, and they sent in the 18th ARVN Division to kick the bad guys out, but that took a while. You could tell things were going from bad to worse when all the Vietnamese civilians started packing up and moving out, heading back to the city, and a Vietnamese officer told us we should clear out too, but we didn't, and pretty soon we were surrounded.

Vietnamese air support was nonexistent. To be a helicopter pilot, they had to speak English. That meant they were from affluent upper-class families, sons of government officials, and weren't about to get shot down or killed. Fortunately, we were able to get some excellent close air support from our Air Force, and their "fast movers" saved us. The NVA had gotten very close, not quite to hand grenade range, but close enough. In fact the tactical term was "danger close." What proved to be very effective was the Cessna A-37 "Dragonfly," a small attack jet that the Air Force used for special ops work. The aircraft could carry a lot of bombs and rockets underneath and were very effective for ground support because they were slow and could get in close. In particular, they carried CBU-25 cluster bombs, which was like a group of hand grenades that dispersed and blew shrapnel all over the place. Very effective against infantry.

I was able to climb an old observation tower in the compound to better direct the airstrikes; once the enemy saw me there, they shifted mortar fire toward the tower. Fortunately, their aim was such that I wasn't hit, but some shrapnel did come close. The airstrikes proved to be successful and the NVA were beaten off. Afterwards, we sent out patrols and found 150 blood trails leading away from our compound, which meant we hurt them pretty badly.

As this major battle was raging around us and I was busy calling in airstrikes and putting out one fire after another, I got a call on my tactical net from "Danger 79," wanting a sitrep (a situation report). I had no idea who this individual was, and I was too busy to fool around. I answered, "Danger 79, get the 'heck' off my tactical net and go to the admin channel!" I later found out that he was the three-star general commanding Military Region III, but nothing ever came of it. Years later, I ran into another Academy grad who had been near the Cambodian border at the same time, and exactly the same thing happened. Not everybody gets to blow off a three-star general, but we did. I guess it was karma, or something like that.

Ever since the My Lai Massacre in March 1968 all activities against locals had to be approved by the Vietnamese. You might call it a double chain of command. I was supposed to get a Vietnamese officer's initials on any attack. Fortunately, things were so desperate that all the procedures were expedited, and no one got in our way.

As part of our basic planning, our team had to have an "escape plan." Given the situation, we guessed that meant black pajamas and conical straw hats. Of course given our physical size, trying to sneak away wasn't going to work very well. Fortunately it never came to that. The ARVN 18th Division pushed the NVA and VC units out of the Province, and by late summer things began to calm down.

We were the military side of MACV-CORDS. The other side of CORDS, the Department of State folks from USAID, were working with the government on local economic development. It was a two-pronged approach. If the province senior advisor was a civilian, then his deputy was military, and vice-versa. For some reason, some of the USAID gang didn't think they were part of the war. They thought they were neutral civilians and were safe, and that no one would shoot at them. While I was there, their vehicles were replaced with International Harvester SUVs that were painted gold. One day I came on one of the young USAID men who was about to drive out the gate in his SUV. I saw no weapons and asked him if he was armed. He smiled and showed me a six-shot revolver in his backpack. I looked at him and asked if he had any idea where he was, that there was a war going on, and they'd kill him just as quickly as they would kill me. It was some war.

I rotated back home twelve months and one day after I arrived in Vietnam. I was awarded a Silver Star and a Vietnamese Medal of Honor for my activities during the battle at our compound in the Easter Offensive, which by the way, was known to the Vietnamese as the Ngyuen Hue Campaign.

Upon my return, I had requested assignment back to Fort Carson, Colorado, after I attended the Advanced Course. Naturally, they sent me to Fort Jackson, South Carolina, on the other side of the country. After command and staff time there, I was assigned to the Engineer School at Fort Belvoir near Washington, DC. Unfortunately, the school was in the process of being shifted out to Fort Leonard Wood, Missouri, but my assignment remained at Belvoir. In addition to my BS in engineering from West Point, I was able to earn an MA in Behavioral Science and an MA in Applied Psychology, through programs at the Catholic University of America. After eight years, I was faced with an unaccompanied overseas assignment, in which I'd be out in the field way too much. After long and careful consideration, I opted in favor of my family and resigned my regular Army commission.

As a Reserve Officer, I remained at Fort Belvoir and later joined the Active Guard/ Reserve Program, staying in for a total of 25 years and retiring as a Lieutenant Colonel. Fortunately, when a civilian, I was able to work for a government contractor dealing with weapons systems, automation, training devices and simulators. Some of that was due to connections I made at various duty stations and some of that was due to good luck. In particular, I worked on training simulators, primarily for combat vehicles. I also worked as the Director of Education and Programs at an organization of engineers and surveyors.

Now completely retired, I spend my free time with my family, my 1969 Corvette, and doing volunteer work.

GUY MILLER'S WAR

U.S. Army Captain and Huey Pilot,
60th Assault Helicopter Company, 7-17th Air Cavalry Squadron,
17th Combat Aviation Group, II Corps, 1972–73

I graduated in 1969 from the US Military Academy at West Point as an Armor officer. Like many graduates, I completed Airborne and Ranger Schools and branch officer course, prior to my initial assignment to the 82nd Airborne Division. Following a mandatory year of troop duty, I completed helicopter flight school at Fort Wolters, Texas, and Fort Rucker, Alabama. I arrived in-country in January 1972 and reported to the 60th Assault Helicopter Company, the "Ghost Riders," as a UH-1 Huey aviator. We were based at Ninh Hoa, now a lovely seaside resort along Route 1, twenty miles north of Nha Trang on the South China Sea.

The Army's goal in flight school was to turn out pilots who could take off, fly straight and level, navigate by map, handle emergency procedures and land safely in a variety of conditions. Those who couldn't manage these basic skills didn't graduate. And a lot didn't. There was a war on, and anything more than the basics was beyond the scope of flight school. Once assigned to a combat unit in Vietnam, new pilots soon learned a lot of things that weren't taught in flight school. We learned those from the experienced combat pilots we flew with.

In my assault helicopter company our own stupidity and bad judgment usually posed more serious risks for us than the bad guys. We supported the Republic of Korea [ROK] Army troops of the White Horse and Tiger Divisions operating in II Corps. During early 1972, the ROKs captured a North Vietnamese Army Rest and Recuperation center in a mountainous valley of central South Vietnam, complete with a treasure trove of live pigs and corn. To "win the hearts and minds of the Vietnamese people," the Koreans decided to donate the captured corn and pigs to their adopted local orphanage forty miles away in Nha Trang.

The only way to get the livestock and produce there was for us to fly them out in our helicopter. The Korean troops chopped a tiny clearing in the jungle canopy on the side of the valley, what we called a "hover hole," just big enough for a Huey to land. I was still a "new guy" in-country and was flying copilot that day when our bird got the mission. It was our first sortie of the afternoon, so the bird was heavy with full fuel, and it was starting to get really hot when we arrived and wormed our way down through the hover hole.

There were about two loads worth to haul out, but somehow my Aircraft Commander, the battle-hardened pilot in charge of the helicopter, let the Koreans talk him into trying to fly it all out in a single lift. Bad idea. So the troops packed bags of corn about two feet deep across the entire floor of the Huey, and then threw the five hogtied pigs on top of the pile

and told us to go. I was later to learn that these Vietnam-ese "potbellied" pigs are considered as high-fashion pets by Yuppies, because they are so cute, but I sure didn't think so that day.

We were severely overloaded and air temperature was killing our lift. Naturally, I was given the honors of trying to fly the bird out. As I pulled in power and began to climb through the hole in the canopy, the overloaded rotor was already losing speed and the controls were getting mushy. Understand, our Hueys had no doors. Also understand, pigs do not like to ride in helicopters. What I mean to say is, **_pigs really don't like to ride in helicopters!_** So about twenty feet up, half a ton of tied-up pigs started squealing and thrashing around in the helicopter, making control almost impossible. The blade tips started chopping leaves and branches, swirling loose debris through the cabin, which *really* pissed those pigs off.

By then, the entire platoon of Korean troops on the ground were standing directly beneath the helicopter, staring up at this incredible sight. There was no way I could set the bird back down without squashing a dozen or so ROKs. Fortunately, the pigs got so agitated that they started knocking bags of corn loose from the pile on the floor. Despite the lurching gyrations of the Huey, as loose corn joined leaves and brush raining down on the troops, the aircraft lost enough cargo to regain a little lift. As the rotors finally cleared the jungle canopy, I thought we might actually make it out alive; so I eased the control stick forward, desperate to pick up some airspeed. Too soon. The tips of the skids caught in the branches of the trees, and I thought we were going to nose it in right there.

That was when the Aircraft Commander grabbed the controls away from me and yanked the power control up. This succeeded in breaking the skids free of the trees, but also put an excessive load on the already dangerously slow rotor. The tail rotor had slowed as well, reducing its ability to maintain directional control. We spun a pair of clockwise gyrating rotations as the Huey plunged down the valley side, skimming the canopy, and slinging bags of corn and two of those damn pigs far and wide. Even so, it took about four more hairy minutes for us to nurse enough airspeed and altitude to finally climb out of that valley and start back to Nha Trang. We had nearly lost four American aircrew members and a million-dollar aircraft costing about $1,000 per hour to operate, trying to rescue maybe $50 worth of corn and pigs so the little orphans could appreciate the humanitarianism of our war effort. As it was, we only got about half of the loot to its final destination.

****

Flying north along the South China Sea coast from our home base at Ninh Hoa, before we got to Tuy Hoa and Qui Nhon was the Vung Ro Point, a mountainous protrusion at the easternmost point of Vietnam. It was home to some particularly unpleasant bad guys, which we would avoid by flying out to sea at 2,000 feet elevation. However, if we were working in the Tuy Hoa river valley, where three battalions with 12 companies of the Korean White Horse 1st Regiment were located, we'd try to slip through the Vung Ro pass, a narrow slot through the mountains. There was said to be a radar-guided heavy machine gun there, but I was lucky enough never to confirm that story. Nonetheless, we always traversed that valley either above 2,000' if we could, or else at treetop level, zigzagging as we went.

In May 1972, we were at the end of a really long day flying rations, water, ammo and mail to the ROK units. The weather was low overcast with poor visibility, and I was at the controls as co-pilot, taking us home. The clouds kept us from flying our customary 2,000' safe altitude, so I was nursing the aircraft along as high as we could safely fly, at about 1,600 feet but still within AK-47 range.

The most important single part of the helicopter is the big nut that secures the rotor assembly to the mast. This part is at the highest point on the bird and is affectionately known as the "Jesus Nut." I was flying us along, skimming our Jesus Nut along the bottom of the clouds, still able to see. If we took fire, I could yank us up into the clouds and climb on instruments until we were above the mountains. I was tooling along at 80 knots, already tense, when, **WHOOSH!!!** Suddenly, out of the cloud directly in front of me, just beyond the edge of our rotor blades, I saw the belly of an airplane flying straight down. "**What the hell was that?**" It had an engine in front and another one just behind the cockpit, a "push me-pull you" we called it. This was an Air Force Cessna O-2, the small airplane that Forward Air Controllers flew to call in and control jet airstrikes. That damn FAC was flying **aerobatic maneuvers in the clouds** and had missed a mid-air collision with us by less than 50 feet. He flew on his merry way, completely unaware that his guardian angel had saved him from joining the six of us in the Huey at the pearly gates.

Idiot fixed-wing driver!

****

In August '72, I was an Aircraft Commander and had my own unique call-sign. By this time in the war, the American forces had really been drawn down, and I realized we had not seen another helicopter for several hours. When you're flying over bad-guy country in a single-engine aircraft, the idea that no one is around anywhere to hear a "May Day" call if you find yourself going down is troubling. While my co-pilot continued to fly the mission, I flipped our radio to the universal emergency channel, and called, "Commo check on guard." No response. Again, "Commo check on guard." Absolutely nothing, which was making me more nervous. Once more, "Commo check on guard. Is anyone there?"

Finally I heard a response, "Aircraft calling on Guard, this is Blackbird 081."

"Blackbird 081, this is Ghost Rider 8. Good to hear your voice."

"This is Blackbird 081. You sound like a helicopter. If you're in trouble, I'm afraid I can't be much help. I am at Angels 85, but I could try to relay." That meant he was flying at 85,000 feet, an Air Force SR-71 spy plane, probably flying about 2,000 mph.

"No emergency," I answered. "I just wanted to hear another aircraft."

"Ghost Rider 8, Blackbird 081. Rog…" In the time we were talking, he had already flown over the horizon. Well, at least I knew the Guard channel on my radio worked.

****

An Engineer buddy of mine was a captain heading an inspection team that had to remain overnight one Saturday at Phan Rang airbase. After arranging for bunks and chow for his NCOs, he headed down to the Air Force Officers Club to see to his own needs.

Sitting at the bar, he struck up a conversation with a couple of the "Zoomies," the Air force fighter-bomber pilots, based there. A little before 6:00 p.m., all the guys at the bar began clearing out, and his drinking buddies said, "Come on. You've got to see this."

A whole crowd of people was gathering outside, checking their watches and clearly waiting for something. Finally, someone said, "Here it comes!" Everyone looked northwest, where a rocket plume rose from the hill overlooking the airfield. Dang if a 132-mm Soviet Katyusha rocket wasn't heading directly toward them. It flew straight over their heads, across the runway, and exploded harmlessly in a rice paddy just beyond the base perimeter.

A cheer went up among the gathered crowd, with comments of, "Great shot," and "All right!" and "Better than average," and "Nine point oh, at least." There was even a medic with a Super 8 movie camera filming the entire scene.

As the crowd began to disperse my buddy asked, "What the hell was that?"

Turns out there was a lone Viet Cong soldier camped on the back side of the hill. Every Saturday evening at precisely 6:00 p.m. he fired a single rocket at the airbase, ensuring it always landed harmlessly outside the perimeter. He probably then reported to Hanoi that his rocket had blown up four American fighter jets, two transport aircraft, and a fuel truck. Sometimes he even blew up the control tower. Each week the NVA would send him another heavy rocket, carried by hand all the way down the Ho Chi Minh trail.

My buddy asked, if they knew where this guy was, why didn't they just go out and pick him up? The answer was, then the NVA might send somebody new who would actually do some damage. So, it worked for everyone.

****

The infantry troops we carried considered our helicopters to be giant bullet-magnets and death traps, so on combat assault, a CA insertion, they couldn't wait to get off the Hueys. Almost all of our landing zones were single-ship clearings, which meant we went in one at a time. When there was a slope, we would land parallel to the slope. If the slope was gentle, we would set the uphill skid on the ground so the troops could step off on the uphill side, but on steeper slopes we hovered as low as we could, without risking a blade striking the upslope ground. As the troops jumped off, the shifting weight always made the rotor wobble dangerously, and the troops had to exit toward the nose. The crew chief and door gunner had gigantic screwdrivers they used to bash the helmets of any troops heading the wrong way.

The tail rotor spun so fast it was invisible – essentially a 1,100-horsepower vertical weed eater that could turn a troop into a pink cloud instantaneously. Unfortunately that could only happen once, since the tail rotor would simultaneously disintegrate, leaving the bird to immediately self-destruct. On my first major CA in-country, I saw a bird's rotor blade strike the ground on the uphill side. The Huey rather gently beat itself to death, so all the troops and crew made it out. Mine was the next single ship to go in, so we had to find a different spot to land. After inserting our troops we picked up the four American crew from the downed bird. Our mission commander called for "Big Windy" (the 180th Assault Support Helicopter company) to send out a CH-47 Chinook to sling lift the dead Huey out. That bird would never fly again, but it might have some useable parts, plus the two machine guns were accountable weapons that couldn't be left behind.

While we were flying circles waiting for Big Windy, a grass fire that started earlier from a gunship rocket was creeping up the hill. When it touched the Huey lying on its side, the magnesium and aluminum of the bird began to burn like a trip flare, with brilliant light and a giant cloud of white smoke, blackened by 200 gallons of flaming jet fuel. It took about 45 seconds until there was nothing left of a million-dollar aircraft, not even any ash.

That was one lesson I never forgot. A pilot's greatest fear is fire. If you caught fire more than ten seconds from the ground, it was guaranteed to be a really bad day.

Once in a steep slope LZ, one of the ROK troops couldn't wait his turn, so he jumped off the downhill side, falling about ten feet, carrying all his gear. He had two broken legs; so, on our next sortie we had to Medevac his battered body to the pickup zone. We couldn't stop the CA to take him to the hospital, because the troops already inserted needed all their buddies with them ASAP. Still, that ROK went home early from his tour

****

All the helicopter fueling in-country was "hot," meaning when a bird landed at a refueling station, its engines remained running with the rotor RPM reduced, while the crew pumped jet fuel into the tank. Because of the risk that a spark could ignite the highly-flammable jet fuel, all refueling pads had grounding cables which the helicopter's skids rested upon, and the fuel nozzle had a grounding wire to attach to the aircraft, to prevent static electricity from the flowing fuel from creating a spark and igniting an inferno.

A fueling station made an outstanding target for incoming mortar and rocket rounds, because aircraft were guaranteed to be stationary for several minutes at a precise pre-registered location. The bad guys liked that. All it took was one lucky impact to set fire to several thousand gallons of jet fuel, and possibly some aircraft and fliers as well. Like horseshoes, close enough scored.

One of the pilots remained at the controls of the Huey during refueling, ready to yank the bird into the air in case of incoming enemy fire. A second crewman pumped the fuel while a third stood behind him with a fire extinguisher as fire watch. Refueling was always a messy job, with jet fuel usually spilling on the bird and sometimes on the man pumping the fuel. We had to emphasize to the crew that the fire watch's job was *not* to try to extinguish a burning aircraft, which was hopeless, but rather to extinguish his burning crewmate.

When scout helicopters only had one pilot aboard, he left the engine running while he got out and pumped his gas alone, hoping that neither he nor his little bird caught fire, or that the bad guys didn't choose that moment to start dropping mortar rounds on his location.

One day in 1972 at our squadron fueling station, a scout pilot was standing on the skid of his little bird pumping jet fuel when "Big Windy," a giant CH-47 Chinook helicopter, came in to refuel behind him, coming way too fast. The cargo helicopter pilot flared his rotors to slow down, sending a huge blast of rotorwash that blew the scout bird over on its side, flipping the scout pilot into a back somersault. Fortunately there was no fire while the scout bird beat itself into small pieces. Another aircraft destroyed by "other than combat conditions."

Hueys came equipped with several carbon dioxide fire extinguishers in the cabin. Unfortunately, the troops in the aviation units (usually the ground guys who didn't fly and didn't depend on them) discovered that emptying a CO_2 fire extinguisher was a great way to ice down a case or two of warm beer. They would sneak down to the flight line at night, "borrow" a fire extinguisher off a bird, then return the empty back in place. Part of the morning pre-flight inspection routine was to check all the fire extinguishers onboard, hoping at least one still had a charge of CO_2. By late in my tour, so many units and so much support equipment had been sent home that we couldn't get our fire extinguishers recharged anywhere in-country.

****

At the end of my twelve-month tour in January 1973 I rotated out with a Bronze Star (non-valor) and sixteen Air Medals. I helped a lot of people, was never hurt or shot down, none of my people were hurt, and I did a lot of good that I'm proud of. After I returned home, I branch transferred to the Engineers, commanded a Combat Engineer Company of the 1st Cavalry Division (Airmobile), and served in Latin America. I participated in an officer exchange with the Mexican Army and graduated from the Mexican National War College. After thirteen and a half years on active duty and eight years in the reserves, I retired a Lieutenant Colonel.

Since then, I retired from the Department of Energy as a nuclear weapons program manager. I survived 26 misdiagnosed heart attacks, attributed by the VA to Agent Orange. Since then, I spend my time maintaining my health, singing karaoke with my new bride, and writing down my eroding memories.

XXX

I hope you found this book and its incredibly fascinating stories as interesting to read as I did to put down on paper. If so, the credit belongs to the Veterans who agreed to open up and talk to me about their experiences from fifty years ago. And if you haven't already, I hope you'll check out the 1st and 2nd Volumes of **_Our Vietnam Wars_**, also available in Audio Books from ACS on the Amazon book pages.

My goal with these books has been to cover all the years, locations in-country, the units, and the experiences of the men and women who served there. Through their stories, I hope more of my fellow Veterans, their spouses, and their children will come to realize that they were not alone in what they experienced in Vietnam and what they have suffered the decades since. I also hope that the stories can educate the general public as to what so many good young men and women went through on behalf of a nation that all-too-often rejected, cursed, and even spat on them when they returned home.

When you have completed the read, I would appreciate your returning to the **_Our Vietnam Wars, Volume 3_** Book Page on either Kindle or Amazon, posting an appropriate Star Rating, and leave a comment. It's very easy to do. Just click on the Gold Stars and follow the screens. Both are very important to help the book find a wider audience. Thanks.

I am in the process of completing a fourth volume, which will likely to be my last in the series. So, if you are a Vietnam Veteran and would like me to add your story to our narrative, please send me an email at Billthursday1@gmail.com and I'll be in touch.

Thanks, Bill Brown

MY FINAL THOUGHTS

As Lieutenant General Hal Moore wrote in his 1992 bestseller and movie, _We Were Soldiers Once... And Young_, "Many of our countrymen came to hate the war we fought. Those who hated it the most – the professionally sensitive – were not, in the end, sensitive enough to differentiate between the war and the soldiers who had been ordered to fight it. They hated us as well, and we went to ground in the crossfire, as we had learned in the jungles… We rebuilt our lives, found jobs or professions, married, raised families and waited patiently for America to come to its senses. As the years passed, we searched each other out and found that the half-remembered pride of service was shared by those who had shared everything else with us. With them, and only with them, could we talk about what had really happened over there – what we had seen, what we had done, what we had survived."

No one has ever put it better.

Thanks, again,
Bill Brown

ABOUT THE AUTHOR

With the addition of <u>Our Vietnam Wars Volume 3</u>, I'm the author of twelve books available exclusively on Kindle. The first nine are mystery and international suspense thrillers.

A native of Chicago, I received a BA from The University of Illinois in History and Russian Area studies, and a Master's in City Planning. I served as a Company Commander in the US Army in Vietnam and later became active in local and regional politics in Virginia. As a Vice President of the real estate subsidiary of a Fortune 500 corporation, I was able to travel widely in the US and now travel extensively abroad, particularly in Europe and the Middle East, locations which have featured prominently in my writing. When not writing, I play bad golf, have become a dogged runner, and paint passable landscapes in oil and acrylic. Now retired, my wife and I live in Florida.

In addition to the novels, I've written four award-winning screenplays. They've placed First in the suspense category of Final Draft, were a Finalist in Fade In, First in Screenwriter's Utopia — Screenwriter's Showcase Awards, Second in the American Screenwriter's Association, Second at Breckenridge, and others. One was optioned for film.

The best way to follow my work and learn about sales and freebees is through my web site http://billbrownwritesnovels.wordpress.com,which has Preview Chapters of each of my novels, interviews, book reviews, and other links.

<u>Our Vietnam Wars</u> Volume 1 the Kindle Edition can be found at http://amzn.to/2BOBdu9
    the Amazon Paperback Edition can be found at http://amzn.to/2EjKjg1
<u>Burke's Revenge</u> can be found at http://amzn.to/2ob7qnX
<u>Burke's Gamble</u> can be found at http://amzn.to/2lORmXJ
<u>Burke's War</u> can be found at http://amzn.to/2muFG9C
<u>Cold War Trilogy</u> can be found at http://amzn.to/2mmTweV

The Undertaker can be found at http://amzn.to/2l9Chfg

Amongst My Enemies can be found at http://amzn.to/2lTovlu

Thursday at Noon can be found at http://amzn.to/2ljs1SI

Winner Lose All can be found at http://amzn.to/2lTqRke

Aim True, My Brothers can be found at http://amzn.to/2lPbj0t

HIGH PRAISE FOR THE AUTHOR'S EARLIER BOOKS:

Our Vietnam Wars, Vol 1 as told by 100 Veterans Who Served. 4.7 Stars on 172 Reviews

Our Vietnam Wars, Vol 2 as told by More Veterans Who Served. 4.9 Stars on 55 Reviews

Charles, Kindle Review: "5 Stars! I think it is one of the most interesting books I have read concerning the Viet Nam War. The fact that it is being told by actual combat participants from all over the country at different times of the war paints a very good picture. Personal accounts do much more for one's understanding of Viet Nam than fictional accounts. Anxiously awaiting the next installment."

Edward Koehler, Amazon Reviewer: "5 Stars! Powerful book. The real story of what our service men faced during their time in Viet Nam. Powerful book A must read."

GranJan Amazon Review: "5 Stars! The Truth is in the Telling. This is the most haunting of books! I did not serve, but many of my friends did. My brother-in-law died of Agent Orange 45 years after the fact. Other Vietnam Veterans that I have known didn't last that long. One thing I have learned from my combat-Veteran Marine husband is that we will never know what serving is truly like. And, judging from his PTSD and nightmares, I'm glad for that. This book helped me understand a little more what it was like to be there. I believe that I will re-read this book every so often as it is tough to comprehend in just one reading. Thank you so much for telling their stories!"

Mister Vin, Kindle Review: "5 Stars! Great concept and excellent presentation of person experiences. That it brings back good and bad memories is both good and bad. I can only read and "enjoy" one or two profiles at a time. It is a bit overwhelming but comforting to know that I am not the only one who had my experiences."

Willard J. Bodie, Amazon Reviewer: "5 Stars! It was comforting to read of others who experienced some of the same things I did and can speak of it with honesty and humor."

Dan G. Kindle Reviewer: "5 Stars! As a Veteran of Vietnam, I was eager to read this book. It is absolutely fabulous. A lot of recollections I could relate too on a personal level. If you are a Nam Vet, or if you are into Nam research, GET THIS BOOK, it is priceless. Thanks to the Author for the effort."

Burke's Revenge: 4.6 Stars on 82 Amazon Reviews

Ginny Reader, Kindle Reviewer: "5 Stars! Bob Burke is on the warpath against the "bad guys" once again. No obstacle is too great for Burke and his "Merry Men" as they are ensconced in their own Sherwood Forest. I can highly recommend this book. Be prepared to read it through-it's not easy to set aside."

Ron Paul, Amazon Reviewer: "5 Stars! Mr. Brown continues to write winners with this latest installment of the Burke series. He seamlessly molds current events with the possible, leading to scenarios which could be real if current world affairs took a slightly different turn. It's good reading, so pick up a copy and be prepared not to put it down."

Michael Bon, Amazon Reviewer: "5 Stars! If you like really good action this is the book for you. There are three books in this series, each stands alone well, but reading the first two books first gives the reader great insight into the characters in the books. A great story and never a dull moment. These books are very hard to put down once you start reading so you may lose a few hours of sleep like I have done."

Burke's Gamble: 4.7 Stars on 169 Amazon Reviews

G. C. Whitney Amazon Reviewer: "5 Stars! I can always tell when I'm reading a good book because I am disappointed when the story is over, and I have to say "Goodbye" to the characters in it. That was the case with this thriller by Bill Brown."

Joseph, Kindle Reviewer: "5 Stars! Another home run. Love these two books so far in the Bob Burke series. I think I like them so well because we get lots of old favorites and new characters. Always fast paced and always fun. Keep writing please."

Mack Holbrook, Amazon Reviewer: "5 Stars! Mobsters, Mercenaries, Mystery and Mayhem…What's not to Love? Set aside plenty of time to read this book, once you get started you will not want to put it down!"

Burke's War: 4.5 Stars on 383 Amazon Reviews.

Robert Kruger, Amazon Reviewer: "5 Stars! His characters are perceptively drawn, multifaceted, and fully defined. The prose is smooth flowing, descriptive, and convincing. The final scenes are heart stopping action — among the best."

Amazon Reviewer CAH: "5 Stars! Excellent! Don't know how a follow-up could match it — but I plan to find out."

Robert Smith, Amazon Reviewer: "One of the better books I have read in a long time."

The Undertaker: 4.4 Stars on 282 Amazon Reviews.

Passion Reads: "5 Stars! An awesome must read! This one had me jumping in, headfirst. From the beginning to the end, I was kidnapped and taken for an exciting and thrilling ride. And to top it all off, it was hilarious."

Book Pleasures: "5 Stars! Great fun! It is a thriller with enough action, intrigue, humor and romance to please the most jaded reader. My recommendation? Buy this book and have some quality entertainment time. You won't regret it."

Amongst My Enemies: 4.4 Stars on 282 Amazon Reviews.

Crystal Book Reviews: "5 Stars! This is not just another war story! It takes the reader to the heights and dregs of the human condition... speeds along like a Ken Follett or Eric Ludlum novel of old. For those who love adventure and thrills, this novel will leave you breathless and wanting more from this skillful writer. Splendidly written!"

Book Pleasures: "5 Stars! An entertaining historical thriller! Reminds me of Jeffery Deaver's *Garden of Beasts* and Frederic Forsythe's *The Odessa File*. It provides one answer to the eternal question: What must good men and women do when evil walks among them? Dean Koontz has made a career answering this question."

Thursday at Noon: 4.5 Stars on 147 Amazon Reviews.

The New Yorker: "5 Stars! A thriller in the purest cliffhanger vein... (The) technique is flawless. It could only have been learned by way of a thousand Saturday afternoon matinees."

Publisher's Weekly: "5 Stars! Writing in the vein of Forsythe and Follett, Brown has produced a fast-paced thriller..."

<u>Worldwide Library, Rave Reviews</u>: "5 Stars! (A) mesmerizing tale… Brown is adept at making the unlikely seem all too real… explosive, fast paced action."

Winner Lose All: 4.5 Stars 166 Amazon Reviews.

<u>Glynn Young, Amazon Reviewer</u>: "5 Stars! An exciting, riveting read that explores courage and treachery, love and fear. Another crackerjack novel of World War II, following last year's *Amongst My Enemies*. The reader is right there, carried along for one wild, breathtaking ride."

<u>Tanya, Amazon Reviewer</u>: "5 Stars! If you want a really good story, one that pulls you into the action, then this is the book to read. *Winner Lose All* is a WWII era drama with a strong list of characters, both the good guys/bad guys, and some you just can't decide where they fall in this tale of intrigues. It's a non-stop adventure."

Aim True, My Brothers: 4.7 Stars on 228 Amazon Reviews.

<u>Glynn Young, Amazon Reviewer</u>: "5 Stars! An exciting, riveting read that explores courage and treachery, love and fear. Another crackerjack novel of World War II, following last year's Amongst My Enemies. The reader is right there, carried along for one wild, breathtaking ride."

<u>G. C. Whitney III, Amazon Reviewer:</u> "5 Stars! Another Superb William Brown Thriller! He continues to amaze me with his writing. This story held my interest from beginning to end and, unlike some more famous authors, he didn't jump around from one timeline to another, which confuses the reader. I loved the story and, as is the case with most of his plots, it made sense throughout. Another 5-Star effort by William F. Brown."

Cold War Trilogy: 4.5 Stars on 21 Amazon Reviews

Cold War Trilogy is a boxed set of three of my best-selling action, adventure, thriller novels — "Winner Lose All," "Amongst My Enemies," and "Thursday at Noon." Together they have 262 Kindle Five Star Reviews, an average of 4.4 Stars each. If you like fast-paced spy novels and lots of mystery, and action, this set will prove some great reads. They are three of my favorite stories, with good pacing, twisting plot lines, and some of my nastiest and most evil bad guys. See if you don't agree."

Made in the
USA
Lexington, KY

55154434R00158